QUEENS OF JERUSALEM

QUEENS
OF
JERUSALEM

THE WOMEN WHO DARED TO RULE

KATHERINE PANGONIS

PEGASUS BOOKS
NEW YORK LONDON

QUEENS OF JERUSALEM

Pegasus Books, Ltd.
148 West 37th Street, 13th Floor
New York, NY 10018

ISBN: 978-1-64313-924-1

10 9 8 7 6 5 4 3 2 1

Printed in the United States of America
Distributed by Simon & Schuster
www.pegasusbooks.com

*Dedicated to the memory of my grandmothers,
strong women both*

CONTENTS

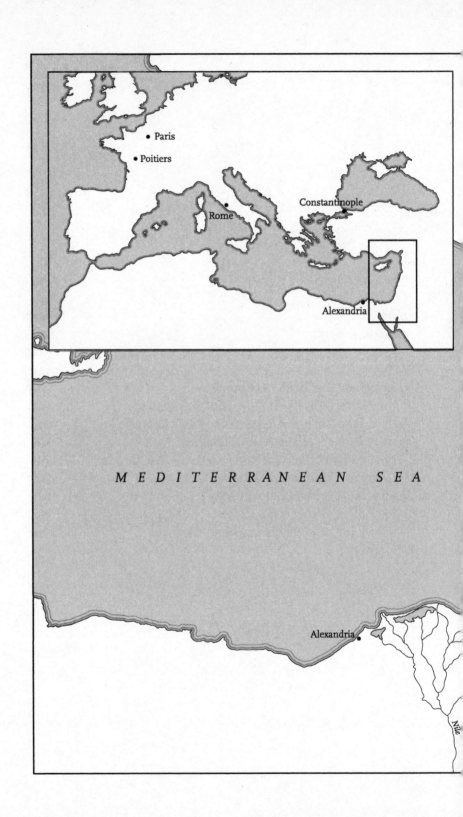

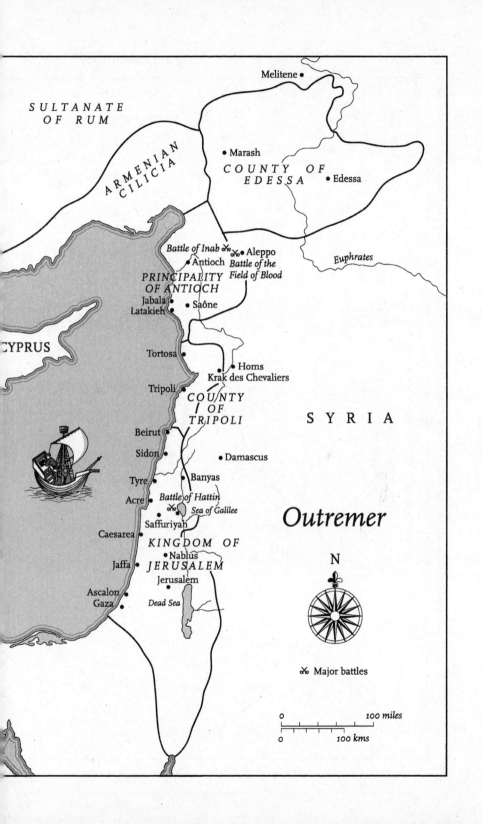

SULTANATE
OF RUM

Melitene •

ARMENIAN
CILICIA

• Marash

COUNTY OF
EDESSA

• Edessa

Euphrates

Battle of Inab ⚔ ⚔ • Aleppo
• Antioch *Battle of the*
Field of Blood

PRINCIPALITY
OF ANTIOCH

Jabala •
Latakieh • • Saône

CYPRUS

Tortosa •

Homs •
Krak des Chevaliers

Tripoli •

COUNTY
OF
TRIPOLI

SYRIA

Beirut •

Sidon •

• Damascus

Tyre •
Acre • • Banyas
Battle of Hattin
⚔ • *Sea of Galilee*
Saffuriyah •

Caesarea •

KINGDOM OF

• Nablus

Jaffa • JERUSALEM

Jerusalem •

Ascalon •
Gaza •

Dead Sea

Outremer

N

⚔ Major battles

0   100 miles

0   100 kms

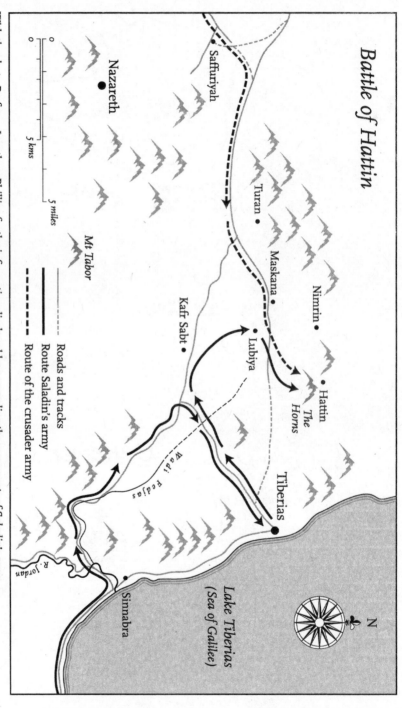

Battle of Hattin

Nazareth

Saffuriyah

Turan

Maskana

Nimrin

Hattin

The Horns

Kafr Sabt

Lubiya

Wadi Redjas

Tiberias

Sinnabra

R. Jordan

Lake Tiberias
(Sea of Galilee)

N

Mt Tabor

Roads and tracks

Route Saladin's army

Route of the crusader army

0   5 kms

0   5 miles

With thanks to Professor Jonathan Phillips for the information displayed here regarding the movements of Saladin's army.

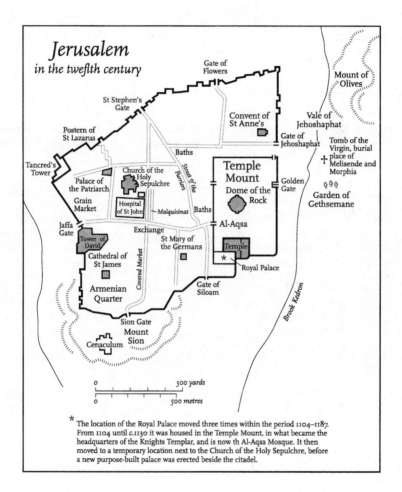

Jerusalem
in the twelfth century

Gate of
Flowers

Mount of
Olives

St Stephen's
Gate

Convent of
St Anne's

Vale of
Jehoshaphat

Postern of
St Lazarus

Gate of
Jehoshaphat

Tomb of the
Virgin, burial
place of
Melisende and
Morphia

Tancred's
Tower

Baths

Street of the Furriers

Church of the
Holy
Sepulchre

Palace of
the Patriarch

Temple
Mount

Dome of the
Rock

Golden
Gate

Grain
Market

Hospital
of St John

Malquisinat

Baths

Garden of
Gethsemane

Al-Aqsa

Jaffa
Gate

Exchange

Tower of
David

St Mary of
the Germans

Temple

Cathedral of
St James

Covered Market

*

Royal Palace

Armenian
Quarter

Gate of
Siloam

Brook Kedron

Sion Gate

Mount
Sion

Cenaculum

| 0 | | | 500 yards |
| 0 | | | 500 metres |

* The location of the Royal Palace moved three times within the period 1104–1187.
From 1104 until *c.*1130 it was housed in the Temple Mount, in what became the
headquarters of the Knights Templar, and is now th Al-Aqsa Mosque. It then
moved to a temporary location next to the Church of the Holy Sepulchre, before
a new purpose-built palace was erected beside the citadel.

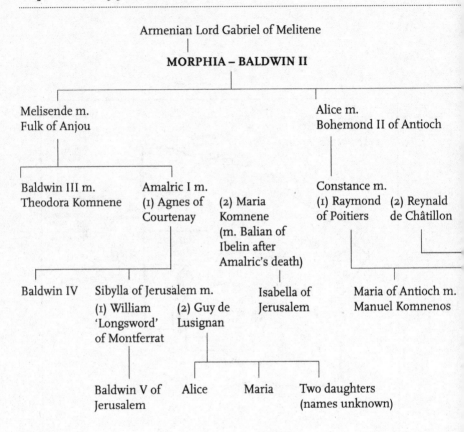

Armenian Lord Gabriel of Melitene

MORPHIA – BALDWIN II

Melisende m.
Fulk of Anjou

Alice m.
Bohemond II of Antioch

Baldwin III m.
Theodora Komnene

Amalric I m.
(1) Agnes of
Courtenay

(2) Maria
Komnene
(m. Balian of
Ibelin after
Amalric's death)

Constance m.
(1) Raymond
of Poitiers

(2) Reynald
de Châtillon

Baldwin IV

Sibylla of Jerusalem m.
(1) William
'Longsword'
of Montferrat

(2) Guy de
Lusignan

Isabella of
Jerusalem

Maria of Antioch m.
Manuel Komnenos

Baldwin V of
Jerusalem

Alice

Maria

Two daughters
(names unknown)

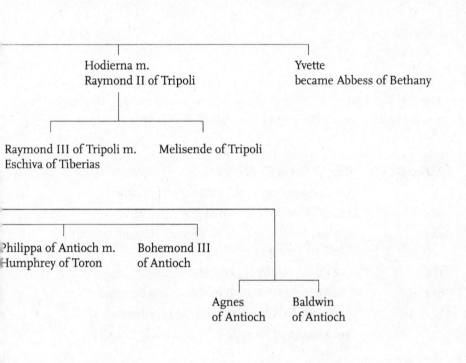

Hodierna m.
Raymond II of Tripoli

Yvette
became Abbess of Bethany

Raymond III of Tripoli m.
Eschiva of Tiberias

Melisende of Tripoli

Philippa of Antioch m.
Humphrey of Toron

Bohemond III
of Antioch

Agnes
of Antioch

Baldwin
of Antioch

Ruling Family of Edessa

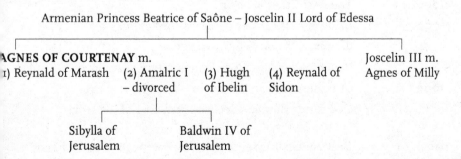

Armenian Princess Beatrice of Saône – Joscelin II Lord of Edessa

AGNES OF COURTENAY m.
1) Reynald of Marash   (2) Amalric I   (3) Hugh   (4) Reynald of
                 – divorced   of Ibelin   Sidon

Joscelin III m.
Agnes of Milly

Sibylla of
Jerusalem

Baldwin IV of
Jerusalem

TIMELINE OF EVENTS

Many of the dates in this timeline are best approximations / disputed. The aim is to give a sense of the chronology rather than precision.

	Capture of Bohemond I of Antioch by Danishmend Turks
	Tancred invested as regent of Antioch
1103–1105	Siege of Tripoli by Raymond of Toulouse
1104	Conquest of Acre by Baldwin I
	Battle of Harran, Baldwin of Edessa and Joscelin of Courtenay captured by Seljuk Turks
1105	Birth of **Melisende**, daughter of Baldwin I and **Morphia**
1108	Baldwin of Edessa released
~1109	Birth of **Alice**, sister of **Melisende**
1109	Tripoli captured by Franks
~1110	Birth of **Hodierna**, sister of **Melisende**
1112	Death of Tancred
	Pons of Tripoli marries **Lady Cecile of France**
1113	Baldwin I marries **Adelaide del Vasto of Sicily**
1113–1115	Baldwin of Edessa conquers eastern Cilicia
1118	Death of Baldwin I, succession by Baldwin of Edessa as Baldwin II, King of Jerusalem, crowned jointly with **Morphia**
1119	Death of Roger of Salerno at the Battle of the Field of Blood
	Regency of Baldwin II begins at Antioch
1120	Birth of **Yvette**, sister of **Melisende**
1123	Baldwin II imprisoned by Balak
1124	Crusaders capture Tyre
	Baldwin II released
1126	**Alice** marries Bohemond II of Antioch
~1127	Death of **Morphia**
1128	Birth of **Constance of Antioch**, daughter of **Alice**
1129	**Melisende** marries Fulk
1130	Birth of Baldwin III, son of **Melisende** and Fulk
1130	Death of Bohemond II
	First rebellion of **Alice of Antioch**
1131	Death of Baldwin II, succession by **Melisende**, Fulk and the child Baldwin III
1131	Second rebellion of **Alice of Antioch**
~1133	**Hodierna** marries Raymond II of Tripoli (exact date not known)

	Baldwin V is crowned co-king
1185	Saladin agrees to truce with Jerusalem
	Baldwin IV dies, succeeded by Baldwin V
~1186	**Agnes** dies (sometime between early months of 1184 and late summer 1186)
	Baldwin V dies
	Sibylla crowned queen
	Death of **Ismat ad-Din Khatoun**
1187	War erupts as a five-year truce is broken
	Saladin defeats main crusader army at the Battle of Hattin, imprisons Guy de Lusignan and executes Reynald de Châtillon
	Jerusalem falls to Saladin s armies
	Pope calls for Third Crusade
1188	Guy de Lusignan released from captivity
1190	Death of **Sibylla** and daughters at Siege of Acre
1205	Death of **Isabella**

AUTHOR'S NOTE

This is a book about women and power. It is about the power noble-women in Outremer struggled for, the forces that limited their power and the power male writers and historians have wielded over their legacies. It tells the stories of an extraordinary dynasty of women-rulers, examining the challenges and triumphs of their lives.

The unique instability and near constant state of crisis in Outremer created an environment in which noble-born women could be propelled to prominence and wield real power. Aristocratic women in Jerusalem, Antioch, Tripoli and Edessa represented a major force in the politics of the medieval Middle East. Despite this, more often than not women of their status in this period have been regarded by historians as little more than transmitters of lands and broodmares for the next generation of kings. They have been remembered as the wives, mothers, daughters and sisters of powerful men, not as autonomous individuals and active leaders with their own political agency. In recent years, great progress has been made to redress this, but these efforts have for the most part been confined to academic works. The aim of this book is to redress this and bring the Queens of Jerusalem, Princesses of Antioch and Countesses of Tripoli and Edessa out of the shadows and into the public eye.

It is not the job of the historian, nor even the feminist historian, to make heroines out of every female figure maligned or dismissed by history. Rather, it is to present the relevant evidence and analysis to give readers the best possible understanding of who that person was and how they functioned within the social, political and religious framework of their society. This book will weigh up evidence and source material where necessary to illustrate something unclear, and present readers with excerpts from source material, inviting them to draw their own conclusions on controversial topics and to test the validity of medieval gossip. It is intended as a work of narrative-driven biography, rather than an academic analysis of female political agency or historiography.

The writing of it has taken me from the reading rooms of the British, Bodleian and Mazarine libraries, across Europe and the Middle East. Much of it was written from the Old City of Jerusalem and various hotel rooms, cafes and draughty ruins in Turkey, Lebanon, Jordan and France. The opportunity to travel in this way and to stand where these remarkable women once stood, to tread the stones they once trod and to look out on the landscapes that they themselves once looked upon, has been a profound joy.

ACKNOWLEDGEMENTS

I owe debts of gratitude to a great many people for the assistance and encouragement I have been given in the creation of this book. The kindness and generosity I have received at almost every turn and in so many countries has been overwhelming. The first thank you I must give is to my editor and publisher, Alan Samson, without whose faith and guidance I would, instead of writing books, be mired in a corporate job to which I was ill-suited. He made this book possible, and has provided invaluable support throughout its writing.

The second thank you must go to my teachers, at school and university, who taught me to love the medieval period, in particular Prof. David d'Avray and Dr Giles Brown. These men gave me the tools, the confidence and the enthusiasm to attempt to write a book. In Jerusalem, I am grateful to the Armenian historian George Hintlian, who went above and beyond in helping make my research trips as productive as they could be. He taught me much about the significance of Morphia's Armenian influence on her daughters, and the multicultural nature of Jerusalem, both in medieval times and present ones. He also made sure I was safe, fed and had places to work and access to source material, and guided me around the remains of the Convent of Bethany. Prof. Adrian Boas of Haifa University was also very kind, meeting me and guiding me around the souks, and later answering my questions and reading chapter drafts with great patience. I must also thank Brother Amedeo Ricci of the Franciscan Friars, who was kind enough to share his PhD research on the Church of the Holy Sepulchre, and give me a thorough and in-depth tour of the space from a Christian perspective. In the UK, particular thanks must also go to Prof. Christopher Tyerman at Oxford University, who, in addition to having valuable discussions with me that caused me to consider the distinction between power and authority, took the time to read and correct my finished manuscript. I am grateful to the convenors and participants of the IHR Crusades and Latin East

Seminar organised by Royal Holloway University, for including me in thought-provoking discussions and sharing material with me. Prof. Andrew Jotischky of Royal Holloway University answered my often ill-formulated questions about various aspects of my research.

My last thank you must go to my parents and my friends, without the support of whom this book would not have been written. My parents gave me the educational opportunities that put me in a position to write history, and my mum read the manuscript countless times. Many of my friends also had the patience to help me, pitching in with everything from reading drafts, to taking photographs, to deciphering handwriting (medieval and modern). Particular thanks must go to Nancy Hervey-Bathurst, who read early versions of the text and encouraged me, and to Fred Shan, César Manivet and Scott Moynihan, who nitpicked the finished manuscript. Martha Bailey tirelessly assisted me with research from the British Library while I was away, critiqued Latin translations and went the extra mile and accompanied me on research trips to Jerusalem and Nablus. In Lebanon, Louis Prosser and Lou'ai Kaakani were generous with their time and good humour, driving me around various ruins everywhere between Tyre and Tripoli. León López Brennan and Okan Çimek assisted me on my trips to Antioch and Edessa, and helped take pictures of these beautiful places. Jo Whitford at Orion has been brilliant in corralling me to get the manuscript and supporting materials into their final shape, and Professor Jonathan Phillips stepped in to give me vital corrections at the eleventh hour.

It goes without saying that any mistakes I've made in the writing of this book are entirely my own, and if anywhere I have allowed myself to be carried away by the drama or romance of the story, it has been against the advice of more level-headed historians.

PREFACE

. . . the coast that has so long sounded with the world's debate . . .
Edward Gibbon

The walls of Acre, beside the Mediterranean Sea

At its easternmost reaches, the clear waters of the Mediterranean Sea lap against crumbling walls of bright stone: the lingering monuments of a forgotten kingdom. These ruined walls are all that is left of once proud fortresses that have guarded the coastline and craggy hilltops from southern Turkey to northern Egypt for nearly a millennium. The land the water touches here, the land on which these citadels are built, is holy. It is the most coveted region in global history, fought over by the three great Abrahamic religions that each view it as their spiritual centre: Christianity, Islam and Judaism. Sprawling across the Palestinian

Territories, Israel, Jordan, Lebanon, Turkey and Syria, rich in nothing but belief and residing under a gruelling summer sun, this land has been the object of bloody warfare down the centuries from antiquity to the modern day. With its protean borders and mercurial rulers, this region has captured the imaginations of generations around the world.

The focal point of this conflict lies inland, some forty miles from the Mediterranean's waters. The magnet at the centre of all these centuries' endeavour, the jewel these coastal castles and ports were built to serve, is the holy city of Jerusalem. A living, breathing city in the middle of modern Israel. Today the streets of the Old City stand much as they did in medieval times. The air is thick with the scent of spices, and the unmistakable smell of frying vegetables. The clamour of vendors vying for customers and haggling over trinkets mingles with the incoherent ringing of many competing sets of bells and Arabic calls to prayer. The throng of pilgrims and travellers is much the same as it would have been a thousand years ago. Spiritual tourists have always clogged the arteries of this city, but are its life-blood nonetheless. Christians, Jews and Muslims of every denomination jostle, pressing towards their separate holy places, which all lie within the same square mile.

The layout of the streets and the landmarks is not much changed either from medieval times, and a medieval pilgrim would not find much difficulty in navigating their way today from the Jaffa Gate to the Church of the Holy Sepulchre. The streets of the souks that wind around the holy places still have the same arched crusader shop fronts, and sell traditional merchandise like leather handicrafts, herbs and religious symbols. These antique streets ring with prayer and the bustle of trade as they did a thousand years ago. Soldiers too loiter here much as they would have in medieval times, a constant reminder of the region's instability. The knights with long swords have been replaced by Israeli teenagers with automatic machine guns, enjoying pomegranate juice and texting.

The architecture of the city has stood witness to its centuries of history, and stands as testament to the many regimes that have risen and fallen within the walls of the Holy City. The arches of the crusader period and the stone walls with their diagonal tooling rub shoulders with Mamluk and Ottoman designs. Crosses, domes and minarets jumble the skyline. When the sun goes down in the Old City, its rays glint on the golden domes of Christian churches before giving way to the pale-green glow of the minarets that illuminate the night sky.

In the Church of the Holy Sepulchre, the holiest site of Christianity and the site of Christ's earthly tomb, columns and plinths from the time of Constantine stand beside medieval and modern additions. In the Armenian chapel, garish modern murals conceal crusader vaulted ceilings, supported by Byzantine and Romanesque capitals with basket-weave and acanthus-leaf designs. The walls that descend to the chapel of the Finding of the Cross are engraved with thousands of rough crosses, the marks made by individual crusaders and pilgrims to mark the completion of their quest.

Here, in what feels like the bowels of the great church, is a rock-cut chapel: the place where Helena, mother of the Emperor Constantine, claimed to have found the True Cross. It was here that she ordered the great church to be built. The Church of the Holy Sepulchre was founded by a woman. This chapel is one of the quietest, most overlooked parts of the church, but it was the culmination of the medieval pilgrimage route. It is cavernous, plain and mostly unadorned, with traces of twelfth-century frescoes permeating the walls. There is no statue of Jesus here, nor Constantine, nor any of the great men later associated with the building, just a serene statue of a queenly woman leaning on a cross above a humble altar, flickering in the light of many votive candles.

Today the key of the Holy Sepulchre is held by a Muslim family, neutral guardians, to quell the bickering of the different denominations of Christians. The key has been passed down, father to son, for generations, and every day at 4 a.m. Adeep Joudeh makes a journey through the shuttered, silent streets and delivers the key that unlocks the door. It is large, iron and arrow-shaped.

This city, with its dispute-riddled streets, and the other lands that surround it have always been the subject of bitter conflict. In generations past this land was referred to by Europeans as 'the Orient' or 'the Levant'. The French still refer to the *Moyen-Orient*, a literal translation of Middle East, which is the term now preferred in Anglophone countries. The terms 'Levant' and 'Orient' both have their roots in imagery of the rising sun. If one traces their respective etymologies back to Latin and French, they mean 'to dawn' or 'to rise': these are Western words for Eastern lands. They are shrouded in mystery and conjure images of men and women in ancient times squinting into the fresh, bright light breaking over the horizon and imagining a world beyond: lands bathed in sunlight, awash in reds and golds, and always out of reach. In Arabic, a similar term is used: *Mashriq*, which derives from the word *sharaqa*, which likewise means 'to rise' or 'to shine'.

Despite their current vogue, the terms 'Middle East' and even 'Near East' are too broad for the region examined in this book, which is narrower. The stories in this work were played out on the sliver of coastline that runs from southern Turkey to northern Egypt, which before it was called the Middle East, and even before it was called the Levant, was known to Europeans by another name: *Outremer*.

The name *Outremer* has nothing to do with the rising sun, but likewise conveys the perceived unreachability and distance of the land in the minds of those that made the word. It comes from French and translates literally as 'over-sea', or 'the lands beyond the sea'. It defines the land by its otherness and exoticism, and in relation to the journey that was made by thousands upon thousands of medieval men and women over land and sea from Western Europe to the Holy Land.

For thousands of years followers of Christianity, Islam and Judaism alike have made pilgrimages to Jerusalem. Pilgrimages are still being made by the faithful today. In the eleventh, twelfth and thirteenth centuries, however, the Christian pilgrimages to Outremer took on a different colour: they became armed, they became organised, and they were rallied by the Pope himself. In 1095, Urban II made a rousing speech at a council of both clergy and the secular elite of France in the town of Clermont. His words electrified his audience as he called upon those assembled to abandon their homes and take up weapons en masse to journey east, to Outremer, to liberate the holy places from infidels. With this speech, the traditional notion of peaceful Christian pilgrimage was overtaken by a thirst for the military ventures that would become known centuries later as 'the crusades'.

To the consternation of many, the First Crusade was met with considerable success. On 15 July 1099, after gruelling years of war and marching across Europe and Anatolia, the crusaders took Jerusalem. The result of this success was that, for nearly two hundred years, Western Europeans occupied Outremer. They created Christian states there, built the fortresses that still dominate the landscape today and, for eighty-eight years, held Jerusalem itself as a Christian capital.

The deeds of men in Outremer in this period are a hyperactive field of study, yet the study of the deeds of the women is comparatively dormant. Women played a key role in both the crusades themselves and the governance of the Kingdom of Jerusalem. When armies marched east from Europe, women marched with them. Men who could afford to often brought their families, and poorer women also travelled with the army. These women prepared meals, washed clothes, nursed the wounded, collected firewood and were the lovers of the soldiers. On rare occasions they even sallied onto the battlefield either to bring water to the men or to fight themselves. In the established territories of Outremer noblewomen organised the logistics of sieges and negotiated with the enemy, and women of the lower classes toiled with the men to undermine fortifications. They endured unimaginable hardships, died alongside the men and also fell victim to rape, imprisonment and slavery. Thousands of European women found themselves traded in the slave markets of Aleppo and Damascus during the twelfth century. When the male rulers of Outremer overplayed their hands and found themselves rotting in enemy dungeons, they were ransomed by their wives.

Despite these clearly documented roles, the vast majority of crusades historians, both medieval and modern, have neglected the roles of women in their histories. This book intends to go some way towards fixing this imbalance by shedding some light on the deeds of women in positions of authority in Outremer: specifically, the dynasty of formidable women rulers founded by Morphia of Melitene, the first crowned Queen of Jerusalem. Her daughters and granddaughters reigned as Queens of Jerusalem, Princesses of Antioch, Countesses of Tripoli, and held many other positions as well. They represent some of the most daring, devious and devoted women that history has ever seen. The source material available on these women is sparse in comparison to what we have regarding their husbands and fathers, but enough survives to construct vivid portraits of these remarkable queens and princesses.

The most famous woman considered in this book was neither a Queen of Jerusalem nor a Princess of Antioch, but rather Queen of France and later of England: Eleanor of Aquitaine. She has a place in this book as the first European queen to undertake a crusade, and for the strange rumours that circulated about her relationship with the Prince of Antioch. Eleanor has perhaps received more than her fair share of fame in comparison to her counterparts in Outremer. This is not to undermine her impact or importance, but rather to contextualise it with the knowledge that there were many other women rulers in the East raising hell for their male relatives and adversaries. Perhaps there was something in the water at Antioch that put fire in the blood, but Eleanor was hardly breaking with tradition when her rebellious nature came into its own within the walls of that storied city. On her journey to Outremer, Eleanor had encountered formidable role models in rule breaking. In Jerusalem she was received by the daunting figure of Queen Melisende, first Queen Regnant of Jerusalem and one of the most powerful women of the age. This meeting with a woman who so excellently embodied female ambition and leadership doubtless influenced Eleanor's later career.

The history of Outremer seems at first glance to be overwhelmingly male, full of masculine rage, zealotry and bloodlust. This, perhaps, is true; but the wrath and wit of women also played their part in shaping the destiny of this region. It is time for this region and this period to be viewed through a female lens. This book explores the lives of the ruling women of Outremer from the year 1099 to Saladin's conquest of Jerusalem in 1187.

INTRODUCTION:
THE BIRTH OF OUTREMER

We who were Occidentals have become Orientals. He who was a Roman or a Frank has in this land been made into a Galilean or a Palestinian. He who was of Rheims or Chartres has now become a citizen of Tyre or Antioch. We have already forgotten the places of our birth [. . .] Some have taken wives not only of their own people but Syrians or Armenians or even Saracens who have obtained the grace of baptism. [. . .] He who was born a stranger is now as one born here; he who was born an alien has become as a native.

Fulcher of Chartres, resident of Jerusalem

View of Jerusalem from the Mount of Olives

The crusaders conquered Outremer city by city and by the sword. Although peaceful surrenders were sometimes negotiated and captives often taken, they still slaughtered and displaced thousands upon thousands of native people as they cut their way across Eastern Europe, Anatolia and the Middle East. Muslims, Jews and non-Catholic Christians alike all fell victim to their zealous ferocity. The Christian states of Outremer grew from a rag-group of sequentially conquered lordships and principalities, with Jerusalem always as the goal. Eventually and against the odds, the crusaders succeeded in conquering Jerusalem, the site of Christ's crucifixion and the holiest city of Christianity. When they at last captured the Holy City they turned it into a city of ghosts. Their bloodlust reached fever pitch as they spilled over the walls and annihilated the inhabitants.

Out of the ashes, blood and filth of the First Crusade, the Kingdom of Jerusalem was forged. Four distinct states were carved out of the territory they claimed: the County of Edessa, the Principality of Antioch, the County of Tripoli and the Kingdom of Jerusalem. Between them, the rulers of these lands controlled the Holy Land and held it in Christ's name. The crusade had achieved its goal and made some of the luckier crusaders rich men to boot.

The news of this triumph reverberated across the Christian and Muslim worlds. Many had given up on the crusade even before the armies came in sight of Jerusalem. After the numerous defeats and setbacks they encountered along the way, the idea of taking the Holy City seemed like a fool's errand. Troubadours and chroniclers of East and West fell on the story of the conquest with unprecedented zeal. Songs, stories and poetry were all written about the adventure, heroism and brutality of the First Crusade. Perhaps most importantly, histories were written too, although the boundaries between history and literature as genres had not yet begun to solidify and the chroniclers used a good deal of artistic licence.

The history of Outremer became one of the best documented areas in the history of the medieval world, and provides a rich trove of sources for historians today. A full list of the primary material used in the research for this book can be found in the Bibliography. We have chronicles written by men in the thick of the political and military arena: Franks, Armenians, Byzantines, Syrians, Kurds, Arabs and Persians. We have charters bearing the seals of those with authority, that give us reliable information as to who was ruling when, and how they were using their power. We have letters from the great men of the West to the rulers of the Latin East, and vice versa. We also have surviving artefacts, and the surviving fortresses of Outremer, alongside the evidence provided by the archaeological record.

However, lucky as we are to have this wealth of information, we are also unlucky in the uniform bias presented across the narrative sources. The majority of surviving chronicles are written by clerics; that is to say patriarchal, religious, celibate men. Men who did not live with women, men who did not love women, and men whose lives featured very little interaction with women. The one notable exception to this is *The Alexiad*, written by the Byzantine Princess Anna Komnene, one of the best educated and most ambitious women of her day. Her chronicle gives some information about the First Crusade and the foundation of Outremer, but even Anna's hand is imbued with much of the patriarchal misogyny of her day: Anna Komnene was certainly no feminist. It all comes down to genre, and Anna Komnene's choice to write a chronicle necessarily binds it with the tradition and attitude of male chroniclers.

Similarly, while the Muslim historians documenting this period were not clerics, they likewise were products of a deeply patriarchal society and did not attribute much importance to recording the activities of women. As a result of this the roles played by women in warfare, sieges, governing and daily life are consistently ignored and underplayed. There appears to be a uniform distaste among male medieval chroniclers for acknowledging and engaging with the importance of women. Where possible, they prefer to ignore them.

The terms 'misogynistic' and 'patriarchal' are both essential for modern considerations of the presentation and treatment of women, and it is tempting to use these terms liberally when describing the lives of the female rulers of Outremer. However, when applied to the medieval world these terms can sound jarringly anachronistic. For this reason I will use them both sparingly. It is always difficult to apply modern terms laden with modern value judgements to the members and attitudes of a long-dead society, distant from us in both time and space, but they can be useful if they are paired with an understanding that the society described in medieval Outremer functioned within an entirely different framework to the modern society in which these terms have developed. The inequality of men and women was accepted as legal fact, built into the fabric and structure of a society defined by the Christian church and warrior ethos. Feminism was an unheard-of concept.

'Misogyny' in the modern usage is taken to mean an irrational dislike or fear of women and discrimination against them. There was much discrimination against women in the Middle Ages. Women had fewer rights with regard to inheritance law and personal freedom, but such measures were considered *rational* in the contemporarily held world view. To deny that men and women had different roles in life would be met with much the same derision as denying climate change in the modern day. This is an important distinction to make. Moreover, much of our perception, as modern readers, of the way women were treated in medieval times filters down to us through the writing of clerics, which comes down to an issue of genre. The way women are presented within chronicles may not actually reflect the reality of their standing in society. With this in mind, the word 'misogyny' can only be uncomfortably applied to medieval society, but it may be more comfortably applied to medieval chronicles.

The chronicle written by William of Tyre, *A History of Deeds Done Beyond the Sea*, is without doubt the most important and exhaustive record of events in the Kingdom of Jerusalem and the Christian states of Outremer. It was written by one of the more astute and thorough historians of the Middle Ages. William of Tyre certainly has a good claim to be the greatest historian of his generation. He was born in Jerusalem around the year 1130, and during his early life was educated at the Cathedral School of the Church of the Holy Sepulchre. Thus, his formative years were spent in the heart of the Old City of Jerusalem and Christianity's spiritual centre. In 1145 he left Outremer for Europe and spent over a decade studying in Paris and Italy. In 1165 he returned to Outremer and was made an ambassador to Byzantium by the then king, Amalric of Jerusalem. From this position he rose through the ranks, becoming Archdeacon of Tyre, Chancellor of the Kingdom and eventually Archbishop of Tyre. While serving in these various offices he became both tutor to Amalric's son and also the court historian to the Kingdom of Jerusalem. With such a varied life experience and education, he was uniquely situated to understand the cultural and political subtleties of the events in Outremer which he recorded. His research was thorough and varied, making use of existing chronicles but also conducting original interviews with eyewitnesses and witnessing many of the events he describes first-hand.

For all his rare enlightenment and relatively modern approach to the writing of history, interspersing his narrative with big-picture analysis, William's chronicle was not immune to the far-reaching influence and symptoms of misogyny, nor indeed political bias. He devotes scarcely five per cent of his one-thousand-plus-page chronicle to the deeds of women. His chronicle, then, must be treated critically, and there is much danger in falling into the trap of assuming everything he writes is a reliable fact. This is particularly true of William's treatment and depiction of women in his writing. Like most medieval chroniclers, he prefers to throw women into one camp or the other: sinner or saint. He does not give much credit to the notion that the women he writes about were individuals as complex as the men, and he prefers to cast women as literary tropes rather than depict them as living, breathing humans.

The Kingdom of Jerusalem and the other states of Outremer were frontier lands living in the shadow of the threat of raids, invasion and full-on annihilation. The customs, topography and climate of the Middle East were unfamiliar to the European settlers. The society was comprised of the conquering military elite, the knights, lords, barons, counts, princes and kings and their vassals ruling over a population that was primarily native Christians.

The female rulers of Outremer were born into a world between cultures, and into a region torn by crisis. The Christian states of Outremer were founded by 'Franks', an indiscriminate term for the Western Europeans who led the First Crusade. The Muslim chroniclers called them *Faranj* or *Franj*, and they also became known as 'the Latins': the phrase 'Latin East' is interchangeable with Outremer. The Franks hailed primarily from Western and Southern Europe and as a result, the culture they imported to the East was Catholic, feudal and military. However, the culture that developed in Outremer differed greatly from Western Europe and was significantly less homogenous, given the instability of the region and the difference in the cultures of the native inhabitants of the Middle East. Jerusalem presented an insatiable draw to people of different cultures from as far afield as Iceland and India. The cities of the Holy Land presented unique ethnic and cultural hubs in the Middle Ages, where people of all faiths were thrown together through periods of intense warfare and uneasy, negotiated peace. It was a period of artistic flourishing and cultural exchange against the backdrop of religious conflict.

The native Christians of the Middle East were primarily Armenians, Greeks, Syrians, Jacobites and Maronites. These groups, often separated along ethnic as well as religious lines, had individual cultures and languages distinctly different to those of the European West. They were afforded fewer rights by the crusaders than Catholic European settlers in the Latin East, and while they certainly ranked higher in the social and legal hierarchy than Jews and Muslims, many were still regarded as heretical. Despite this, cooperation and intermarriage were encouraged at both the highest and lowest levels, particularly in the frontier County of Edessa.

Such cooperation was essential to the survival of the Christian states of Outremer. The occupying force was small, many crusaders returned to the West after the capture of Jerusalem, and although a new wave of crusaders did journey east to swell the ranks of the Franks in Outremer during the reign of Baldwin I, it was not enough to successfully occupy and populate the entirety of the lands they had claimed. The victorious army of the First Crusade that conquered Outremer did not constitute a population for their newly won lands. They were primarily soldiers, and although a great many women did travel with the army, they had been greatly depleted during the gruelling march across Europe and Asia Minor. Immigration was not confined to the main crusading expeditions. Bit by bit, however, native Christians returned: Armenian and Syrian Christian communities formed alongside the Catholics in Jerusalem, and tax breaks were given to encourage settlement and trade across the newly won lands.

Gradually the Franks began to assimilate their new conditions and incorporate elements of local culture into their own. One of the most popular anecdotes relating to this is of a particularly enthusiastic Frankish knight who, upon learning of the custom of some Arabs of shaving pubic hair, demanded that a male bath attendant shave both him and his wife in like style, scandalising both the attendant and the chronicler Usama ibn Munqidh, to whom he related the tale, and doubtless his bemused wife as well.

Despite the preference for viewing Muslims and Christians as mortal enemies in Outremer, always determined to kill each other on sight, this was simply not the case. In the cities of Outremer, particularly those on major trading routes, Christians and Muslims mixed with relative freedom, with the Muslims only having to pay taxes and fees for the right to trade and live in Christian territory. Diplomatic negotiations regularly took place between Christian and Muslim leaders.

The relationships between men and women followed the pattern of Western Europe. In the eyes of the men writing the laws, noblewomen primarily served the purpose of childbearing and transmitting lands and titles to husbands and children. However, the instability and lack of military security in Outremer threw their roles and capabilities into greater prominence. Life expectancy was short for a fighting man in Outremer. If he were not struck down by disease or mishap, he might well be slaughtered on the battlefield or in an unexpected raid. Noblewomen were generally safer than their husbands, fathers and brothers: they lived behind the high walls of the citadels and convents that sprang up across the Middle East during the crusader period. We have no records of a noblewoman being killed in action: the task of physical fighting rarely fell to them, although they did have the challenges of childbirth to contend with.

Women in Outremer began to outlive the male relatives who normally would have controlled them, and to become lynchpins of power and political loyalty in their own right. Beyond this, by pure chance the kings of Jerusalem found themselves blessed with daughters rather than the sons they desperately craved. This forced society in Outremer to adapt to the concept of queenship and swallow the bitter pill of female rule.

The two central figures of this book are Queen Melisende of Jerusalem and Queen Sibylla of Jerusalem. These women, grandmother and granddaughter, served as Queens Regnant of Jerusalem, and consequently there is considerably more source material written about them than the other noblewomen of Outremer. However, the lives of their mothers, sisters, nieces and cousins, ruling variously as Queens Consort of Jerusalem and Princesses of Antioch, are also worthy of note, playing pivotal roles in the internal politics of Outremer.

MORPHIA AND THE FOUR PRINCESSES

On Christmas Day 1118, a royal couple sat enthroned in the Church of the Holy Nativity in Bethlehem. The man was fair-haired with piercing blue eyes and a long beard. The woman was of a different race – Eastern with dark hair and eyes. They were resplendent in intricately embroidered coronation robes made of the finest silks the East could offer, heavily stitched with gems that winked in the candlelight. Seated beneath the dome of the Byzantine basilica which glowed with mosaics that spread across it like molten gold, they were waiting to be made monarchs. In front of the hushed congregation, the man swore an oath before Christ and his angels to conserve law and peace in the Kingdom of Jerusalem for both the church and his subjects. A ring was placed on his finger symbolising his loyalty, a sword was buckled to his waist representing his role as the Kingdom's military defender, and finally an orb and sceptre were placed in his hands to represent the justice he would dispense and his God-given power on earth. The woman beside him swore to support her husband in his task.

With great solemnity the man and woman sank to their knees and the Patriarch of Jerusalem anointed them with holy oil, transforming them from simple mortals to God's representatives on earth. The Patriarch solemnly raised and lowered two golden, gem-encrusted crowns onto their brows. The man had been an adventuring knight from France, a second son unlikely to inherit anything. To reach this moment he had traversed Europe and Asia Minor, fought in countless battles and endured years of imprisonment. He had leapfrogged barriers and grasped opportunities to propel himself to this most exalted position. His name was Baldwin, Count of Edessa. The person kneeling beside him was the woman who had stood by him, defended his interests and raised his children for almost two decades. She had borne him three daughters and protected his lands while he languished in Saracen prisons. Before long she would give him a fourth daughter, who would be the first child to be born to a king and queen in Jerusalem. A mysterious woman, a princess of an ancient Armenian kingdom, she was private, strong and dutiful. Her name was Morphia of Melitene: she was the first woman to be crowned Queen of Jerusalem.

Their choice to be crowned in Bethlehem on Christmas Day was steeped in significance. Not only was it the day of Christ's birth and thus one of the holiest days in the Christian calendar, but it was also the day which Baldwin I had chosen for his coronation, and the day when Charlemagne had himself been crowned Holy Roman Emperor in Rome in the year 800. Not only was Bethlehem the place of Christ's birth, but it was also the site where David had been anointed King of Israel. In choosing Christmas Day for their coronation, the new king and queen were symbolically associating themselves with the three most important kings of both the sacred and the secular worlds: Jesus Christ, King David and the Emperor Charlemagne.

Coronations were events of unparalleled importance in the Middle Ages and in the newly formed Kingdom of Jerusalem in particular. This was an age before the printing press: there were few forms of mass communication and propaganda available to rulers, and some of the primary ways of communicating power to one's subjects was through the images on coinage and public spectacles. The coronation of a new monarch was a golden opportunity for the latter. The grandeur of the coronation would set the tone for the reign of the monarch and was an opportunity to win the admiration of the monarch's new subjects and assert his or her authority and supremacy over the nobility. It was a highly ritualised and meticulously planned affair. Crowds from miles around descended on the area surrounding the Church of the Nativity in the hope of catching a glimpse of the newly crowned couple when they made their exit from the church.

There exists no contemporary description of the festivities surrounding Baldwin and Morphia's coronation, but we do know that the Franks of the Latin East knew how to throw a lavish party and loved the opportunity to mount displays of wealth and accomplishment. Descriptions of other celebrations in Outremer refer to acrobats twisting and tumbling to music from Armenian musicians, dancing in the streets, mouth-watering banquets and jousting tournaments.

The setting was certainly splendid: the Church of the Nativity in Bethlehem was built over the site of Christ's birth, in a cave grotto that had housed a stable just over a millennium previously. Over these humble origins a basilica had been built by Saint Helena, mother of the Emperor Constantine, when she made her tour of the Holy Land in the early fourth century. During this expedition she 'discovered' the True Cross and founded numerous places of worship. Helena's church was rebuilt by the Emperor Justinian in the sixth century with his customary flourish.

Justinian was famous for his ambitious building projects, and the Church of the Nativity was no exception, boasting a soaring domed basilica decorated with gleaming tesserae and frescoes. Among these decorations were depictions of the three magi who brought gifts of gold, frankincense and myrrh to the newborn baby Jesus. This had been an auspicious addition: when the Holy Land was conquered by Zoroastrian Persians in 614, the invaders were moved when they saw a depiction of the magi dressed in traditional oriental clothes so very like their own, and thus preserved the church.

In the echoing nave of the church cheers rang out for the new King Baldwin II and Queen Morphia. The great and the good of the Kingdom had turned out to witness the coronation, and the leaders of the clergy and the surrounding states were present. Among the spectators watching in awe as sovereignty was conferred upon this unlikely couple were three sisters: Melisende, Alice and Hodierna. They were Morphia's daughters, aged thirteen, eight and seven, and with the coronation of their parents all three became Princesses of Jerusalem. Their fates and that of Outremer were changed forever.

Princess Melisende, watching the coronation of her parents alongside her young sisters, would become the strongest queen the Kingdom would ever see. Alice and Hodierna would also grow into firebrands and become two of the most prominent political players of their day. Morphia and her daughters were the beginning of a formidable line of women rulers in Outremer.

Morphia, however, was Queen *Consort* of Jerusalem rather than Queen *Regnant*. This meant that her position as queen derived from her marriage to Baldwin II, rather than hereditary right. This in turn meant that her role was primarily to support her husband in his rule rather than to wield authority or influence of her own in political matters. Thus the authority wielded by queens consort differed greatly from queens regnant, who ostensibly held the same authority as reigning kings. A distinction must be made, however, between authority and power. Whether either a queen consort or a queen regnant had power depended entirely on the force of her personality and her ability to play the game of politics amid the climate of the time. Morphia wielded more power than any other queen consort in the Kingdom of Jerusalem, until perhaps Queen Maria Komnene some fifty years later.

Morphia was the first woman to preside as queen over the Kingdom of Jerusalem for any length of time, from 1118 to 1127. She was the first to wield influence in the Kingdom, and she was the first to provide heirs to inherit. Technically speaking, however, Morphia was only the third Queen of Jerusalem.

Baldwin II was the third crusading Frank to rule Jerusalem. The first had been Godfrey de Bouillon, who led the armies of the First Crusade over the walls of the city. He had refused the title 'King' out of deference to Christ, the only true 'King of Jerusalem', and was unmarried and had no heirs. He was succeeded by his brother, the wily Baldwin I, who likewise was childless, thus passing his throne to his cousin, Morphia's husband Baldwin II.

Morphia's predecessors as Queen Consort of Jerusalem were the unhappy wives of Baldwin I: one an Armenian princess like herself, named Arete;* and the other a powerful Sicilian countess, Adelaide del Vasto. Baldwin I shared his successor's name but not his temperament. He was married no fewer than three times, each more expediently and briefly than the last. He burned through wives at record speed, even for a medieval warlord, more preoccupied with extracting wealth from his brides than wooing them and making heirs.

Baldwin I had a long-standing record of being self-serving and deceitful when it came to personal relationships. During the First Crusade he captured the County of Edessa through a rather dishonourable act of skulduggery. He was welcomed by the city's ruler Thoros of Edessa, who was childless and took a liking to the charismatic and well-armed crusader from the West. Thoros adopted Baldwin I as his heir, and Baldwin I undertook the somewhat embarrassing ritual of joining his prospective and distinctly middle-aged parents naked under a hair shirt to complete the process of adoption. With this ceremony Baldwin I became the heir to the wealthy county. Just weeks later, his adoptive father Thoros was brutally killed in a civilian rebellion. As the riot progressed he appealed to Baldwin for aid, but Baldwin stood by and watched without lifting a finger to help. The people of Edessa, their bloodlust sated, allowed the succession to follow the writ of law and Baldwin was invested as Count of Edessa just days after Thoros' death.

This was only the beginning of Baldwin's political career. Not only was he Thoros' heir, but he was also his brother Godfrey's, and Godfrey died

---

* Traditionally, this woman has been known as 'Arda' by historians, despite there being no known primary evidence for this. Susan Edgington has argued convincingly that 'Arete' is more likely to be accurate.

less than a year after being invested as ruler of Jerusalem. A chronicler wrote that when Baldwin I learned of Godfrey's demise, 'he grieved a little for his brother's death but rejoiced more at his inheritance.' Power and glory meant more to Baldwin I than familial relationships, and this would demonstrate itself clearly in his treatment of his wives.

Godehilde, a Norman noblewoman and Baldwin I's first wife, died during the First Crusade on the journey to the East. Her brief marriage to Baldwin was full of adventure and intrigue. She was one of the very few noblewomen permitted to accompany their husbands on the First Crusade. Caught up in the fervour of the original expedition, she had been held as a hostage in Hungary alongside her husband as surety that the crusaders' armies would not pillage the Hungarian king's lands. This was unlikely to have been a life-threatening situation but the couple protested vehemently at being forced to stand hostage. They were released quickly and Godehilde finally made it to Asia Minor. She was received at the glittering court of Constantinople, presided over by the fiery-eyed Alexios Komnenos and under the watchful gaze of his daughter Anna. Godehilde's expedition to Jerusalem was destined to be cut short: she died before the campaign left Asia Minor, in 1097, in Marash in modern-day Turkey. Little can be said of Godehilde's relationship with her husband, except that it must have been more successful than his later marriages: she accompanied him on crusade when he was under no obligation to bring her. This indicates that he intended to continue his life with her and settle in the East.

Baldwin I does not seem to have been struck down by grief at Godehilde's death. He promptly remarried mid-crusade, following his acquisition of the County of Edessa. A council was summoned and advised Baldwin to strengthen his position in his new territory by marrying a local woman of noble birth and with connections to the Armenian rulers. Baldwin followed this advice and chose a local Armenian noblewoman as a bride: Arete. She was the daughter of a lord named Taftoc, and niece to the still more powerful leader Constantine who held a strategically important and well-fortified stronghold in the Taurus mountains and had large armies of elite soldiers at his disposal. Constantine and Taftoc, on account of their great wealth and power, were the most significant Armenian lords of the region and were tantamount to kings.

It was this wealth and power that attracted Baldwin I to Arete. This was a marriage of political convenience, and the bride brought with her the hefty dowry of 60,000 gold bezants. Bezants were minted in the Byzantine Empire and were in this period valuable coins – approximately

4.45 grams of 20.5-carat gold. This dowry was a significant sum of money and could easily pay an army or rebuild a city's defences. It was, however, never paid in full; only the initial instalment of 7,000 bezants made it to Baldwin's coffers. This insult would cause problems for Arete further down the line.

Less than three years after their marriage, Baldwin I was made King of Jerusalem and journeyed there to take the throne. Arete was therefore the first Queen of Jerusalem in name, but in practice she was nothing of the kind. When he travelled to Jerusalem, Baldwin left Arete behind in Edessa. The marriage was childless and so far under great strain: Arete's father had since lost his lands in battle and had fled to Constantinople and had never delivered the remaining sum of Arete's dowry. As such the marriage had brought neither the wealth nor the sought-after allegiance that had been promised.

After some years apart, Baldwin eventually summoned Arete to join him, no doubt under pressure from his nobles to at least try to father an heir for the Kingdom. She travelled overland to Antioch and then took a ship from the port of St Simeon to Jaffa. When she did arrive in Jerusalem, there is no suggestion that Baldwin I made much effort with his long-absent wife.

There is no record that Baldwin I ever bothered to have Arete crowned and before too long he began the process of repudiating her and having their marriage annulled. They had been married eight years when Baldwin I demanded the annulment based on the claim that Arete had been unfaithful to him on her voyage to join him in Jerusalem. The French chronicler Guibert of Nogent told a rip-roaring tale of rape by pirates during the journey. Despite the gusto with which Guibert relates the tale, it is unlikely to be true: such a scandal would have been more widely reported.

Despite its spurious authenticity, this alleged infidelity, consensual or otherwise, became the reason for Baldwin I to put Arete aside. These were flimsy grounds, and it is likely the true reason why Baldwin wanted rid of her was because her father had failed to deliver her promised dowry and she had produced no heirs. Beyond this, it was simply the case that an alliance with Taftoc of Armenia had been a tactical advantage in the partly Armenian County of Edessa but was politically useless in the Kingdom of Jerusalem. Medieval brides were expected to bring their husbands rich dowries, useful allegiances and heirs. Arete had done none of these things, and consequently she was forced to take the veil and enter a nunnery – the only respectable option for cast-off wives.

The nunnery in question was particularly grim. It was the newly consecrated Convent of St Anne, and while today it stands as the most peaceful and beautiful church in Jerusalem, in the early twelfth century it was a far from pleasant or lively place. Only very recently founded and without a superfluity of rich widows, it had only a handful of other nuns living there and so represented an austere and lonely life for Jerusalem's first queen. It seemed Arete would be expected to live the rest of her life in a glorified prison with scarcely any company. It was also a Catholic establishment, rather than Armenian or Greek Orthodox, and as such it would further alienate Arete. She had been raised an Eastern Christian, and while it is likely she would have adopted her husband's faith on marriage, it added insult to injury that even after his disposal of her she was imprisoned within a house dedicated to Catholicism.

Unsurprisingly, Arete was not pleased with this prospect and eventually exerted some pent-up will-power to secure a brighter future for herself. She managed to obtain permission from her former husband to leave the convent and travel to join her father in Constantinople. Perhaps seeking to make the most of her new-found freedom lest it be snatched away again, Arete led a colourful life at the Greek court once free of the controlling stare of her husband. William of Tyre asserts that when she reached the city she 'prostituted herself to men of both high and low rank'. There are subtle implications across several sources that Baldwin I was a homosexual, and it appears that the combination of three years in Baldwin I's bed followed by a stint in a convent had left Arete sexually ravenous.

Following this embarrassing debacle of a marriage and separation, Baldwin I married for a third time in 1112. This time his bride was Adelaide del Vasto of Sicily. This was a significantly advantageous match and perhaps this is why members of the court and church were willing to overlook the fact that any marriage undertaken by Baldwin I while Arete was still living would be both bigamous and illegal. The king ploughed ahead with the marriage because the Kingdom of Jerusalem, following a rocky first few years of existence under continuous harassment by enemies at the borders, was in dire need of a wealthy new queen. As a rich widow and the mother of the King of Sicily, Adelaide del Vasto would fill the vacancy nicely.

As the reigning King of Jerusalem, rather than the Count of the somewhat obscure Edessa, Baldwin I was now a far more attractive quantity as a bridegroom. Thus he was able to secure for himself a Western noblewoman of high rank and wealth. Adelaide was an odd

choice for a childless king who needed an heir; she had a grown-up son
and was well into middle age. However, when she travelled to Jerusalem
she came armed with both gold and fighting men, exactly the resources
Baldwin's administration in Outremer lacked. William of Tyre described
Adelaide as 'a wealthy woman of great influence . . . rich and possessed
of everything in great abundance', and compared her wealth to the
king's penury, writing, 'Baldwin on the contrary was poor and needy, so
that his means scarcely sufficed for his daily needs and the payment of
his knights. Hence he longed to supplement his scanty resources from
her super-abundance.'

Albert of Aachen similarly described the booty that Adelaide brought
with her and the great style in which she travelled:

> she had two trireme dromonds, each with five hundred men very expe-
> rienced in warfare; seven ships laden with gold, silver, purple and an
> abundance of jewels and precious garments; weapons, hauberks, hel-
> mets, shields resplendent with gold, and all the other weaponry which
> powerful men are accustomed to carry for the defence of their ships
> . . . [on the countess's ship] the mast was clad with purest gold and put
> forth rays from afar like the brilliance of the sun, and both ends of the
> ship, covered by craftsmanship with gold and silver, were a sight to
> wonder at . . . In one of the seven ships Saracen men who were very
> strong archers and glittered with the brilliance of their precious gar-
> ments were brought as a gift for the king, and their skill at archery was
> considered inferior to none in the region of Jerusalem.

In his eagerness to get his gauntleted fists on Adelaide's wealth,
Baldwin I agreed to the unusual condition that if their marriage were
childless, the throne of Jerusalem would pass to Adelaide's son from her
first marriage, Roger of Sicily. This agreed, Adelaide set sail for Outremer, laden with gold, grain and a fresh horde of Sicilian-Norman soldiers,
and the pair were quickly married.

Given Baldwin I's track record, it is unsurprising that this relationship ended just as disastrously as his previous marriage. Adelaide did
not produce an heir, and the marriage was widely (and correctly) criticised as bigamous, given that Arete still lived. Under pressure from
his nobles, fearing for his life and the fate of his immortal soul after
a period of serious illness, Baldwin I agreed to annul the marriage
after just five years and summoned Arete to return to Jerusalem. Arete
ignored his summons, but Adelaide was sent packing nonetheless. She
returned 'highly indignant' to Sicily, 'sad and sorrowing over the insult

offered her as well as over the futile waste of her wealth'. Baldwin I made sure to relieve her of both her wealth and her Sicilian soldiers, thereby swelling the ranks and coffers of the Kingdom of Jerusalem.

This was a public disgrace, and an unforgivable insult to the ruling house of Sicily. Adelaide's son, the young Roger of Sicily, was so incensed by this insult to his mother that he refused to send aid to the crusader states in Outremer for as long as he lived, a policy maintained by generations of his successors. William of Tyre expressed great sympathy for Adelaide, whom he describes as a 'noble and honourable lady'. He claims she was deceived in this venture by the machinations of the wicked and dissolute Arnulf, Patriarch of Jerusalem.

Baldwin I, despite his personal qualities as a leader, ultimately failed as king in securing the succession. He created a stable Kingdom but died without an heir, and the throne of Jerusalem passed to his cousin Baldwin, Count of Edessa.

MORPHIA AND BALDWIN II

Morphia was born in the Armenian region of Melitene to its ruler Gabriel and his wife. Melitene is now known as Malatya, an obscure city in eastern Turkey, famous only as the capital of the apricot-growing region. It lies in the south of the Anatolian Plateau near the banks of the Euphrates, and is one of the earliest continuously inhabited places in the world, situated on the edge of the Fertile Crescent. Malatya holds little draw for tourists, and amid its modern buildings few of the splendours of its medieval past remain. Once the capital of the medieval kingdom of Armenia Minor, at the time of Morphia's birth it was an important and prosperous city, strategically located and protected by the surrounding Tarsus Mountains and the Euphrates.

Morphia's parents, while Greek Orthodox Christians in religion, were Armenian in race, culture and language. Morphia would have grown up speaking Armenian, and possibly reading biblical Greek.

The Armenian Kingdom of Cilicia was an area of pivotal importance during the crusader period. It straddled the south of the Anatolian Plateau, controlling the mountain gateways through Asia Minor to the Holy Land. Beyond the strategic importance of the land, ethnic Armenians made up the bulk of the populations of the Christian settlements of Edessa and Antioch, and had a considerable presence in Jerusalem as well. When the Christians tried to encourage settlement in the remoter parts of Outremer, such as the desert Lordship of Oultrejourdain, there is evidence of them encouraging Armenian settlers to travel there. Baldwin II would also eventually pass a law granting Armenians special trade privileges in Jerusalem in order to promote their settlement. There is evidence of flourishing Armenian communities in every significant Christian city in Outremer. Beyond this, they were expert, specialist soldiers. Armenians had been variously co-existing with and fighting Muslims in the Middle East for centuries, and their expertise and advice would prove invaluable to the crusader armies at various points over the next two centuries, and were arguably 'most accomplished military architects in the Levant at the time of the first crusade.'*

In Jerusalem itself the Armenians also had a strong presence and great influence. The Armenian Apostolic Church had been founded in the first century AD and the Kingdom of Armenia had been the first nation to formally adopt Christianity as the state religion. From the birth of the Church, Armenian pilgrims had been travelling to Jerusalem to visit the Holy Places. Floor mosaics in Jerusalem bearing Armenian inscriptions date to the fifth century, and the Armenian presence in Jerusalem can be clearly documented still earlier than this. Moreover the Armenian church and the Armenian Christians had an identity and influence distinct from the Greek church of Constantinople, and even under Islamic rule had maintained influence and status within Jerusalem.

Morphia, then, was a princess of proud heritage. Her father Gabriel was a wealthy man, and in 1101, the twenty-five-year-old Morphia made a powerful marriage with Baldwin of Bourcq, one of the heroes of the First Crusade who, a year earlier, had been enfeoffed with the County of Edessa. Edessa was one of Outremer's most significant territories, and shared a border with Gabriel's territory in Melitene. Beyond this, it was a city of great significance to the history of Christianity, and this carried weight among the Western Christian armies.

Edessa is situated between the Tigris and Euphrates rivers, in the land known in ages past as Mesopotamia, or 'the land between the rivers'. It lies slightly to the north of the modern Turkish–Syrian border, in the centre of the Fertile Crescent. William of Tyre described its boundaries in crusader times as '[beginning] at the forest called Marrim and [extending] out toward the East beyond the Euphrates.' It was a land rich in history long before the crusaders made their marks on the

* George Hintlian, *The History of the Armenians in the Holy Land.*

territory. It was the first city to convert to Christianity and, occupying a strategic position at a crossroads between Europe and Asia, it stood once as one of the most important cities of the Christian East. Today, Byzantine cave tombs sit matter-of-factly in the rock beneath a stretch of modern houses, and the archaeological museum holds the world's earliest life-sized sculpture of a human. A stone's throw from the city is the archaeological site of Gobekli Tepe, the earliest known human temple, predating Stonehenge by some 7,000 years and casting fresh light on the relationship between the development of agriculture and that of religious worship. Many followers of Abrahamic religions believe Edessa to be the historic birthplace of Abraham, and the place in which he was burned by Nimrod. Legend has it that the flames turned to water, and formed the famous 'Pool of Abraham' that still exists in the city centre to this day and is a place of pilgrimage for Muslims.

Citadel of Edessa

For a medievalist the central point of interest in this city must be the great fortress that rises on an acropolis within the city, dominating the horizon. A deep moat surrounds the fortress, carved from the basalt on which the city stands, and above this are warm-coloured stone walls, restored in modern times but built by the Abbasids in the ninth century, who in turn were building on the remains of an even older structure dating back to antiquity. This was the citadel that Melisende, Alice and Hodierna were born in, and the marital home of Baldwin II and Morphia.

There is now not a single Christian church in Edessa – all were converted to mosques. Edessa is now called Urfa, or Sanliurfa ('glorious

Urfa'), because of the significant part it played in the Turkish wars of independence following World War I. The modern city, however, does not feel glorious, whatever its heritage. Even though it is an important site of pilgrimage, many of its inhabitants are held in the grip of poverty. But in the twelfth century Edessa was a bustling, heterogeneous centre filled with people from a variety of faiths and ethnicities, and situated on an important trade route. As a result it was a rich city, and that made its ruler a powerful man.

Baldwin was thus one of the most eminent noblemen in Outremer and marriage to him was doubtless a good match. Morphia's father paid well for this marriage and the valuable alliance it brought with it, shelling out a king's ransom of 50,000 gold bezants as her dowry. William of Tyre emphasises the importance of this gold: 'with her he received as dowry a large sum of money, of which he stood in great need'. In his entire chronicle William only mentions Morphia twice, and on each occasion emphasises the great dowry she brought with her, spending more time describing Morphia's money and relatives than Morphia herself.

Baldwin II proved to be the antithesis of his cousin when it came to human relationships. He was a loyal husband to Morphia and the proud father of four headstrong daughters. He never took action to put her aside once it became apparent that she would not give him sons.

Baldwin II had made his way to the East with the other princes of the First Crusade, had fought at the legendary sieges of Nicaea and Antioch, and had stormed the Holy City itself. He had a reputation for being a genuinely pious man, with knees calloused from prayer. He ruled well, defending his borders and rising to the many challenges that were hurled his way during the course of his reign.

He was an active soldier and was taken captive by the enemy on two occasions, on both of which his wife Morphia moved to be nearer to his place of imprisonment, and personally helped with the negotiations for his release. Besides his propensity for getting captured, Baldwin II's only shortcoming as a ruler was his genuine devotion to this same wife who failed to provide a male heir to continue his dynasty. The lack of sons did not prove a stumbling block in his marriage to Morphia, and the chronicles give the impression that he was as devoted a husband as it is perhaps possible to find in the medieval world.

At the time of his cousin's death and his sudden accession to power, Baldwin II was ruling comfortably as the Count of Edessa, a position he had occupied for eighteen years, since his cousin had vacated the office to take the throne in Jerusalem.

The gold that Morphia's father had offered and the promise of the

Armenian alliance were doubtless what attracted Baldwin to Morphia, who by medieval standards was decidedly over the hill at twenty-five. However, the gold was soon spent on soldiers, building work and other resources, and the early years of their marriage, while the couple ruled Edessa, were far from smooth.

Shortly after the wedding, Morphia's father Gabriel lost his territory of Melitene to Danishmend Turks and died soon after. Despite this blow, Morphia became pregnant in 1104 with the future Queen Melisende. Shortly after this baby was conceived, Baldwin II rode out to besiege the fortress of Harran in an effort to expand and secure his territory. Despite back-up arriving from Antioch, Baldwin II had overplayed his hand. The Christian armies were almost annihilated, and Baldwin was captured alongside his kinsman Joscelin of Courtenay, who had recently joined him in Edessa. This was a decisive blow against the Christians of Outremer and threw the states of Edessa and Antioch into turmoil.

Baldwin II remained in captivity for four years, during which time Morphia remained in Edessa, carrying her pregnancy to term, giving birth, and raising her infant daughter. This was her first child and, given the recent death of her father, the loss of her husband and the precarious position of Edessa in his absence, these years undoubtedly presented a steep learning curve for Morphia. Baldwin was ransomed in 1108, returning home to greet his wife and meet his daughter. Melisende was three years old when she first met her father, but the pair formed a close bond and he would fight her corner from that day forward. She would grow to be a woman after his own heart: strong, wise and reckless in equal measure.

Morphia and Baldwin's separation did not derail their marriage, and roughly a year after his return from captivity they welcomed their second daughter, Alice, and not long after that their third, Hodierna.

The strength of the bonds within this unusual medieval family unit can be clearly discerned through the honour and respect that Baldwin II paid to his wife and daughters on an ongoing basis. When he ascended the throne of Jerusalem in April 1118, he delayed his coronation until December, when his wife and daughters had been conveyed safely to join him. Morphia and Baldwin II were crowned together on Christmas Day 1118 in the Church of the Holy Nativity in Bethlehem.

Morphia was a wisely chosen wife, being thoroughly Christian and thoroughly Eastern, thus giving Baldwin a legitimacy and connection with the region that his predecessors had lacked. His children were half Armenian, daughters of both the crusade and the Eastern Orthodox church, which would position them uniquely well to govern the multi-cultural Kingdom of Jerusalem.

A KING IN CAPTIVITY

Despite Baldwin's clear regard for his children, their upbringing was far from smooth. Even following his release from captivity, his time as Count of Edessa was turbulent. Baldwin frequently fought not just with Muslim enemies but with other Franks, also quarrelling bitterly with the Armenian populations of his own territories, who plotted against him on numerous occasions. These difficulties meant that he was frequently separated from his family, owing to the need to lead his soldiers in battle.

A fourth daughter, Yvette, was born to Morphia two years after her coronation, the first child to be born to reigning monarchs in the Kingdom of Jerusalem. In 1123, when Yvette was three years old, the four sisters saw their father captured and imprisoned for a second time, while making a raid in eastern Anatolia. This was far more significant than his previous stint in captivity, since he was now the King of Jerusalem and the spearhead of the Christian military presence in Outremer. His captor was a Turkish emir named Balak.

Morphia distinguished herself both as a wife and as a queen in the months that followed. Not content to let her husband rot in a Muslim prison and their Kingdom and their family disintegrate around them, she devised a daring rescue mission. Favouring the skills of her own countrymen over the Antiochene Franks, she sent one hundred Armenian men to infiltrate Balak's fortress at Kharpart during Balak's absence. These Armenians travelled to Kharpart disguised as monks but wearing daggers and swords under their robes. Upon reaching the gates of the city, they put on an elaborate performance, saying they needed to speak to the governor to complain of the ill treatment they had received along their journey. The credulous guards unbolted the doors of the city, and as soon as the 'monks' were admitted, they began to slaughter every Turk in sight. They then released Baldwin and Joscelin from their chains and gave them weapons with which to fight their way out. Somehow Joscelin of Courtenay managed to slip away into the night, but Baldwin remained caught up in the struggle.

Despite her men having freed the prisoners, Morphia's rescue mission was far from complete. While her retainers had reached her husband and killed the guards, they still had to get themselves safely out of the city and across the border into Christian territory, and this proved far more problematic than the first phase of the operation. They had blown their cover, and by this point the alarm had been raised. The city was now awake and Turks were pouring forth from every barracks to prevent them escaping before Balak's return.

Balak meanwhile sensed that something was wrong in Kharpart and woke from a vision, determined to return to his fortress and his high-status prisoners. Baldwin II and Morphia's Armenian agents had by this point succeeded in taking control of the citadel at the city's centre, and while they had bought themselves momentary safety with this manoeuvre, they were still no closer to freedom. Balak's forces swooped down on the city and besieged them. They held out as best they could, rejecting Balak's honeyed words and promises of freedom in exchange for surrender, but were ultimately recaptured by the Turk. Balak spared the life of his valuable royal prisoner and contented himself with transferring him to the more secure fortress at Harran, but he was not so lenient with the audacious Armenians who had hoodwinked his guards and come so close to freeing his valuable hostages. He killed them viciously, variously flaying, burning and burying them alive.

Balak did not long outlive these victims, and on his death a few months later the guardianship of Baldwin transferred to his kinsman Timurtash. Timurtash did not like the responsibility or liability of having to contain the restless King of Jerusalem, and so let it be known that for the right ransom, he would release him.

Meanwhile, Morphia had journeyed north to be as close to her captive husband as she could. She – along with Joscelin of Courtenay, who had escaped and joined her – entered negotiations with Timurtash.

Timurtash demanded a ransom of 80,000 dinars for Baldwin II, 20,000 of which were to be paid up front. In addition, he demanded that the territories of Athareb, Zerdana, el-Djezr, Kefer-thab and Azaz be yielded to him, and that King Baldwin promise to support him in his wars against the Bedouin. The lands Timurtash demanded belonged to the Principality of Antioch rather than the Kingdom of Jerusalem, and thus were not legally Baldwin's to resign, but nevertheless the king acquiesced to Timurtash's terms. Despite this ready agreement, such a complex and expensive ransom could not be handed over all at once, and if territory were to be released and troops sent, Baldwin II had to be free to give commands. The 20,000 dinars were duly paid, but it was arranged that high-status hostages would be given as a guarantee that the other terms of the ransom would be honoured in due course. Timurtash demanded

Yvette, the King's youngest daughter, as hostage and would brook no opposition.

THE ORDEAL OF PRINCESS YVETTE

Why the infant Yvette was demanded as a hostage remains unclear. It may be that she was the least important of his daughters and thus the one he was most likely to agree to part with. More likely, however, is the explanation that she enjoyed a special status within the royal household. Perhaps she was her father's favourite, the cherished youngest daughter. This tallies with the evidence we have that Baldwin II made arrangements to visit Yvette at Shaizar during her time in captivity. Moreover, Yvette was the only one of Baldwin's daughters to be born when her parents were the reigning monarchs of Jerusalem, and thus was the only one of the princesses to enjoy the status of 'porphyrogeniture'. Her steely mother, for the sake of her husband and the Kingdom, agreed. This separation must have taken a toll not only on the girl and her mother, but also on her three elder sisters, Melisende, Alice and Hodierna.

Baldwin II, after sixteen months in captivity, was released on 29 August 1124. While the Kingdom breathed a sigh of relief at the return of its king, Baldwin was not yet in a position to relax. While he had escaped his gruelling imprisonment, during which time he had only been fed twice a week and had seen his comrades tortured, his youngest daughter had essentially traded places with him and, for all he knew, now suffered similar torments. Joscelin had also been forced to give up his ten-year-old son as a hostage. The two fathers now had the grim task of choosing between securing their territories and bringing their children to safety.

Despite his apparent love for his daughters, Baldwin's next moves took a serious gamble with Yvette's life. Instead of returning to Jerusalem to Morphia and his remaining daughters, he broke the terms of his ransom and ran a great risk in doing so; two of Timurtash's other hostages were put to death as a result of this. Instead of allying with Timurtash against the Bedouin, as promised, Baldwin allied with the Bedouin against Timurtash and marched on Aleppo. Fulcher of Chartres claims that one of his motivations in doing this was to try to force Timurtash to release Yvette. The siege was a long drawn-out fiasco, and after four months of futile effort the king finally returned to Morphia in Jerusalem, two years after being taken captive. It is unclear why Timurtash did not execute Yvette in retaliation for the Siege of Aleppo, but perhaps he knew that such a blow would move matters from the political to the personal. If he harmed her, not only would any prospect of the rest of the ransom disappear, but he would bring the full fury of the Kingdom of Jerusalem down upon himself.

While ultimately no harm came to Yvette, despite her father flagrantly disregarding the terms of his ransom, and indeed going so far as to ally with the Bedouin against Timurtash, it was an episode that would cast a shadow over the rest of her life. One contemporary chronicle claims that Yvette was 'violated' by the Saracens who held her. This text may have been written with the intent of inspiring more Western knights to become crusaders and travel to the East, and therefore it is likely that this claim of sexual abuse was an invention designed to shock and appal Western readers. However, the fact remains that Yvette was ostensibly 'tainted' by her time as a hostage. While her three sisters Melisende, Alice and Hodierna made important marriages and became the premier noblewomen of the region, Yvette instead entered a convent. The *Estoire d'Outremer*, a thirteenth-century French chronicle, implies that this decision was due to Yvette's time in captivity. In the eyes of medieval knights, a Christian girl who had been held hostage by Muslims was tainted by the experience and rendered unfit for Christian marriage.

The fact that Yvette was subjected to this treatment and traded in this way raises some serious questions about the image so far gleaned of Baldwin II as a devoted father and family man. If we do believe this image of him to be genuine, then it gives a far stronger indication of the desperation that Morphia and Baldwin must have felt if they were persuaded to part with their youngest child. While Baldwin might have trusted Timurtash's honour not to hurt her, he chose to break their agreement, which could have resulted in Timurtash killing the girl. This episode casts a bleak shadow on the otherwise exemplary legacy of Baldwin II.

In 1125, after almost a year in captivity, Yvette was returned to her family. She was five years old. Following the successful sieges of Tyre and Azaz,* by plundering the city of Azaz her father had raised funds to pay a cash ransom for his daughter. Morphia was able to welcome her youngest daughter home at last. However, within a few years of being reunited with Yvette, Morphia died of natural causes in the Kingdom of Jerusalem.

In the last years of her life, her relationship with her husband must have been under considerable strain. Yvette was the last child she

* The Siege of Tyre occurred and was won during Baldwin's captivity.

conceived, and this was likely due both to Morphia's advancing age but also because, in the later years of her life, she and her husband were once again separated for months and years at a time. The quality of tireless military campaigner that made Baldwin II so successful as a king must have made him a difficult man to be married to.

Morphia was mourned by her husband and daughters. Beyond this, her death was significant in that there was now no hope of her conceiving a son to inherit the Kingdom. Baldwin II did not, as one might have expected, remarry following the death of his wife of twenty-five years. His decision not to remarry meant firstly that his daughters were now the undisputed heiresses to the Kingdom of Jerusalem, and secondly that for five years, between Morphia's death and the accession of her daughter, there was no queen in Jerusalem. Baldwin's decision must be seen as a mark of his devotion to his late wife. According to the custom of the time, as a man still in good health, it was his duty to remarry and father more heirs for the Kingdom – hopefully a male child, at long last. Instead he remained single until the end of his days, and never entered into negotiations for a new wife.

Morphia was interred at the Benedictine Abbey of St Mary in the valley of Jehoshaphat. This abbey had been founded by Godfrey de Bouillon on the site believed to be the place of the Virgin Mary's tomb. Morphia's choice to be buried here set a precedent for the Queens of Jerusalem to be buried apart from their husbands. Baldwin II would follow the tradition of his predecessors and be buried in state in the Church of the Holy Sepulchre. Morphia's choice to be buried separately from him was an odd one for a queen who enjoyed such a long relationship with her husband. It is possible their relationship had deteriorated in the final years of their marriage, with his renewed captivity and the loss of Yvette.

This is not necessarily the case, though. Anyone visiting the chapel will understand why Morphia may have chosen this particular religious site to be her resting place over the great Church of the Holy Sepulchre. The abbey stands at the foot of the Mount of Olives, beyond the walls of the Old City of Jerusalem. The Church of the Holy Sepulchre, standing as it does in the heart of the Old City, on the edge of the souk, and inundated with pilgrims and tourists, can feel to a visitor more like a bustling religious marketplace than a place in which to reflect and commune with a higher power. It must have been the same in the twelfth century, for then, as now, it was the global centre of Christian pilgrimage and an object of warfare. St Mary's Abbey, on the other hand, is quieter, darker and filled with incense. Morphia's chosen resting place is a small side chapel, off to the left of the monumental staircase, beneath several other chapels, and with a modest dome overhead. Her tomb is no longer visible to visitors, hidden by smooth stone walls and altars to saints built over it. The tomb of Mary mother of God seems a fitting burial place for a queen who was not vocal in political life but was truly religious and a mother of four daughters.

Whatever Morphia's reasons for choosing this location, it was a fortuitous decision. The tombs of the Kings of Jerusalem in the Holy Sepulchre were destroyed, but St Mary's Chapel survives. It is still possible to visit the chapel where Morphia was buried and see the alcove where she lies. The date of her death is recorded in an elaborate psalter belonging to her eldest daughter Melisende, and is remembered as 1 October. Although the year is not given, it is likely it was 1127. Morphia's legacy was profound, leaving behind four formidable daughters, and the imprint of Armenian culture on the crusader kingdoms.

Steven Runciman, a beloved and imaginative historian of the crusades, described Baldwin and Morphia as the 'perfect image of conjugal bliss'. It is easy to detect a note of ironic cynicism in this statement, as this analysis of their relationship is certainly sweeping and superficial. While it may be tempting to see the length and success of their marriage as proof of harmony, to do so would be to ignore the complexities of their relationship and the many hurdles they had to overcome. Baldwin married Morphia for money; in 1114 he threw the Armenian population – Morphia's people – out of Edessa; and he twice got himself captured on arguably unnecessary raiding trips, leaving Morphia isolated and vulnerable with their young children. They were separated forcibly for over five years while Baldwin was imprisoned, and eventually Morphia was forced to give up Yvette as part of the hostage negotiations. The pressure Morphia must have been under and the strains that these events put on their relationship can only be guessed at.

In spite of this, it is clear that there did exist a strong and deep bond between the couple. Their fidelity to one another, the lengths to which Baldwin went to include his wife in his coronation, and the initiative Morphia took to attempt to secure his release from captivity speak volumes about their relationship.

HEIRESS TO A KINGDOM

For all his risk taking with his youngest daughter's life, Baldwin II took no chances with his daughters' futures when he returned to Jerusalem following his two-year absence. Yvette was recovered, and he took care to ensure that his elder daughters married suitable husbands. He took particular care with the betrothal of his precocious eldest daughter, Melisende. Whoever was chosen to be Melisende's husband would be the next King of Jerusalem, and thus the priority was not to find a 'good match' for the princess but rather to find a competent ruler for the Kingdom. Melisende needed a husband who could offer wealth, soldiers and leadership expertise.

Melisende's father made his regard for her clear throughout her childhood. She was thirteen when Baldwin II ascended the throne, and from that day forward she stood as heiress to the Kingdom of Jerusalem. In March 1129 Baldwin II issued a charter for the Holy Sepulchre, to which Melisende gave her consent: *Milissenda filia regis hoc laudat et consentit.* This demonstrated that Melisende was taking an active role in politics, was present at meetings of the Haute Cour (High Council), and was being groomed for succession. A short time after this, her status had clearly increased, as she was referred to in a similar document as *Milisenda filia regis et regni Ierosolimitani haeres* – daughter of the king and heir to the Kingdom of Jerusalem. This was an uncommon honour and position to be afforded to a medieval princess, and more than this, it gives us a glimpse of Baldwin's ultimate intentions regarding the succession.

No rules had yet been developed in the Latin East with regard to succession, and indeed the specific conundrum of female succession. Thus far, the crown had passed to brother and then to cousin, based on convenience and the logistics of who was present with a decent claim at the death of the king. Given that the first two rulers of the Kingdom of Jerusalem had died childless, there was no precedent for the crown to be handed down the generations from parent to child. Baldwin II made it his mission to establish this tradition, and leave his Kingdom to his daughter.

No matter what Melisende's personal qualities, or her relationship with her father, it would have been impossible for Baldwin to name her sole heir to the Kingdom of Jerusalem. Despite the greater freedoms beginning to be enjoyed by women in Outremer and the more liberal inheritance laws of the region, unmarried women did not inherit thrones. The Kingdom of Jerusalem was a military state under continual harassment. The monarch had to be a military leader as well as a political one, able to wear armour and lead vassals to war. This was a step too far, even for Melisende. Therefore a husband had to be found for her, and he must be such a man whom the barons would accept, and a strong enough man to defend the interests of Melisende and any children they would have. The barons of Outremer were unruly and motivated by self-interest. They were variously manipulatively calculating and rashly foolhardy, and they needed a strong monarch to keep them in line. The decision as to who would be Melisende's partner was a matter of state, a decision to be made by the leading barons of the realm as well as Melisende's father.

It was decided that a Westerner with strong ties to the aristocracy of France and the ability to bring a new influx of fighting men to the East with him would be the most beneficial choice for the Kingdom. The Haute Cour conferred and dispatched an embassy to the West to search out suitable candidates. Baldwin baited the hook for Melisende's husband with the promise of the two rich coastal cities of Acre and Tyre to hold during his lifetime. This was a very generous settlement, as these two cities together made up most of the wealth of the Kingdom of Jerusalem, valuable trading ports as they were.

The man eventually chosen for this job was Fulk, Count of Anjou. He was a great magnate of medieval Europe and an experienced crusader and soldier. He was also considerably older than his royal fiancée, and considerably less attractive. Despite the attractions that marriage to Melisende presented, Fulk would not have been tempted to resign his powers in France to journey to Jerusalem to wed a girl he scarcely knew for anything less than the promise of the throne of Jerusalem. This may have been why, when beginning to search for a husband for the princess, her status was increased in charters and court documents, explicitly naming her as heiress to the Kingdom. The men considering marriage to her wanted to be quite sure they were marrying into the line of succession.

To confirm this, the agreement drawn up on the occasion of Fulk and Melisende's wedding, signed by the barons, stipulated that Fulk would inherit Baldwin's power. Melisende was side-lined, or so it seemed. Fulk wanted to be assured that both Baldwin's kingship and Melisende's status as the sole and undisputed heir were confirmed before he gave up his lands in France. In addition to Melisende being named as the heir in official documents, the Pope of the day, Honorius II, issued a letter to Baldwin that both formally confirmed his kingship and recommended Fulk to him.

Fulk arrived in the East 'attended by an honourable retinue of nobles and with a magnificence and pomp which surpassed that of kings', and the wedding was celebrated with great style on 2 June 1129. William of Tyre and other court chroniclers did not deem it necessary to record the details of the royal weddings of Outremer, in all likelihood because they assumed their readers would be familiar with the style of celebrations. In contrast, a Muslim travel writer, Ibn Jubayr, who travelled from Andalusia to the Holy Land in the twelfth century and witnessed a Christian wedding there, was so struck by the spectacle that he gave a detailed description of the event, from which we can deduce something of what Melisende's must have been like. He describes the bride emerging from her door, escorted by two male family members. To Ibn Jubayr, usually so hateful towards the Christians in his writing, she was a vision of loveliness that moved him to awe at her beauty:

> She was most elegantly garbed in a beautiful dress from which trailed a long train of golden silk. On her head she wore a gold diadem covered by a net of woven gold, and on her breast was a like arrangement. Proud she was in her ornaments and dress, walking with the little steps of half a span, like a dove, or in the manner of a wisp of cloud. God protect us from the seduction of the sight.

In front of this beguiling bride walked a group of musicians, playing jubilant music in honour of the occasion. Behind them came a procession of noblemen dressed in their finest clothing, next the bride and her male kin, and behind them the female nobility and her female kin, all richly attired as well, preening and proud in their trappings of wealth. This elegant and lavish procession led the bride to the house of the groom through crowds of dazzled onlookers, Muslim and Christian alike. There the wedding was celebrated with a feast that lasted all the day. This was merely the wedding of a wealthy woman, rather than royalty, and it was still enough to stun Ibn Jubayr with its beauty and sense of occasion. He was anything but provincial, hailing from Granada, the richest city of Moorish Andalusia, and recently having travelled through the splendours of Damascus, Baghdad and other great cities of the East.

Melisende's wedding to Fulk doubtless followed a similar pattern but would have been even more gorgeous and of still greater opulence. Melisende too would have worn a dress of golden silk, but one also richly adorned with gems in the Eastern style, and she would have been bedecked with jewels testifying to her status as heiress to a Kingdom. The nobles that witnessed her wedding would have been the highest of the land, including the king, her father, and the women that followed in procession behind her would have included her sisters Hodierna and Yvette, likewise displaying their wealth and status through jewellery and fine silks. The church she was led to would not have been the cathedral of Acre, but the Church of the Holy Sepulchre, and the house from which she was escorted would have been the palace of the Kings of Jerusalem. It would have been a wedding of rare splendour.

Melisende was the second of Baldwin's daughters to marry, wedding Fulk in 1129, three years after her younger sister Alice had married Bohemond II and become Princess of Antioch. When Melisende did wed at last, it was at the age of twenty-four. Her marriage to Fulk began well, with Baldwin II carving out a position for him in the governing of the realm. The surest sign of the success of their marriage was the birth of a son within a year of their nuptials. He was named Baldwin for his grandfather: Jerusalem had a direct male heir at last.

EMPRESS MATILDA

Among the illustrious connections that Fulk brought with him from his power base in the West was the fact that he was father-in-law to the heiress of England – Matilda, eldest daughter of Henry I.

Matilda had left England as a child in 1114 to live in Germany and marry the Holy Roman Emperor. When she left, her older brother William stood as the heir to her father's crown and there seemed little question of a struggle for the succession. Catastrophe struck, however: a ship taking Matilda's brother across the English Channel sank off the coast of Barfleur in the winter of 1120, catapulting England into an unprecedented succession crisis. Rumour has it that the captain of the ship managed to keep his head above water, but when he saw that the king's son had drowned, he let himself sink back beneath the waves rather than face the wrath of the prince's father. There was now no male heir to inherit King Henry I's crown. Moreover, no one was willing to consider Matilda an heiress to England while she was married to Emperor Henry V, as to leave England to the wife of the German Emperor would result in the independent Kingdom of England being absorbed into his empire.

This objection was circumvented by Henry V's sudden death in 1125, which left Matilda a widow, available for remarriage and a viable candidate to be heir to her father's kingdom. In 1127, after being summoned to join her father's court, Matilda was proclaimed heiress to the English crown, and all the nobles of the realm were compelled to swear an oath to support her.

As with Melisende, the choice of Matilda's husband became an extremely important one. Henry I, like Baldwin II, was impressed by the qualities demonstrated by the Counts of Anjou, and thus arranged a marriage between Matilda and Fulk of Anjou's son and heir, Geoffrey. As with the marriage between Melisende and Fulk, there was a disparity in ages between the couple, except in this instance Matilda at twenty-four was the older party, marrying a boy of just fifteen. The nuptials were celebrated at Le Mans on 17 June 1128. Three weeks before, Fulk had publicly taken the cross and vowed to travel to Jerusalem.

Henry I's settling of his kingdom on his daughter served as the model for Baldwin II proclaiming Melisende his heir. She was only formally recognised as Baldwin's heir *after* Matilda was recognised as Henry's. Fulk of Anjou endorsed both declarations; the first concerned the marriage of his son, and the second concerned his own proposed marriage to Melisende. It is possible that he insisted Melisende receive the same recognition as Matilda had in England, in order to guarantee her succession. The recognition of female succession in the West paved the way for Melisende's inheritance in the East.

However, despite Matilda's marriage to Geoffrey and her father's support, she was not a popular choice among the Anglo-Norman barons. They rankled at the notion of accepting female rule and an Angevin king. Moreover, Matilda was regarded as more German than English, given that she had spent her formative years at the German court. Thus, despite Matilda's inheritance serving as a model for Melisende's, Matilda had far more trouble in claiming hers. Matilda's throne was usurped by her male cousin Stephen of Blois in 1135, which set the wheels in motion that would plunge England into a fourteen-year civil war from 1139 to 1153, whereas Melisende and her husband would claim their throne almost without a hitch. That said, the matter of their succession to the throne did not go quite as smoothly as Fulk had anticipated.

A KING'S DYING WISH

In August 1131 Baldwin II was gravely ill. The old king was dying, worn out by a life of incessant warfare and travel. He was moved from the royal residence to the palace of the Patriarch next to the Church of the Holy Sepulchre. As he received the last rites and confessed his sins, Baldwin II's thoughts once again turned to the succession.

He summoned to his bedside Melisende, her husband Fulk, their baby son and a small council including the Patriarch of Jerusalem. With these people standing witness, a new document was drawn up. This, signed only by the hand of the ailing king and by none of his barons, nor by the church, changed the future of the Kingdom of Jerusalem and the position of women in the medieval Middle East forever.

Baldwin II's new will dictated that the inheritance of the kingship of Jerusalem was bestowed in equal measure between Princess Melisende, her husband Fulk and their infant son, the future Baldwin III. Any objection Fulk of Anjou may have raised to this unsanctioned and shocking change was quietened by the solemnity of the situation. A king was dying, surrounded by his family and supporters. It was not the time for his son-in-law to start grumbling about previous agreements. Perhaps Fulk did not expect the new will to be legally binding, given the circumstances, but the document held strong despite its dubious creation, which had ignored virtually every legal procedure and convention.

This was an event of almost unparalleled significance with regard to the standing of women in the society of Outremer. Fulk had doubtless believed that the crown and its power would pass solely to him. The notion of shared power was wholly foreign. Why else would he have turned his back on rich possessions in France in favour of marriage to Melisende in unstable Outremer? The fact that Baldwin chose to bequeath the power of a king to a woman alongside his son-in-law (his adopted *male* heir) gave credibility to the 'distaff' line and the idea of cognatic succession, as opposed to agnatic succession. Beyond this, it was a formal acknowledgement of women's abilities beyond the domestic. Melisende had been raised at her father's side, she had the support of the Haute Cour and had taken a position of political importance from a young age. Her father knew her quality, and this was his formal acknowledgement of this. While it can certainly be argued that Baldwin II was simply ensuring his grandson's inheritance with this manoeuvre, and that Melisende's rights were merely a vehicle for securing little Baldwin III's, Baldwin II was a steely and pragmatic ruler. Even if his end goal was the succession of Baldwin III, he must have believed his daughter was capable of defending both the Kingdom and the interests of her family when making this decision and leaving power jointly to her as well.

In practice, Baldwin II's division of the Kingdom between three heirs had little consequence in the immediate aftermath of his death. It certainly did not mean the Kingdom would be divided into three parts between a man, a woman and a baby. Even if each of the three were equally entitled to a share of power, the Kingdom would not be carved up, and Fulk would still enjoy nominal rule. Baldwin's will gave Melisende authority, but it did not necessarily give her power. However, in an age and region where symbolism was given such importance, it was still a highly significant tactic to have deployed, and the dying king must have known this.

It seems several concerns were weighing on Baldwin II's mind, and it seems likely that he felt he could not get away with so sly a political manoeuvre in any other context than the solemnity of the deathbed. He thus waited until such a moment when Fulk could not decently raise opposition, and when many of his most vocally argumentative barons were absent.

The question must be asked: what prompted Baldwin to make this deathbed alteration to his will? There are two main reasons. The first is straightforward: he wanted to ensure that the power of kingship remained within his bloodline, and within the bloodline of the original crusaders. The second is more complex and hinges on the instability and fragility of the Kingdom of Jerusalem and the surrounding principalities. The threat from Muslim foes was too great to risk leaving rule solely to such a divisive figure as Fulk had proven to be. Despite his pedigree, wealth and experience of Outremer, he was to the local nobility little more than an interloper who failed to understand the intricacies of the region's internal politics. Fulk, to the end of his days, would remain more Western than Eastern in spirit and loyalties. Baldwin must have seen that it would be wiser to bequeath power also to Melisende, a Princess of Outremer from her first breath, who had grown up as heir of Jerusalem.

Fulk had impressed the nobility of the Kingdom with the vast retinue of knights he had brought with him, but that retinue also brought with it complications. All these men would expect to be given lands, titles and other privileges in the East as reward for their loyalty and service. This influx of immigrants to Outremer resulted in mixed feelings among the Palestinian barons, who began to fear that their wealth, jobs and lands were under threat. They were wary of Fulk and his followers and probably came to regard them as an unwanted intrusion.

Baldwin II was well aware of these potential conflicts and consequently deemed it imprudent to confer the kingship on Fulk alone. In allowing Melisende to share the throne, Baldwin II ensured that the succession was not as stark a change in ruler as it otherwise might have been, and would safeguard unity among the nobility of Outremer.

The need for such unity was great. The foes of the Kingdom of Jerusalem were beginning to unite under the Atabeg Zengi, and posed a far more significant threat than previously. With the rise of Zengi and the extension of his influence from Mosul to Aleppo, the disparate Muslim groups in the region began to unite under one commander and structure their resistance to the Christians far more cohesively.

Zengi was rumoured to be the child of a German princess, Ida, Magravine of Austria, captured at the Battle of Heraclea in 1101 and carried off to a harem to be the sex-slave of a Muslim lord. Although this is hardly plausible, it was part of crusading legend and folklore, and demonstrated the mystique surrounding this warrior-prince of the Muslims. In his lifetime, Zengi would garner himself a ferocious reputation, not only on the battlefield but within his own court. He was a tall man with 'melted eyes'. Zengi was one of three Muslim heroes known for their efforts in undermining and defeating the Franks in the East, the other two being his son Nur ad-Din and Saladin himself.

Muslim sources, which usually tend to err on the side of cliché and praise of their heroic figures, make no such efforts on Zengi's behalf and uniformly portray him as a brutal and tyrannical leader from the start. Usama ibn Munqidh related that for every soldier that deserted, two innocent men would be cut in half as punishment. Another chronicler recorded how, in a drunken fit of rage, Zengi cast off one of his wives and watched while the grooms in his stables gang raped her. He was feared as much by his own people as his enemies.

That said, the chroniclers are also admiring of his achievements: a tirelessly effective military leader, during his lifetime he earned such epithets as 'the hero', 'the warrior of the faith' and 'the falcon prince'. Ibn al-Athir believed that Zengi was the leader that the Muslim world had been awaiting, and would spearhead the resistance to the Franks and cause Islam to unite, to rise up and repel them from the East. He wrote passionately in his chronicle: 'Allah wished to set over the Franks someone who could requite the evil of their deeds [. . .] he did not see anyone more capable of that command, more solid of inclination, stronger of purpose, and more penetrating than the lord.' This man was the main antagonist against the Franks in the final years of Baldwin II's reign and in the early years of Melisende's. He would prove to be a ferocious adversary.

In 1128, Zengi had managed to take possession of the strategically important Syrian city of Aleppo, which confirmed his status as a true threat to the Christians. Fear of Zengi's expansion and its implications may well have been what prompted Baldwin II to accelerate Melisende's marriage to Fulk in the first place. Baldwin was anxious to secure his succession, to have a strong partner for his heir and to ensure that she would produce a male child. Beyond this, there was a chronic manpower shortage in Outremer in the final years of Baldwin II's reign. Ten years earlier, in 1119, the previous ruler of Aleppo had won a decisive victory against the Principality of Antioch in a battle so ferocious, it is known to history as the Battle of the Field of Blood. This was a military fiasco with serious long-term ramifications for the Christians of Outremer, as the vast majority of the Antiochene military elite was wiped out and the city was turned into a city of widows overnight.

Baldwin II did not want to further weaken the position of the Christians in the East by leaving his realm in the hands of the unpopular Fulk. It would be better to leave power also to his daughter, the half-Armenian and thoroughly Eastern Melisende, who would have the loyalty of the native nobles and links with the indigenous Christians of the region through her mixed heritage.

Female succession was a touchy subject in the medieval world. It contradicted the highly patriarchal principles by which society was governed, and consequently the idea of putting forward a woman as the heir to a kingdom was deeply unusual in both Europe and the Middle East. It was a risky business in both locations, and it is a mark of the difference in the circumstances of the two regions that Baldwin II of Jerusalem's will held, while Henry I of England's did not. This clearly demonstrates that one of the main factors enabling Melisende to become a Queen of Jerusalem in her own right was the instability of the region she was living in. The desperation for stability and continuity in Outremer, alongside the shortage of male heirs, proved the difference between Melisende and Fulk's smooth accession and the struggle of Matilda and Geoffrey.

Baldwin II had another key reason for dividing power equally between Fulk, Melisende and his infant grandson. He may have been troubled by the very real possibility that Fulk would try to put Melisende aside and marry another woman, and so Baldwin wanted to invest her with her own distinct hereditary right. Since the triumvirate he instigated included the infant Baldwin III, if Melisende were to die or be put aside, and Fulk remarried, then the throne could not pass to any offspring of Fulk's next union.

Baldwin II and Joscelin of Edessa (who both died in 1131) represented the last of the original crusaders, the founders who built and defended the Kingdom of Jerusalem. These men abandoned the lives they had been given in the West to undergo a perilous journey and forge new lives. They had gone through extreme hardship and risked death on numerous occasions, and seen friends and comrades die in order to carve out Christian territory where there was none, and to maintain it against constant attacks from Muslims. Fulk was an outsider. Despite his visit to the Holy Land in 1120, he did not have Jerusalem in his blood as Melisende did, nor had he bled for it as Baldwin had. It would have seemed inappropriate both to Baldwin and his barons to let the hard-won prize of Jerusalem pass to a Western knight who had not suffered for and earned the privilege.

Beyond this, we should return to the original and perhaps most obvious reason why Baldwin left his Kingdom to his daughter: he was proud of her and recognised her abilities. Melisende displayed strength, charisma and 'uncommon wisdom' during her tumultuous reign, and these qualities would doubtless have begun to be present in her youth.

Beyond her personal qualities, Melisende had several natural advantages over Fulk. She already commanded the loyalty of the Haute Cour and of the local populations, which included Western Christians, Armenians and Greek Orthodox, given her connection through her mother both to Armenians and the Greek Orthodox faith. For the vast majority of Melisende's childhood Baldwin had either been imprisoned or away fighting, and so her upbringing would have been left primarily to Morphia, no doubt resulting in a close familiarity with Eastern Christian customs.

More important, however, than Baldwin's reasons for allowing Melisende's inheritance was Melisende's ability to safeguard it and maintain it. A lesser woman would simply have bowed to her husband's will and the customs of the time and allowed power that was rightfully hers to simply meld with her husband's, never daring to voice or enforce her own opinions. Melisende would adopt a distinctly opposite approach, and took no prisoners when it came to defending her hereditary right to Queenship of Jerusalem.

Despite the legal objections to Baldwin's deathbed will, Melisende and Fulk were anointed and crowned jointly on 14 September 1131 in the Church of the Holy Sepulchre.

2

ALICE, THE REBEL PRINCESS OF ANTIOCH

ALICE AND BOHEMOND: A MATCH MADE IN HEAVEN?

Morphia's second daughter, Alice, carried three names during her life. She was born Alice of Edessa, came of age as Alice of Jerusalem and died Alice of Antioch. She was the first of her four sisters to marry, and at the time of her mother's death in 1127 she was seventeen years old and living hundreds of miles north of Jerusalem, at her marital home in the city of Antioch.

Antioch was the jewel of the Christian East. Once the capital of the Roman Orient, founded by a general in the army of Alexander the Great, in the medieval period the city and its territories formed an important frontier state between the Byzantine Empire, the Seljuk Turks and the Armenians of Cilicia. Despite the decline of the Byzantine Empire's power in the wake of the Arab invasions, Antioch still remained a city of great importance. It had been won by Bohemond of Taranto after a gruelling siege during the First Crusade. It was the second crusader state to be created in Outremer, and Bohemond had installed himself as its first prince. Nestled in a valley of unusual and enduring beauty on the banks of the Orontes, the medieval city was a cosmopolitan hub of culture. With an imposing hilltop citadel and colossal walls encircling the city, Antioch was a haven in the war-torn frontier region of the Nur Mountains. The same remains true today. It is no longer protected from war and raids by the high Byzantine walls, but rather by the closed Turkish–Syrian border that lies just twenty kilometres to the east of the city.

Medical staff, soldiers, journalists and NGO workers who venture into Idlib regard the city as a safe place and a welcome respite after the instability of Syria. The city's glory, that shone so brightly in antiquity and the Middle Ages, has all but worn away, but modern Antioch (Antakya) is still rich in atmosphere: the air is thick with history. If one ventures out of the city and into the more remote areas around it, ruins of the once impregnable walls can still be found clinging to the mountainsides. The most impressive remains are those of the Iron Gate which forms a bridge across the now trickling Orontes. Over one thousand years old, this structure gives a sense of the massive scale of the walls: three metres thick, made of solid stone, and inestimably high. It is the one surviving gate of the walls of Antioch, blocking one of the more passable ways through the challenging Nur Mountains. If one looks up from the valley straddled by the Iron Gate, the ancient walls of the Byzantine fortifications can be seen running along the tops of the mountains on either side, creating a formidable frontier. Antioch may have been a haven for trade and culture, but the citizens were only kept safe and businesses allowed to flourish thanks to the protection of these high walls. The more dedicated traveller can still scramble up the mountainside to these highest points and walk along the remains of the Byzantine walls and arches far above the city. The mountains are daunting but they are not impassable, and the walls afforded necessary protection.

Antioch

In the autumn of 1126 a young man set sail in search of this city. He departed from Apulia in southern Italy, crossing the Mediterranean Sea for Outremer. His mother was a French princess famed for her beauty, and his father was the crusading conqueror of Antioch, Bohemond of Taranto. William of Tyre described this young man in detail:

> He had blond hair and well-made features. His whole bearing plainly showed the prince even to those who did not know him. His conversation was agreeable and easily won the favour of those who listened to him. He was generous of nature and, like his father, truly magnificent.

This affable young man brimming with promise was Bohemond II, the prodigal heir to the Principality of Antioch. Though the city had passed through the hands of numerous regents, the true heir was Bohemond of Taranto's only son, Bohemond II. Following a series of humiliating defeats, Bohemond I had retired to Italy in a state somewhere between exile and retirement. He died when his son was a small boy and so Bohemond II found himself raised by his mother, the formidable Constance of France. A Capetian princess by birth, she was famed both for her beauty and her iron disposition.

Constance had wielded more power than was usual for a woman in Western Europe. She had demanded a divorce from her first husband, and remarkably received it, before marrying Bohemond I and settling down with him in southern Italy. Following her husband's death, she ruled as regent on her son's behalf during his childhood. Eventually she lost control of much of their Italian lands due to the uprising of Grimoald Alferanites in 1120. She was captured and imprisoned, and only released following the intervention of the Pope and the King of Sicily. However, a condition of her release was that she forfeit her claims to Bari and relinquish her right to be regent for her son.

Bohemond II was raised on legends of his father's exploits and the knowledge that Antioch was waiting for him across the sea. By the time he came of age, he was eager to claim his inheritance.

Constance of France took great care with her son's upbringing and she was reluctant to let him leave for Outremer. From a practical perspective, this trepidation makes perfect sense: the life expectancy for young men in the East was not encouraging, and in Antioch it was even worse. Since it was a frontier state, fatalities were higher there, and the sheer number of castles and fortifications that survive in the region to this day stand as testament to its instability and need for defences. When Bohemond was eleven years old, word would have arrived in Apulia of the devastating Battle of the Field of Blood between the Antiochene army and the armies of Aleppo, which was a crushing defeat for the Christians. Virtually every able-bodied man from Antioch was slaughtered in one day. The extent of the carnage and the news of this defeat brought horror to all of Outremer. Not long before this, another disaster had struck Antioch: the city was devastated by a terrible earthquake. It is no surprise that Constance of France had little enthusiasm for sending her only son out to rule such a volatile region.

Orderic Vitalis, a contemporary Anglo-Norman chronicler, writes of Constance that 'the anxious mother held him back, until [he] escaped from her fetters'. Indeed, Bohemond only succeeded in realising his dreams of travelling to the East following the death of his mother in the autumn of 1125. After a due period of mourning, Bohemond set out for Outremer with a fleet of twenty-four ships, laden with soldiers and horses. At last the apron strings had been cut and he was setting out to claim his hereditary lands and rule independently, without the meddlesome influence of female relatives.

Princess Alice of Jerusalem must have awaited Bohemond's coming with a mixture of anticipation and trepidation. This prodigal prince was to become her husband. News of his arrival in the Holy Land had circulated many times but each time proved to be a false rumour. In 1126, however, Bohemond II and his fleet did indeed materialise on the shores of Outremer, and Baldwin II and Alice were waiting to greet him in Antioch.

The long-awaited meeting between Baldwin II and Bohemond II was set to be politically charged. Since the Battle of the Field of Blood in 1119, Antioch had been rudderless. King Baldwin II had taken over as regent, but his attention was divided between Jerusalem and Antioch, and just as he was eager to relinquish the burden of responsibility for Antioch, so too were the population desperate for a dedicated leader. The arrival of this golden prince, the blood of the original conquering hero, must have seemed a godsend to them and a restoration of order at last.

As King of Jerusalem Baldwin II occupied the highest secular position in Outremer, and had proven himself both as a ruler and a diplomat. He held both authority and tangible power, commanding loyalty from all of his vassals and the nobility of the region. He could give Bohemond II invaluable advice and insight on how to rule Antioch and defend the lands against the forces of Aleppo, but he was also tired. Baldwin II needed to turn his attention back to the affairs of Jerusalem, and the issue of his own succession. As such he needed Bohemond, not so much for his personal qualities but for the knights he brought with him from Apulia, and the loyalty he would command from the citizens of the city as Bohemond's heir. Equally, Bohemond needed Baldwin. He needed his expertise, his protection, and if he wanted to accede to his patrimony without bloodshed, he also needed Baldwin's goodwill and cooperation. The fate of the Kingdom rested on the meeting between these two men, a generation apart in age.

Depending on how Baldwin managed his diplomacy, Bohemond II of Antioch could become either the greatest ally or the greatest rival to the King of Jerusalem. If the prince was anything like his father, he would require very careful handling.

A seasoned soldier and diplomat, Baldwin II took these challenges in his stride. He summoned his second daughter Alice and travelled with her to Antioch to await the arrival of Bohemond II and to extend to him every compliment and courtesy, to ensure their relationship started on the right foot. The meeting went off without a hitch. The prince arrived by ship into the port of St Simeon, and then travelled up the Orontes from the sea. When he reached the city of Antioch, the population of the city, led by Baldwin and Alice, greeted him joyfully with great pomp and ceremony, delighted and relieved to have Bohemond's heir among them at last. He was welcomed by a state procession and a great feast.

Following the lavish festivities, King Baldwin II formally offered Bohemond II his daughter Alice as a wife, although it is likely these negotiations had been concluded long before Bohemond arrived in Antioch, given the speed of their wedding. Any twinges of parental anxiety Baldwin II may have felt about the first of his children to marry must have been assuaged by the fact that it was such a good match. There was scarcely two years between the young couple in age, and Bohemond was good-looking, likeable and impressive.

William of Tyre sang the young man's praises, as did Matthew of Edessa, describing him as 'a beardless youth of twenty years, but a valiant and mighty warrior, tall with a lion-like face and blond hair'. Matthew was an Armenian chronicler with every reason to detest Bohemond II, given his aggressive military campaigns against the Armenians of Cilicia, so his favourable depiction of the young prince is striking.

In marrying Bohemond II, Alice would overtake all of her sisters in status and become Princess of Antioch at sixteen years old, far earlier than Melisende could dream of becoming Queen of Jerusalem. Alice may have already been showing signs of her great ambition, and this match may have served to temporarily satisfy her desire for rank and power.

Regardless, Bohemond II was evidently delighted with his bride, and the wedding took place with all haste, celebrated in Antioch with much jubilation. After the ceremony Bohemond II sat on his throne and was invested and crowned as Prince of Antioch. With this ceremony, Alice became Princess Consort of Antioch. Baldwin II, pleased with a job well done, returned to Jerusalem, doubtless relieved that he could give up the regency of the troublesome principality and once again turn his attention to the affairs of Jerusalem.

A perusal of medieval records would suggest that the marriage was a good one. Their similarity in age, appearance and breeding all contribute to this, as does the fact that a child was born a year or so into the marriage – a daughter, named Constance for Bohemond's mother. However, the happiness and success of the marriage should not be taken for granted. Indeed, William of Tyre emphasises the political nature of the union: 'This alliance was arranged under conditions approved by both the King and the Prince, that the friendly relations and esteem between them might be increased.' It was not a love match, but an important political alliance between the ruling families of Jerusalem and Antioch. The young couple had never laid eyes on each other or exchanged a letter before Bohemond II arrived in Antioch, and the marriage marked the end of Alice's life with her mother and sisters. All accounts suggest that Baldwin II's four daughters were close to one another.

Despite this, Alice was certainly better off than most medieval princesses in the husband her father chose for her. He was young, handsome, of royal blood, and her father and his had been sword brothers of the First Crusade. Furthermore, Antioch was not so very far from Jerusalem, and many royal princesses were packaged off to marital homes across seas with very little prospect of ever seeing their family again.

Prince Bohemond was her equal in every way, but problems arose between them because he failed to recognise this. All the qualities that caused chroniclers to catch their breath at the advent of this young man and lavish praise upon him, were the very qualities that would make him a less-than-ideal husband. Bohemond II arrived in the East an ambitious man eager to make his mark on the world and honour his father's legacy through great deeds. His vision of his life as a conquering Prince of Outremer did not allow space for sharing power with an ambitious wife.

Bohemond II showed little enthusiasm for personal and domestic affairs. While he certainly impregnated Alice with great speed, he spent remarkably little time with her in Antioch. Contemporary chroniclers praise his tireless appetite for war and his boundless energy, but a tireless appetite for war means little time spent at home. Alice saw little of her husband after their honeymoon, and their infant daughter saw even less of him. Like many energetic newcomers, Bohemond II had a hunger for slaughtering 'the other' that was not satisfied by the ongoing religious conflict with Muslims, but also extended to territorial conflict with the local Christians – the Armenians who were his wife's own people.

All these characteristics, while roundly praised by chroniclers, did little to endear him to his equally ambitious wife. He ceded no power to her and her role was entirely limited to that of consort. Only one charter survives from Bohemond II's reign, and Alice is not listed in the witness list. This strongly implies that she was given little political standing, certainly nothing like that her sister was enjoying in Jerusalem, or even that her aunt Cecilia had enjoyed as the consort of the ruler of Antioch before her. All the evidence points to a conservative and unequal marriage, and it is little wonder that when an opportunity to seize autonomy arose, Alice jumped at it.

Regardless of the tenderness of feeling, or lack thereof, between Bohemond II and Alice, the relationship was never given the chance to either flourish or flounder: Alice was widowed just four years after making her marriage vows.

Bohemond II made an excellent start as Prince of Antioch, recapturing the city of Kafartab in Syria from the Emir of Homs. His indefatigable campaigns against his Muslim neighbours were reflected in the bitter testimony of Usama ibn Munqidh, who wrote of him: 'that devil, the son of Bohemond, proved a terrible calamity to our people'. However, Bohemond II also began a series of punishing feuds with Joscelin of Edessa, which led to infighting between the Christian armies of Antioch and Edessa, much to the anger of his father-in-law King Baldwin II, who had worked so tirelessly for peace in the region. This enmity led to a missed opportunity to capture Aleppo.

Following a series of raids, of limited success, along the Aleppan frontier, Bohemond turned his attention to Armenian Cilicia. His enthusiasm for slaughter was not sated with the Muslim forces, as he wished to restore to his principality all the lands that it had held during his father's reign. With this in mind, he waged war against the Armenian ruler Levon, Lord of the Mountain and King of Cilicia. Several regions that had been under Bohemond I's control had since been reabsorbed by Cilicia, and Bohemond II wanted them back. This could not be disguised as religious warfare as the Armenians were a Christian people, and more than this, Bohemond's own wife was half Armenian. This campaign cannot have gone down well with Alice.

Bohemond II, expecting a relatively routine campaign against a far inferior enemy force, evidently did not expect great risk in the endeavour.

He brought no allies with him, but did march the bulk of his household guard, foot soldiers and cavalry, into Cilicia to confront Levon. This unit was annihilated to a man.

On hearing of Bohemond's intentions, Levon had sought an alliance with the Emir of the Danishmends. The far larger Muslim army had quietly marched to Cilicia and lain in wait for the Antiochenes and ambushed them. The battle raged but there was no hope for the Christian army, and Bohemond II was slaughtered among his cavalry, unrecognised by his attackers. Had they known who the particularly striking blond knight was, they doubtless would have spared his life and extorted a princely ransom from his city. When they realised their error, they rooted among the fallen corpses and carnage on the battlefield to find his body. Once found, the Prince's beautiful and lion-like head was struck off and sent to the Caliph of the Abbasids in Baghdad – a grisly token of victory. It was a sudden and anticlimactic end for the heir of Bohemond of Taranto.

THE FIRST REBELLION OF PRINCESS ALICE

The demise of Bohemond II heralded the rise of Alice of Antioch.

The news of her husband's death did not come as a blow to Alice, but rather spurred her to action. Losing scarcely a day to mourning, she immediately set about hatching a plan that would turn his death, a devastating loss to the city, to her advantage. She saw the death of Bohemond II as perhaps the first opportunity she had had in her life to decisively throw off the oppressive influence of her male relatives and achieve personal independence. A chance for real personal and political agency was at last within her grasp.

Her position as a widow and young mother was not an enviable one. The laws and customs of Outremer, while more forgiving than those of France and Western Europe, were still rigid. A condition of Alice's marriage contract with Bohemond II had specified that in the event of his death, she would receive the strategically important coastal cities of Latakieh and Jabala, on the coast of modern-day Syria, to be her own and held under her control. While this was a generous settlement and the law dictated that these lands now belonged to Alice, it also decreed that as a widow she was obliged to remarry and transmit her dower lands to a new husband, should her suzerain lord demand it. Bohemond II had implicitly accepted Baldwin II's suzerainty over Antioch, thus accepting the overlordship of Jerusalem over the people of Antioch, including

Princess Alice, and giving Baldwin II the right to force his daughter to remarry.

Given Alice's position as mother of the heir of Antioch and the possessor of such important lands, she was too valuable a commodity to be allowed to remain single. According to the laws of the land, she should have been given a choice between three suitors, but she would have had no say in who these options were and would have been forced to marry one of them very quickly. The only consideration given to the match would be who would be the best ruler of Antioch, rather than the best partner for Alice. It is unsurprising that Alice was keen to avoid this fate. Within days of her husband's death, with the grim reality of her position becoming apparent to her, she decided to rebel.

In the political culture of the time, personalities were far more important than policies in running state affairs and forming and acknowledging allegiances. This is why the death of one lord and the accession of another was such an unstable time for any region, particularly in Outremer. Any notions of suzerainty would be expressed between the individual rulers of two states rather than as a result of custom or precedent. Thus while Alice's husband might have readily acknowledged Baldwin II as his suzerain lord, Alice was not obliged to do the same if she could take up the reins of the Principality. These were matters of politics rather than legality, and if Alice asserted that Antioch was an independent Principality, as indeed it had been at its conception, then Alice had no lord to whom she was beholden. If she were to reject Jerusalem's suzerainty, then all of a sudden she was the highest-status noble in the city, and her two-year-old daughter was the undisputed heir to the Principality. With her father and his armies far away in Jerusalem, the chance was Alice's to seize Antioch and claim control of her own life. Thus, in an act of open rebellion against Jerusalem and her father's authority, she assumed the regency of Antioch and proclaimed herself in control of the city.

While it was not particularly shocking for rulers of one area to reject the suzerainty of another, it was shocking indeed for a daughter to reject the authority of her father, as this challenged the patriarchal fabric of society and transgressed established gender roles and the Christian doctrine of deference to parents. This is perhaps why William of Tyre so emphasises and criticises Alice's role in this rebellion:

> As soon as [Alice] learned of her husband's death, and in fact, before she was aware of her father's intention to come to Antioch, an evil spirit led her to conceive a wicked plan [. . .] whether she remained a widow

or remarried, Alice determined to disinherit her daughter and keep the principality for herself in perpetuity.

Although William of Tyre condemns Alice and her motivations, she was acting within the framework of the law. Moreover, in order to take control of the city in the way that she did, she must have had support from powerful nobles within the city, and indeed from a sizeable chunk of the population as well. While her actions would certainly have appalled the King of Jerusalem and his supporters, they cannot have been altogether outlandish or outrageous, or else the population of Antioch would never have accepted them. No matter how fiery Alice's temper, it is unlikely she could have subdued an entire city of mutinous noblemen with glares and petulant threats alone.

While the newly empowered princess was lining up her defences and planning her strategies, her opponents were beginning to move against her. Her father Baldwin II and her brother-in-law Fulk of Anjou had also been notified of the death of her husband, and understood all too well the power vacuum that the young Prince's demise had created in that most problematic Principality. They mustered an army and set off for Antioch in haste, anxious to stabilise the situation, appoint a *male* regent, and doubtless rush Alice into the arms of a new and politically advantageous husband. They did not reckon on the headstrong Alice having other plans. When they left Jerusalem, they had no idea that she was preparing to resist them and had claimed control of Antioch.

Despite demonstrating her savviness and gumption in seizing the window of opportunity created by her husband's death, Alice made the key mistake of underestimating the weight of the powers she was dealing with. She overplayed her hand through panic. Hearing of her father's approach, she realised that despite the support she had in Antioch, she could not hope to resist the King of Jerusalem in battle: Antioch had next to no army left, as the bulk of its knights had been killed alongside her husband in Cilicia. She needed a powerful ally with the military might to challenge Jerusalem. Frankish lords in other territories in Outremer were unlikely to take her side against the well-established King Baldwin II, and in desperation Alice, doubtless terrified of her father's approach, sent a messenger to none other than the fierce Atabeg Zengi, whose unification of Mosul and Aleppo was proving such a threat to the Christian states in Outremer. Alice offered homage to Zengi in exchange for assistance in repelling her father and maintaining control of Antioch. This offer ultimately boiled down to ceding Christian territory to a Muslim lord for the purposes of personal gain. Any

Frankish support she had within the city was doubtless alienated by this manoeuvre.

In reaching out to Zengi and suggesting an alliance, Alice did not break fresh ground – it was not the first time a crusader noble had allied with a Muslim to achieve their own ends, and it would not be the last. An alliance with a Muslim lord was not in itself shocking, and the leaders of the First Crusade had had to cooperate with Muslims in order to reach Jerusalem; however, the act of allying with a Muslim lord against the Christian king was still taboo. This move also revealed Alice's naivety. She did not appreciate that Zengi was no more likely to allow her to rule Antioch as her own Principality in her own right than her father was – indeed, he was even less likely to, because while female agency was beginning to be recognised more and more in the laws of Outremer, it was nowhere near this point in Islamic custom.

As part of her embassy to Zengi, Alice arranged for an elaborate and symbolic gift to be sent to the atabeg. She commanded that a fine horse, snow white in colour, should have its hooves shod with shoes of silver. She adorned it with a saddle and bridle made of white silk and decorated with silver, and she ordered a messenger to convey this princely gift to Zengi. Western horses were prized in the East and the workmanship on the horse's tack was exceptionally fine. It was a handsome gift and one that she hoped would please the infamous atabeg and demonstrate to him her refined character, respect and good intentions. The messenger and palfrey never reached their destination, so we cannot know what Zengi would have made of Alice's gift or her offer of cooperation. The man and the horse were intercepted by Alice's father's men, marching to Antioch themselves. After a brief interval of brutal torture, the messenger revealed his mission and Alice's intentions. He was put to death. History does not relate what happened to the lovely white palfrey.

Once he understood the gravity of the situation in Antioch and his own daughter's rebellion, Baldwin II hastened his progress to the city, now no longer with the aim of finding a husband for Alice, but of confronting her and thwarting her ambitions. When he arrived at the city, brimming with fury at his daughter's audacity, he found the gates barred against him and the recalcitrant Alice resolutely refusing to allow him entry without the promise of independence and the rule of Antioch. Baldwin II could certainly not tolerate such brazen insubordination from any of his vassals, least of all his twenty-year-old daughter. Such a concession would have been emasculating and would have completely undermined the authority of the crown of Jerusalem.

At the sight of the assembled fury of Jerusalem at the gates of Antioch and their princess grasping at straws, many of the Franks within the city began to have second thoughts about supporting Alice's rebellion. A Frankish knight named William of Aversa together with a monk known as Peter the Latin ignored the orders of the princess and opened the gates to Baldwin II and Fulk. In desperation Alice retreated to the citadel of the city and barricaded herself inside. She was not long there before she accepted that further resistance was futile. She first received the assurance of her life from her besiegers, then, shame-faced, came out and publicly threw herself on her knees before her father, weeping, repenting, surrendering the city and begging for forgiveness.

Perhaps more due to weariness than anything else, Baldwin II granted Alice the leniency she sought. She received no specific punishment such as imprisonment, but she was promptly banished from Antioch, a sentence which carried with it necessary separation from her young daughter Constance, who would remain behind as heiress to the Principality. Constance's grandfather appointed his old ally Joscelin of Courtenay, Lord of Edessa, to be the little princess' regent and guardian in her mother's absence. William of Tyre asserts that due to personal munificence and stirrings of parental tenderness, Baldwin allowed Alice to retain her dower lands in Jabala and Latakieh, but this apparent display of generosity is unlikely to have been anything of the kind, but rather a result of Baldwin II's hands being tied by the law. Alice's dower lands were hers by legal right, left to her by Bohemond II. Baldwin II, the man who had traded his five-year-old daughter Yvette's safety for his own, was not a man to be moved by Alice's tears.

It is possible that, had Alice assembled strong support within the city and petitioned her father for regency of the city, rather than challenging him through open rebellion and attempts to ally against him with Zengi, she might have been met with more success. However, it is unlikely that she would have been able to remain single, and it seemed that Alice had been so disenchanted with the idea of marriage by her brief relationship with Bohemond that she would not settle to strive for the more achievable option of regency under Jerusalem's overlordship, but wanted to throw off the suzerainty of her father and act as the regent of Antioch as an independent Principality. The danger of accepting regency for a female child while under the control of a male overlord was that the King of Jerusalem could compel either Alice or Constance to marry when it suited him: if he forced a husband on either of them, Alice's power would be immediately superseded by the new Prince of Antioch.

While Alice had some support within the city, no one believed she could hold out in a siege against the Kingdom of Jerusalem. The Armenian inhabitants of Antioch likely welcomed the rule of the princess, but the Frankish population, who held the positions of power, were unwilling to tolerate the rule of a woman over that of the King of Jerusalem or the Count of Edessa.

William of Tyre writes: 'by [Zengi's] aid, she hoped to acquire Antioch for herself in perpetuity, despite the opposition of her chief men and the entire population' and 'in that very city were God-fearing men, contemptuous of the impudence and foolishness of a woman.' However, William offers no explanation of how a woman opposed by her entire population managed to take control of the city single-handed, and makes no specific mention of either the Patriarch or the Constable opposing her, and it stands to reason that she must have had, at the very least, their begrudging cooperation in order to close the gates of the city against the king. Moreover, had Alice gone a step further and imprisoned them, then such an act would certainly have made it into the chronicles.

Indeed, William of Tyre's whole treatment of Alice's first bid for independence is deeply problematic. Despite glossing over the vast majority of female achievements, William is notably generous in his descriptions of women such as Queen Melisende and various others. However, he has little time for women who upset the balance in the Kingdom and lays into Alice with uncharacteristic venom.

The most effective way of discrediting a woman in the Middle Ages was to undermine her femininity. In describing Alice's actions in this rebellion, William is at pains to state that she was a bad and unnatural mother. He asserts that the little girl Constance 'did not stand high in the favour of her mother' and that 'whether she remained a widow or remarried, Alice was determined to disinherit her daughter and keep the principality for herself in perpetuity.' It is unlikely that Alice had such intentions, even though William makes the point twice during his diatribe. It is more likely that she wished to claim her legal right to rule as regent on her daughter's behalf until Constance came of age, and have a strong influence over her choice of husband. There was a precedent of female regency on behalf of underage children, as evidenced by Constance's own grandmother and namesake, Constance of France, ruling on behalf of Bohemond II in southern Italy.

In any case, William of Tyre certainly did not approve of Alice's actions, dubbing her an 'extremely malicious and wily woman'. This kind of verbal attack is usually the recourse of a man against women threatening the social structure in which his gender has the advantage. William further describes Alice's crimes in these words: 'she was intriguing to wrong the principality. Her plan was to disinherit the daughter whom she had borne to her husband and thus secure for herself the principality; she intended to marry again according to her own pleasure.' He argues that in seeking to rule herself, she was attempting to subvert the interests of Antioch, but this is highly contestable. If she had been planning to disinherit Constance, this would have been a crime, but there is little evidence of this animosity towards her young daughter. And William seems to take equal exception to Alice wishing to choose her own husband. He attacks her femininity in order to defame her to the patriarchal audience for which he was writing; this excerpt is perhaps one of the least balanced and least substantial in William's chronicle.

However, the details of Alice's rebellion against her father and the fact that it did take place are corroborated in multiple sources, including that of the Muslim chronicler Kemal ad-Din. It certainly brought the wrath of her father down upon her head. Baldwin II admonished his daughter before banishing her forcibly from Antioch. She marched in shame to Latakieh, where the men of the Kingdom hoped she would lead a meek existence, out of sight and out of mind.

THE SECOND REBELLION OF PRINCESS ALICE

Alice did not remain in exile for long. This can hardly be surprising, given what we know of her character. Her first rebellion had exhausted her father, and Baldwin II returned to Jerusalem just in time to make his peculiar will, before succumbing to the exhaustions of a long and battle-weary life, dying in his bed watched over by his devoted eldest daughter, his son-in-law and his little grandson.

Alice did not attend her father's deathbed, and it is impossible to know if pangs of regret were felt by either of them for their treatment of the other, or if there was any sadness that their last encounter had been that of lord and rebellious vassal rather than father and daughter. If Alice did feel remorse or melancholy at her father's passing, she was remarkably brisk in her dismissal of it.

Shortly after Baldwin II's death and the coronation of her elder sister and brother-in-law, Alice set to scheming again. Indeed, in the charters she issued from Latakieh she took pains to emphasise her connection to Antioch, despite having been long since banished and deprived of the fief. She begins a charter granting land to a religious order, emphasising not only her own pedigree, but also her links with Antioch and her claim to the city:

> I, Alice, second daughter of Baldwin King of Jerusalem, once wife of Lord Bohemond, son of Bohemond the Great, most excellent prince of Antioch, by the grace of God princess of Antioch, for the love of God and for the soul of my Lord Bohemond and my parents and also for my own salvation and that of my daughter Constance . . .

Even to a medieval audience, this might have appeared to be laying it on a bit thick. Beyond this, the fact that Alice was issuing charters from Latakieh at all is particularly telling of her ambition. It means she had opened a scriptorium there, which was not common for a dowager landowner in a relatively small coastal city. By running her household on this grand scale she was maintaining her status as a princess and reminding the world that, banished as she was, she was still a key player in the politics of Outremer.

Just as the death of Alice's husband presented an opportunity to her, so too did the death of her father. The transition between rulers was always a delicate time in Outremer, and the death of a king or prince, or a huge battle against the Muslims, marked the time when the Kingdom was least stable and least likely to resist an attempt to change the political order. Thus, almost immediately following the death of her father, Alice struck again.

Her second rebellion would focus on contesting the suzerainty of Jerusalem, not only over Antioch but over the two other crusader states, Tripoli and Edessa. In simple terms, suzerainty equated to overlordship, and if the King of Jerusalem held suzerainty over Antioch, it meant that while, technically, the Principality was recognised as independent and enjoyed aspects of self-rule, the practicalities of this independence were limited.

Bohemond II's father, Bohemond of Taranto, had captured Antioch long before the rest of the crusaders captured Jerusalem, and never recognised any of the Kings as his suzerain lord, although he did pay homage to the Byzantine Emperor, following an embarrassing defeat. His regent and successor, his nephew Tancred, was even more vocal in his refusal to accept the suzerainty of Jerusalem, and rejected that of the Byzantine Empire as well, fighting hard to retain Antioch's independence. However, on his arrival in the East, Bohemond II had failed to accept the mantle of resistance from his predecessors. He fell into the arms of the royal family of Jerusalem as soon as he arrived in Outremer, accepting Baldwin II's hospitality and marrying his daughter.

Alice had a far more cynical view of the bargain that was struck between her husband and her father. She had been used as a gift to seal a deal between the two men, and she understood the implications of her husband's acceptance of her father's offer of 'friendship'. She saw it as undermining the independence of Antioch. Alice would hang her second rebellion on correcting this mistake.

To add to the suitability of the moment following her father's death, another death occurred within months of Baldwin II's, which created a golden window of opportunity for Alice to flex her muscles once again: Joscelin, Baldwin II's successor as Count of Edessa, also died. He had been the last of the original heroes of the First Crusade who held power in the East, and crucially, he was the man whom Baldwin II had appointed as guardian of Constance of Antioch following Alice's exile. With him out of the way and her stubborn father dead, Alice could once again demand the regency of Antioch. The power in Outremer now lay firmly in the hands of the next generation.

With her father's death and her brother-in-law's accession to the throne, Alice was given a gift. The people of Outremer did not like Fulk. He was a newcomer, and brought all his power-hungry friends with him. Given the personal nature of politics in this period, this was a hugely destabilising factor for Fulk's new regime. While Baldwin II, a hero of the First Crusade, had been a King of Jerusalem to whom his vassals were willing to pay homage, Fulk of Anjou was not.

Baldwin II and his predecessor Baldwin I had held suzerainty over the counties and principalities and lordships of Outremer through sheer force of personality, but this was something Fulk could not emulate: he was an outsider, and the local barons would not accept him as overlord. With her father's death, the lynchpin tying the loyalties of the local barons to the throne of Jerusalem had vanished and Alice was in a far better position to win allies.

The new generation of lords did not owe the King of Jerusalem the same debt of gratitude that their fathers had. The inheritors of the other main territories of Outremer – Tripoli and Edessa – owed the new King Fulk nothing on a personal level. Where their fathers had owed a great debt to Baldwin I and Baldwin II, who had made them lords and granted them territory, their sons had inherited their rights to their lands by right of blood, and did not want to pay homage to this interloper from the West who appeared to have swanned in, married a Princess and begun handing out local honours to his foreign friends. They were resentful, and Alice capitalised on this.

Joscelin II, a weak and ugly man who probably had a lot to sulk about in this land full of heroes, was denied the right to become Constance's guardian on the death of his father. This was a sensible decision on Fulk's part. While Joscelin I had been a veritable lion and therefore a good man to hold the reins of Antioch, his son and successor was by all accounts an ineffectual young man, and it made no sense at all to allow him to inherit the guardianship of such a volatile Principality. Nevertheless, from Joscelin II's perspective, this was a serious insult, and it pushed the young man into the arms of the scheming and smouldering Princess Alice.

Likewise, Alice's neighbour to the south was already disenchanted with the idea of Fulk of Anjou as his overlord. Pons of Tripoli had already tried to extricate his lands from the authority of Jerusalem on several occasions, and the opportunity to do so again was extremely attractive. The most uncooperative barons in the history of Outremer had been Bohemond I and Tancred of Antioch; they had both firmly refused to recognise the overlordship of Jerusalem. Pons had been raised under Tancred's tutelage at Antioch and had been thoroughly indoctrinated with the ideology that Antioch, Edessa and Tripoli should be independent territories. He went a step further in his connection to Tancred by marrying Tancred's young widow upon his mentor's death. Thus, when Alice contacted him to test the water and see if he would join her, she cannot have been surprised when he jumped at the opportunity to ally with her and rebel against the crown.

CECILE OF FRANCE

The story of Pons' wife, Cecile of France, widow of Tancred of Hauteville, was a peculiar one. She had been an excellent match for Pons, as Tancred had bequeathed with her some of the most valuable fortresses of Antioch. She and her mother, in fact, had an interesting story of their own.

In addition to being the wife of Pons, who would rebel against King Fulk, Cecile was also the half-sister of Fulk, which added to the sting of her husband's rebellion. While Cecile's father was the King of France and Fulk's father was the Count of Anjou, they shared their mother, Bertrade de Montfort.

Bertrade had married Fulk's father, the Count of Anjou, as a young woman and Fulk was born soon after. However, in 1092, still aged only twenty-two, she left her husband and her son, having fallen in love with the King of France, Philip, who had become similarly enamoured of her.

Indeed, it is his love of Bertrade that dominates Philip's legacy, and he became known to history as Philip the Amorous (and Philip the Fat). He repudiated his fat wife Berthe to marry the beautiful Bertrade, an act that would see him excommunicated by Pope Urban II at the very same Council of Clermont at which he first preached the Crusade and set Europe on fire. Philip and Bertrade had three children, the last of whom was the Lady Cecile. Bertrade outlived her husband, and when her potentially vengeful stepson Louis of France came to power, she wisely withdrew from public life and became a nun, prompting William of Malmesbury to write: 'Bertrade, still young and beautiful, took the veil at Fontevraud Abbey, always charming to men, pleasing to God, and like an angel.'

Cecile seems to have inherited her mother's angelic qualities, even if Fulk did not. She came to the East in 1106, aged only nine, to wed Tancred of Hauteville, the Prince of Galilee and regent of Antioch. Tancred was more than twenty years her senior but doubtless an impressive man. The nephew of Bohemond of Taranto, he too was steeped in glamour from his exploits and achievements during the First Crusade. They were married for only six years, as Tancred died in 1112, and were childless – doubtless on account of the princess' young age, and hopefully because the marriage was not consummated. With his last breaths, Prince Tancred did his young wife a great favour, arranging her next marriage for her, to Pons of Tripoli. While this might seem an unusual final action for a husband, it was in fact an act of kindness. Pons was the same age as Cecile, and a young man whom Tancred held in high esteem and knew well. Pons had been raised and educated at Tancred's court, and Tancred was confident that he would become a great leader and be a good husband and protector for his young widow. Tancred was certainly aware that a fifteen-year-old widow in Outremer, far from her family, and with vast territorial possessions, was in danger of being torn apart by greedy and vulturous suitors anxious to acquire her lands and wealth. He was keen to make sure that Cecile's second marriage was a happy one. She and Pons had grown up together under Tancred's protection, and it is also possible that he decided to arrange this marriage because he had begun to observe the strong affection that would evolve between them.

However difficult her first marriage had been, tearing her away from her family across the sea to marry a man more than three times her age, her husband certainly provided well for her future. In addition to arranging the marriage, he also bequeathed Cecile and her husband the valuable fortresses of Arcicanum, Rugia, Tortosa, Maraclea, Safita and the world-famous Krak des Chevaliers. In those days, however, the castle did not have the impressive fortifications that survive to this day. Back then it still went by its original name, Hisn al-Akrad, which translates as 'Castle of the Kurds'.

Krak des Chevaliers is one of the best examples of the brilliance of crusader military architecture ensuring its own survival. Various crusader churches and shrines have been destroyed, most sadly William of Tyre's great cathedral by the sea in Tyre, of which only rubble remains today in an overgrown field. However, Krak, like so many other crusader fortresses, has stood the test of time and weathered the ages, standing to this day as testament to the determination of its creators. The Syrian civil war caused damage: there are signs of bombardment of some of the walls and bullet holes are sprayed here and there, but for the most part it survives intact. The crusaders only lost control of the fortress to the Mamluks due to trickery in the form of a forged letter, not because the defences failed them.

Thus, King Fulk's half-sister Cecile found herself remarried in her late teens to a man of her own age alongside whom she had grown up. A few years after the wedding she gave birth to her first son, Raymond, the future Count of Tripoli. The couple had two more children, Philip and Agnes.

Despite being well matched as a couple, Cecile and Pons were not exempt from the fate of all ruling families in Outremer, and had a rocky and hazardous life together. After a marriage of twenty-five years, he was captured by native Christians, whom he had alienated over the years. He was handed over to Bazwaj, the Mamluk commander of Damascus, and was killed in 1137, leaving Cecile a widow. The earlier years of their marriage had been just as tumultuous. In 1131 Cecile's half-brother Fulk ascended the throne of Jerusalem, and one of the first challenges he faced was securing the obedience of the other Princes and Counts of Outremer. Cecile's husband was keen to have autonomous control of his County of Tripoli, and thus allied himself with Alice of Antioch in her rebellion against Jerusalem, and thereby set himself against King Fulk, despite Fulk remonstrating with him and Cecile on the grounds of kinship.

In Pons of Tripoli Alice had found a powerful ally, and the time was ripe for her to once again attempt to throw off the overlordship of her male relatives in Jerusalem and claim Antioch as her own. William of Tyre, continuing his efforts to undermine Alice, asserted that she had only won the allegiance of Pons and Joscelin through spending her husband's hard-saved gold: 'by lavish gifts and promises she had secured certain powerful nobles in her plot: namely, William de Sehunna, brother of Guarenton; Pons, count of Tripoli; and Joscelin the younger, count of Edessa.'

The Western chroniclers minimise this episode in their accounts of the history of Outremer, and try to present it as a second unsuccessful rebellion by Alice, but it was a great deal more than that and deserved a great many more pages of explanation than any of the contemporary chroniclers saw fit to give it. This rebellion represented a serious uprising and civil war that split Outremer in half, the local barons rejecting the authority of the newcomer, Fulk of Jerusalem. Alice of Antioch was just one player in a far larger drama.

A plot was hatched between the new generation of rulers in the states of Outremer, to rid themselves of the suzerainty of Jerusalem once and for all. Alice must have attempted to win support from her own nobility within the city of Antioch, for news of the plan reached the ears of certain Frankish noblemen who were not sympathetic to Alice's cause, and who tipped off Fulk in Jerusalem. The king immediately began to move his army north, to put down Alice's rebellion and neutralise the unrest in Antioch for a second time.

Antioch lies on the banks of the Orontes River, in the southernmost part of modern Turkey. To reach this city from Jerusalem, one has to pass through modern-day Lebanon, which in the twelfth century was the County of Tripoli, and the domain of Pons. When Fulk's army reached the city of Beirut, the king found that his way was barred by Pons' army. The rebellion was more serious than he had realised if Pons, too, had declared against him. Fuming at this insubordination from a young man so many years his junior, and indeed married to his own sister, Fulk and his army were forced to take the sea route. The army was loaded onto ships and sailed up the coast of Tripoli and put into port in St Simeon. Here they were met by the same anxious noblemen who had warned Fulk of Alice's plans, and led overland to the city of Antioch.

The king had little difficulty in subduing the city. Alice was not a military leader and had no great army to speak of. Antioch's fighting men had been annihilated in the Battle of the Field of Blood and the battle with the Danishmends in Cilicia that had killed Bohemond II, and the armies had not yet been restored. Furthermore, Alice had once again failed to ensure the cooperation of the nobles of the city, and so Fulk was able to take control with relatively little difficulty.

Despite the capitulation of Antioch, this rebellion was far from over. On hearing of the capture of Antioch, Pons of Tripoli marched his army north. When he had married his mentor Tancred's widow, Cecile, he had received as her dowry vast possessions in Antioch, and thus, despite being Count of Tripoli, he was also one of the most powerful landholders and barons in Antioch. He ordered his fortresses of Rugia and Arcicanum to be fortified to resist the king. Hearing of this and at the urging of the Antiochene nobility, Fulk mustered his army to move south and meet Pons in battle.

The armies clashed in a pitched battle in a plain in the region of Rugia, south of the city of Antioch. They fought bitterly, but Pons' losses were greater and eventually he was forced to surrender. William of Tyre does not record how many soldiers lost their lives in this battle, but the fight was significant enough to earn mentions in Muslim chronicles. Pons' men, exhausted by the battle, were led in chains to Antioch. However, despite Pons' flagrant insubordination, a wary peace was brokered between the two nobles. The fate of Outremer hung in the balance: if the Christians in the East did not remain united, then they would not maintain their territories for long. Together, Pons and Fulk advanced towards Antioch, where Alice waited for news.

On hearing of this defeat, she once again retreated to Latakieh. Fulk took no punitive action against her, perhaps due to the intervention of his wife, or simply because he had bigger fish to fry. Alice's plans were foiled, but her spirit was not yet broken.

Fulk remained in Antioch for some time, continuing his predecessors' efforts to stabilise the region. William of Tyre writes:

> From this time, the king enjoyed full favour with the people of Antioch, lords and common people alike. The Princess hated him and resented his presence at Antioch, and, up to this time, some of the nobles who favoured her cause by reason of the lavish gifts which she distributed had been opposed to him. Now, however, the hearts of all were completely won over to him.

THE FINAL DEFEAT OF ALICE OF ANTIOCH

Alice's second bid for independence had been far more threatening than her first. It had resulted in a short-lived and hastily patched-up civil war that had nevertheless left dents in the armies of both Tripoli and

Jerusalem. Fulk and his advisors decided that Alice's dreams of regency and rule in Antioch needed to be extinguished once and for all.

Surprisingly, Alice was permitted to return to Antioch not long after this conflict. Her sister Queen Melisende had intervened on her behalf and Fulk had relented. It seems she also had the sympathy of the new, more practically minded Patriarch, Ralph, who may also have spoken for her. Alice was allowed back to Antioch but not as regent, and under a new government installed by Fulk, headed by Rainald Mazoir, Lord of Maqab and Constable of Antioch. Demonstrating clearly his uneasiness with the situation, Fulk remained in the city himself for some time, doubtless to keep a watchful eye on his recalcitrant sister-in-law. Alice hated his presence; to her he was the embodiment of male, Frankish oppression and she loathed him with fierce intensity.

Before long, however, the affairs of the Kingdom of Jerusalem summoned him home, and Alice was once again left in Antioch. She began marshalling her forces for one final attempt to take control of the city and Principality with which she had become obsessed: it was her life's ambition to rule Antioch.

It seems that Alice became mistress of the city in practice, if not in name, when Ralph, the new Patriarch, lost favour with the rest of the clergy. Once again, she claimed regency and brought the great gates of the city swinging shut and declared herself against Fulk and Jerusalem. This time no powerful allies like Pons would come to her aid, but the princess remained resolute. Her main supporters were the native Armenian Christians, and she didn't care much about traditional Frankish loyalties and allegiances. Antioch had a long and bitter history of war and enmity with the Byzantine Empire, but this didn't stop her offering her daughter Constance, now seven or eight years old, in marriage to Manuel, the son of the Byzantine Emperor John Komnenos, in 1135 as part of a bid to win his support.

Many have read this proposed match as a flagrant disregard on the part of Alice for the last century of her daughter's heritage and a flouting of traditional Antiochene foreign policy and loyalty. However, if Alice had succeeded in bringing about this match, it might have been the most significant and salient political union in the history of Outremer. For all that her testy brother-in-law read it as Alice overplaying her hand, her own daughter Constance clearly was of a similar mind when she came of age. While she did not follow through on her mother's early scheme of marriage to the future Emperor Manuel, she considered Byzantine suitors of her own, and eventually went so far as to revive Alice's original plan and arranged a marriage between her own daughter and the very same Manuel some decades later. Thus, Alice's granddaughter Maria would, with the full consent of the Antiochene nobility, wed Manuel and become the first Antiochene Empress of Byzantium.

Despite this and perhaps due to Alice's gender and her history of making trouble and attempting to forge treacherous alliances, Fulk of Jerusalem saw this as the last straw. In order to prevent Alice from creating an unsavoury alliance through the marriage of her daughter, he set out to broker his own match for the girl. While all these schemes simmered around her, Constance was only eight years old.

If she had married Manuel, it might have created a Byzantine–Frankish alliance in Antioch and might also have bolstered the Principality's defences against the growing Muslim threat in the East. From Alice's perspective, it might also have got her daughter out of the way so that she could rule.

Political tensions aside, there was also great enmity between the Greek Orthodox church in Antioch and the Byzantine Empire. This fraternising with the Byzantines alienated Alice once and for all from the Patriarch of Antioch – a mistake which would prove to be her undoing.

Alice's negotiations with Emperor John Komnenos had still come to nothing by 1136, and while her scandalous dealings with the Empire had been known about in Jerusalem for some time, Alice had still felt no repercussions from this scandal. This eerie calm should have put her on her guard but it did not, perhaps because she believed the respite was due to the intervention of her sister, who had intervened on her behalf previously, and by this point had her husband Fulk wrapped tightly around her little finger.

During this brief period of quiet a suitor arrived at the gates of Antioch and offered to wed Alice, who had not had many proposals since her previous disgrace. The young man in question was Raymond of Poitiers, 'of noble blood and ancient lineage'. According to those chroniclers who knew him, he was a charming and elegant prince. He was devout, skilled in war, good-looking and generous. However, with all these wonderful qualities he had been given some fatal flaws: overconfidence, recklessness and impulsiveness. The result was a cocktail of good and bad traits that would eventually lead to his demise.

In spite of this tendency to hubris, Raymond was undoubtedly an attractive prospect for Alice, single as she had been for many years. He was only a few years her junior and it may have seemed like a blessed compromise when this man showed up out of nowhere to pay her suit.

While Alice had once sought to rule Antioch in her own right, her position had deteriorated in the wake of two failed rebellions, and perhaps she could now see the wisdom of marrying a powerful lord of attractive countenance who could help her retain control of her beloved city. Indeed, he did seem to appear from nowhere, as he had travelled in disguise to Antioch, and Alice knew nothing of his arrival until he was on her doorstep. The Patriarch Ralph, anxious no doubt to restore order to the Principality under a traditional male ruler, assured her that Raymond was a good match, handsome as he was, from a good family, a similar age to her and offering promises of co-rulership. Alice, under Ralph's guidance, consented, and the young man was admitted to the city. The princess set about making preparations for her long-awaited second marriage.

However, no sooner was Raymond admitted and Alice's wedding preparations commenced, than another wedding took place in secret, unbeknownst to Alice. The bride was Alice's daughter, the little Constance of Antioch, and the groom none other than Raymond of Poitiers. While Alice had been busy preparing for what she imagined to be her own wedding, no doubt ordering food and decorations for a feast, her assumed fiancé had married her eight-year-old daughter instead. Beyond the personal mortification this must have caused Alice, this marriage effectively cut her out of the line of succession and positioned Raymond to be the next Prince of Antioch. This scheme had been Fulk's brainchild, and it had been his emissaries who had proposed the match to Raymond in England and smuggled him out to Antioch.

Alice had been duped. This was her final defeat. Consumed with rage and humiliation, she fled the city, retiring to Latakieh where she would pass the rest of her days in quiet isolation. With the marriage of Princess Constance, any claim Alice had had to regency was nullified with immediate effect: Constance was the heir to the city, Alice only a guardian, and a mother is second place to a husband. Alice was publicly humiliated, and her daughter wed to a man four times her age.

This should not have been possible. The legal age of consent for marriage in Outremer was twelve years for girls, and Constance was not more than eight at the time of her wedding. Moreover, the Patriarch had previously sworn to support Alice, and it was he who solemnised the marriage. This was a dramatic change in allegiance. Raymond, it seems, not only tricked Alice, but tricked the Patriarch too. He had sworn him an oath of fealty in exchange for his assistance, and indeed the entire charade would not have been possible without Ralph's complete cooperation. Ralph had convinced Alice that Raymond was her suitor and persuaded her to accept him; it was Ralph that gave permission for

Constance to be wed, despite her extreme youth; and it was Ralph that took the couple to the altar and pronounced them man and wife.

In spite of this, once Raymond's position was secure, he swiftly made it clear that he had no intention of honouring his pledge of service to the Patriarch, and indeed did everything in his power to have him deposed. The type of priest who would participate in skulduggery to depose a ruler was not the type of Patriarch Raymond wanted serving in his new city.

Despite this devious and duplicitous start to his reign, Raymond would govern the Principality well. At least, he did until his fiery and beautiful niece Eleanor of Aquitaine arrived to pay her uncle a visit. What transpired between them is related in Chapter Five.

It is neither a tragedy nor a surprise that Alice was finally thwarted in her attempts to take power in Antioch. She had played a dangerous game, and made crucial mistakes along the way. She also demonstrated ample helpings of the same megalomania exhibited by her father-in-law and other crusaders, and while she may not have deserved the ill-treatment she received, she was far from blameless. That said, she should not be portrayed by history as the weak-minded villain that William of Tyre presents us with. Rather, she was a woman of immense ambition and reasonable intelligence who came up against opponents within a system to which she was not equal.

Alice had spent six years attempting to take over Antioch, which ended in a humiliation and a defeat. Alice is a model of frustrated female ambition. She did not have the patience to wait for windfalls to come to her, but wanted to use her own skills and ideas to win autonomy and power – she should not be discredited for this. Had a man taken these steps, as indeed Bohemond of Taranto and Pons of Tripoli did, history would have been more forgiving. The treatment of Alice in the chronicles and modern history books is the result of a multitude of patriarchal voices drowning out truth. Alice's name and memory have been repeatedly dragged through the mud because she tried to claim power for herself and rule as a woman. She may have been egocentric, but she was following the example set by men of her time. Alice wanted more from her life than to sit quietly and bear children in the hope of one day winning freedom as an elderly widow, and that is an admirable thing.

It is our task as modern readers to take a more balanced approach to the memory of Alice. To take examples of respected crusades historians of both the modern and medieval periods, Hans Eberhard Mayer and

William of Tyre both fail in their treatment of Alice, respectively calling her 'disgraceful' and 'wicked'. It is a mistake easily made. William of Tyre was a wise man, and a brilliant historian, matchless in his age; but he was also a product of an inherently patriarchal society and way of thinking. This coloured his writing and his opinions, as did the martial society in which he was writing. Writing eight centuries later, Mayer was too willing to accept William of Tyre's assessment of the princess and dismissed her as 'domineering and given to politicking'.

More recently, highly respected historians have variously described Alice as 'flighty', 'meddlesome' and 'silly': how often are these gendered terms applied to male leaders? Alice had the audacity to display free thought, and while she was part of a deeply questionable society, she deserves no more condemnation than any of the princes, and probably a good deal more praise.

Alice was the first of Morphia's daughters to die, shortly after her retreat to Latakieh in 1136. She and her three sisters were close, and aided each other in their quests for agency and power whenever they could. Melisende had intervened on Alice's behalf when she clashed with King Fulk, and would similarly step in to help her sister Hodierna in the second part of her reign. Yet for all the sisterly feeling between the four Princesses, it is clear that Alice reviled her sister's husband, Fulk. During her short and unhappy adulthood, Alice became a figurehead behind which other disaffected nobles rallied to express their discontent with the Angevin monarch, and during the height of her exile, she had played host to one of the most powerful lords in the Kingdom, Count Hugh of Jaffa, at Latakieh.

Hugh was her cousin, and a close confidant of Queen Melisende, and the historical record attests that he spent enough time at Alice's satellite court in Latakieh to have his name included in the list of witnesses in some of the charters she issued from her scriptorium. His mere presence at the disgraced Alice's court is enough to attest that he was an enemy of Fulk, and Hugh would soon come to lead a rebellion of his own, fighting not for Alice's rights as regent of Antioch, but for Melisende's rights as hereditary Queen of Jerusalem.

3

MELISENDE OF JERUSALEM

History has remembered Melisende very differently to her sister. The blame for this can be laid squarely on the shoulders of William of Tyre, who managed to be a staunch supporter of Queen Melisende while being utterly disdainful of Princess Alice. All we can reliably glean from William's depictions of the women is that he liked, or at least felt loyalty to Queen Melisende, but disliked and felt no loyalty to Alice.

Where William condemns Alice as malicious and willing to trade her daughter's happiness for her own, he presents Melisende as an astute politician, a loyal friend and an excellent queen. In his account Melisende succeeds in surpassing all others of her sex, and indeed many men, in her governance of the Kingdom of Jerusalem.

Despite the evident admiration William of Tyre felt for Melisende, this esteem did not go so far as to compel him to write a physical description of the queen for posterity. He never felt it necessary to furnish his audience with detailed descriptions of women, although he frequently did so with men. In spite of this, in his description of Melisende's eldest child Baldwin III, William unwittingly gives us a glimpse of this mysterious and formidable queen. He writes of Baldwin III: 'His features were comely and refined, his complexion florid, a proof of innate strength. In this respect he resembled his mother.' He goes on to write that Baldwin's build was on the heavier side, 'not spare, like his mother'. From this, we can clearly discern that Melisende was a thin woman, with attractive features, who emanated strength of character. She had European colouring, a pink-tinted skin tone, suggesting that she took after her Frankish father in colouring rather than her Armenian mother. Given that on top of this, both of her sons were fair-haired with flashing eyes, perhaps we can assume with relative safety that the same was true of Melisende.

A distinct portrait of the medieval queen begins to emerge. She was an athletic woman who loved horse riding and nature, and was easily bored when confined to women's tasks inside. She was not afraid to go head to head with men in debate. Like her sister, she was a woman of high passion whose emotions sat close to the surface, and she had no qualms about expressing her anger when it was roused.

Baldwin II left Melisende a share of the Kingdom of Jerusalem on his deathbed. The transition of power was not as smooth as he intended, but Melisende did eventually succeed in coming into her own to take power in the Kingdom.

The greatest treasure from the reign of Queen Melisende is housed not in an ancient building in Jerusalem, under vaulted ceilings and stately arches under which Melisende herself would once have passed, but in the vaults of the British Library in London. Here, in the bowels of this modernist building near King's Cross station, reside the ornate manuscript and the ivory bindings that once made up Queen Melisende's personal prayer book (see pp.1–2 of the plate section).

If you can find the right words, the curators will yield it up for inspection. Up close, one can discern the subtle intricacies of the intertwined carvings decorating the ivory covers which tell the story of King David, surrounded by hunting motifs. The age-darkened ivory is inlaid with winking garnets and demi-orbs of turquoise, and the temptation to try to carry the book out into sunlight is great, to see the red-stone eyes of the frozen hunting animals come to life in natural light. Given the value of the manuscript, this is not possible, and it can only be viewed under supervision in a carefully controlled environment. The ivory plates were once bound at the spine with fine Byzantine silk and contained the lavishly illuminated pages of Melisende's personal psalter. Today, the ivory plates are separated and enclosed within Plexiglass sheets for protection, and the woven silk spine is mounted separately. The pages of the manuscript have been rebound in red leather. Embossed in gold on the spine are the tantalising words: 'Melisende Psalter'.

The bone covers are carved with scenes of religion and scenes of violence, and the history of Jerusalem. There are hunting animals, frozen mid chase in perpetuity, biting, snarling, pursuing. Superimposed above them all, at the centre of the back cover, is a carved falcon, with red eyes, surveying the ornate chaos around him. This bird is often interpreted to be a symbol of Melisende's husband Fulk and suggested as evidence that the book was given as a gift from him to his wife. This cover represents perfectly the different elements comprising the early years of Melisende's reign: religion, violence, passion and Fulk. Indeed, the prevalent opinion among historians is that this glorious and deeply personal book was a peace offering from Fulk to Melisende, following a devastating scandal that almost undid their marriage.

Melisende's psalter is one of the finest surviving examples of craftsmanship from Outremer and is the only surviving artefact that we can be sure belonged to Melisende herself. It was made in the scriptorium of the Holy Sepulchre and the illustrations inside were created with the richest materials and most sophisticated craftsmanship of the day. Gold and lapis lazuli were not spared in the illumination.

It is only when viewing this manuscript in person that it makes its full impact, and the inspirational and spiritual values of the illuminations become evident. The act of turning a page causes the gilding to catch the light, giving an otherworldly quality to the illustrations and energy to the figures depicted. Basileus, the Greek artist who made the illuminations, also scratched subtle details into the gold, including the feathers of angels' wings and his own signature, that cannot be glimpsed on the digitised images.

Beside the exquisite and inestimable artistic value of this object, it also stands as a testament to the multicultural nature of both Jerusalem and Queen Melisende herself. It is a glorious synthesis of Orient and Occident; a unique fusion of Eastern and Western philosophy and art. At least six different artists, all of different training, specialities and probably also ethnicities, contributed to the creation of the book, blending Greek, Frankish, Armenian, Anglo-Saxon and Islamic influences.

The psalter does not carry Melisende's name, but there are several signals that this was a gift to her from a contrite Fulk, due to several key clues we find amid the intricate decorations and contents. At the front of the psalter is a calendar and in it are marked two key dates – the dates of the death of Melisende's mother Morphia (1 October), and of her father Baldwin (21 August). These are marked to remind the owner to pray for their souls on the anniversary of their deaths. The emphasis on these dates makes it clear that this psalter was commissioned for a daughter of Baldwin and Morphia. However, there were four daughters. We can deduce that it was created specifically for Melisende, however, because looming large on the ivory cover is Fulk's carved falcon. There is one other viable option: that it was created for Melisende's sister Yvette by the queen herself. However, the overwhelming opinion among academics is that it belonged to Melisende.

It is an object that reflects Melisende's importance, piety and personality. It is possible to examine the illuminations in the text for signs of medieval use, and it is significant that on some pages there is evidence of increased damage to the paint and gilding around images of Christ's feet and hands. Psalters were devotional aids, and it is possible to imagine Queen Melisende kissing the hands and feet of Christ as part of her personal worship.

In many ways the calendar is similar to Western illuminated manuscripts, and it appears to be a copy of one used in Winchester, but the individual artworks created by Basileus are distinctly Eastern in style and execution. They have more in common with the art of the Byzantine Empire and the Greek Orthodox church than Roman Catholicism. While Melisende was the Latin Queen of Jerusalem, her mother was Armenian Morphia who had been raised in the Greek Orthodox faith. So this style of art would likely have appealed to Melisende on a personal level.

If Fulk did indeed create this unique object for his wife, he did well in his choice of gift. It was one that celebrated their relationship, and demonstrated to her that he understood her, and cherished her piety and her heritage, and respected her link to the throne of Jerusalem and to her parents. The third key date inscribed in the calendar alongside that of her parents' deaths is 15 July 1099, the day Jerusalem fell to the first crusaders – Melisende's cousins Godfrey de Bouillon and Baldwin I, and her father Baldwin II.

Understanding this book gives us a keen glimpse into the life of Melisende, her cultural background, and the scandal that rocked the first years of her reign. At the centre of it all was a beautiful young man with a fiery personality: Hugh, Count of Jaffa.

INTRIGUE IN THE KINGDOM

Baldwin II died not long after quashing Princess Alice's first rebellion, and not before making a will that gave his eldest, favourite child hereditary rights to the throne of Jerusalem. In making this will, Baldwin II insulted Fulk and robbed him of sole rulership. Fulk had ruled efficiently and with an iron fist in Anjou, and had not been tempted to the East to share power with his decades-junior wife.

Three weeks following her father's interment in the Chapel of Adam in the Church of the Holy Sepulchre, Melisende and Fulk were jointly anointed and crowned with great splendour in the nave of that same church. It marked the beginning of a new age in Outremer, with rule passing to the next generation. Fulk and Melisende were the first monarchs of the Kingdom of Jerusalem to be crowned together in this location, Melisende's parents and their predecessors having been crowned in Bethlehem. With this, they started a tradition that would endure until the loss of Jerusalem and the collapse of Outremer. Regardless of location, the coronation broke new ground, as it was the first time a woman was crowned as queen *regnant* rather than queen consort. During this ceremony, Melisende became an anointed *ruling* Queen of Jerusalem, albeit sharing her power with her husband and her son.

As demonstrated by Alice's rebellions, two of which occurred during the early years of Fulk and Melisende's joint rule, the new ruling couple's reign did not get off to the smoothest start. They had their work cut out for them in persuading the northern states of Outremer to recognise their suzerainty. Outremer was not a country; countries in the sense we know them today did not exist in the medieval age. Allegiances were to Lords, to families, to benefactors, to those who spoke the same dialect, rather than to an overarching national identity. Fulk also made the mistake of angering the established nobility of Outremer by bringing with him an influx of French retainers whom he rewarded with wealth, lands and offices. The local baronage resented this intrusion.

The contemporary Muslim chronicler Ibn al-Qalanisi, an important Damascene noble who was twice mayor of Damascus, viewed Fulk in a dim light when compared to his predecessor on the throne. He wrote that after the death of Baldwin II,

> there was none left amongst [the barons of Outremer] possessed of sound judgement and capacity to govern. His place was taken after him by the new Count-King, the comte d'Anjou [. . .] but he was not sound in his judgement nor was he successful in his administration, so that by the loss of Baldwin they were thrown into confusion and discordance.

Ibn al-Qalanisi was writing with the benefit of hindsight, and perhaps his judgement of Fulk is harsh, given the intensely complicated political situation he inherited. Nevertheless, he is correct in his analysis that Fulk's time as king cannot be viewed as a success. Perhaps history judges Fulk unfairly. Baldwin II was a hard act to follow, and Melisende proved to be a far more dynamic figure from early on in their reign.

Fulk received a messy inheritance from his father-in-law alongside the international glory and renown that came with the throne of Jerusalem. It seems that in the beginning of his reign, he further took it upon himself to claim both the work and the glory for himself alone, and to sideline his younger, more legitimate co-ruler. Although they were crowned jointly, the early charters of their reign were issued in Fulk's name alone with no mention of Melisende's agreement or consent. This implies that Fulk wanted to hold all the reins of Outremer in one hand, and keep his wife at bay with the other. Melisende, mourning her parents, as she was, and perhaps preoccupied with her first child, seems to have let this slight slide for several years. This, however, was a complacency she would soon be forced to jump out of with an uncomfortable jerk.

In addition to the grief Melisende must have experienced following the death of her father and the responsibility of raising her infant son, she also became responsible for looking after her two youngest sisters, who were several years her junior, unmarried and suddenly orphans. Hodierna was around twenty years old, and little Yvette only ten. Both needed supervision and for their eldest sister to take the initiative in brokering either marriages for them or some other kind of future.

On top of these domestic responsibilities, two crises faced the new monarchs. The first was the second rebellion of Alice, alongside Pons and Joscelin of Edessa, as previously discussed. This rebellion certainly put Melisende in a difficult position, caught as she was between her sister and her husband. She clearly felt sympathy for Alice, as it was her intervention that prevented harsher penalties being imposed upon Alice.

The second crisis was still more personal, and arose as a result of a tension and jealousy between her close confidant and her increasingly angry and manipulative husband.

Among Melisende's companions in the Kingdom of Jerusalem was a young man of similar age to her. He was an exceptionally handsome youth, and given his high status, age and closeness of kin with the royal family, he was a fitting companion for Melisende both during her father's lifetime when she was a princess, and after his death when she was a young queen. Hugh of Jaffa was Melisende's second cousin, and as such was entitled to spend time with her *en famille*. However, it seems that whenever men and women spent time together alone in Outremer, regardless of kinship, sparks of gossip began to catch.

A generation earlier Hugh's parents, high-ranking nobles in France, decided to brave the long journey and undertake a pilgrimage to Jerusalem. Hugh's father, also named Hugh, was a cousin of Baldwin II, and his mother Mamilia was a niece of Bohemond of Taranto. Mamilia was pregnant when they set out from France and went into labour when the pair reached southern Italy. There she gave birth to Hugh. The baby was not strong and his father took the decision to leave him behind in the care of Bohemond's household. Any objections that Mamilia might have made to this plan have not been recorded by the chroniclers.

When Hugh senior arrived in Outremer, his cousin King Baldwin II invested him with the County of Jaffa to be his hereditary Lordship in the East. This is where the elder Hugh's good fortune ended: he died just months after settling in Jaffa. Mamilia did not enjoy any better luck than her husband. As an important widow with significant lands, she was quickly married off to another man, Albert of Namur. Shortly after their nuptials, they both died too.

Hugh and Mamilia's child, having been left in Italy, escaped the disease and ill-luck of his parents and grew to manhood in relative tranquillity. Around the age of sixteen he journeyed to the East to lay claim to the Lordship of Jaffa, which Baldwin II granted him without demur as his birthright. The teenage Hugh was treated with much the same courtesy as Alice's husband Bohemond II had been when he arrived in the East, and quickly found himself a favoured guest at court.

Baldwin II had clearly been pleased with the arrival of his cousin's son and allowed him to spend much time with his family. It was here that Hugh met the four Princesses of Jerusalem and struck up a particular friendship with Melisende and Alice. These sisters were so close to him in age that this seemed only natural. Hugh's familiarity with Melisende would soon develop to become the greatest scandal of their generation.

Baldwin II lavished further favour on Hugh, perhaps encouraged by his evident rapport with members of his family. The old king gave Hugh one of the wealthiest widows in the Kingdom to be his wife. Her name was Emelota and she was nearly twice his age with two grown-up sons, but she brought to the marriage wealth and land in abundance. She was also extremely well connected, the niece of the Patriarch of Jerusalem himself.

Hugh and Melisende's affection for each other was strong, and neither Baldwin II's death, Hugh's marriage to Emelota, nor Melisende's own marriage to Fulk disrupted their relationship. The marriages they each made to significantly older spouses, both of whom already had adult children, and the death of Melisende's father, seemed only to push the pair closer together.

Baldwin II's death left Melisende isolated: both her parents were gone; Alice, her sister nearest to her in age, had left Jerusalem to become Princess of Antioch; and her youngest sisters, little Hodierna and Yvette, were perhaps too young to be proper companions for her. Similarly, her husband was much older than her, and her son was only an infant. Hugh must have been one of the few confidants remaining to the young queen.

Fulk was fifteen years Melisende's senior, and Hugh's wife Emelota was twenty years older than him. While Emelota appears to have adored her energetic young husband, her grown-up sons were less than enthused with the union. Their names were Eustace of Sidon and Walter of Caesarea, and their dislike of Hugh was not unreasonable given that he, a man of their own age, had married their middle-aged mother and taken over her lands, which otherwise might have passed to them.

Also, there were widespread rumours that Hugh was unfaithful to their mother. While this on its own was not necessarily enough to cause scandal, it soon began to be whispered that Hugh's affair was with none other than Queen Melisende herself, a rumour far more sinister than simple infidelity. An affair with the queen could impugn the parentage of the prince and heir to the Kingdom and thus compromise the succession. Hugh's close relationship with Melisende was widely known, and this gossip was dangerous indeed. An accusation of this kind could be enough to dissolve the royal marriage, deprive Melisende of her crown and see her carted off to a nunnery – as Arete, the first Queen of Jerusalem, had been.

The truth of this rumoured affair cannot be established or disproved by modern scholarship. Any private communication between the pair has been lost, and all that remains to us as evidence is the gossip reported by William of Tyre, which William himself did not believe. Indeed, there is a strong case to be made that the rumour was in fact started by none other than King Fulk, in an effort to discredit his wife and push her off the throne. The person with the most to gain from this rumour would in fact have been the cuckolded king. If he could repudiate Melisende, then he could rule alone and replace her with a dimmer and more docile consort.

Moreover, beyond simply seizing Melisende's power, on the basis of this rumour Fulk would have the power to sentence Hugh to death and seize for himself the County of Jaffa and the rich revenues that came with it. This was exactly the sort of scheme that Baldwin II had sought to guard against in his will.

Regardless of whether Melisende and Hugh were sexually attracted or involved with one another, Fulk had every reason to dislike and envy Hugh. He was younger than Fulk, in the prime of life, and of equal wealth and nobility. William of Tyre remembered Hugh thus:

> young, tall of stature, and of handsome countenance. He was distinguished for military prowess and was pleasing in the eyes of all. In him the gifts of nature seemed to have met in lavish abundance; without

question, in respect to physical beauty [. . .] he had no equal in the kingdom.

Any husband would feel threatened by such a man spending many hours in the company of his wife, and Hugh was threatening not just Fulk's marriage, but the legitimacy of his successors and his claims to the Kingdom. William of Tyre wrote:

> the king cherished a deep distrust of the count, who was rumoured to be on too familiar terms with the queen, and of this there seemed to be many proofs. Hence, spurred on by a husband's jealousy, the king is said to have conceived an inexorable hatred against the man.

Those who did not believe the rumours of Melisende's infidelity with Hugh chose instead to believe that Fulk's violent hatred of the man came rather from a fury at Hugh's arrogance, for Hugh 'refused to be subject to the king like the other nobles of the realm and obstinately declined to obey his commands.' This suggests that Hugh took issue with Fulk's sidelining of the local nobility, and perhaps due to his youth and friendship with the queen, he was part of a minority that was not afraid to voice their opinions and distrust of the new monarch.

While Hugh had in many ways landed on his feet when he arrived in Outremer, quickly enfeoffed with the rich County of Jaffa, he was complacent in cementing the human relationships and winning loyalties that could have kept him out of trouble. He had been quick to befriend Alice and Melisende, but failed to win over his stepsons Eustace and Walter. These men were powerful barons in their own right, ruling over important coastal territories with formidable defences. The sea castle of Sidon stands to this day in modern-day Lebanon, and represents one of the most beautiful and impressive crusader-era coastal ruins.

Eustace and Walter resented Hugh, as they perceived his marriage to their mother as usurping their inheritance. This hatred ran deep, and the tensions between the three men came to a head when Walter stood up one day in a bustling and crowded assembly of nobles and accused his stepfather Hugh of high treason and conspiring to kill the king. If Hugh were found guilty of this charge, he would be punished by either exile or execution.

It was thought that this accusation was not merely the product of a stepson's angst, but rather that King Fulk had put Walter up to it in an attempt to dishonour and neutralise the threats posed by Hugh. This seemed all the more likely when Walter challenged the understandably shocked Hugh to trial by combat. If Fulk had wanted to ensure Hugh's death while keeping his own hands clean, he had certainly picked the right method and the right man. In this most idiosyncratic method of medieval justice, a man's guilt or innocence could be decided by hand-to-hand combat between the accused and the accuser, rather than a rational and impartial assessment of evidence. The theory went that God would influence the battle so that if the man was innocent he would survive, and if he was falsely accused then the slanderer would be punished by death. Walter was famous throughout Outremer for his great strength and it seemed there would be little contest between the hulking Walter and the lean Hugh. Walter had every reason to dislike Hugh and would go to the task of slaughtering him with impassioned vigour.

Hugh immediately denied the charges made against him and agreed that he would fight Walter to clear his name. A date was set for the combat between the two men. When the day arrived and Walter prepared for battle, no doubt gleeful at the prospect of simultaneously killing his stepfather and earning the King's gratitude, Hugh was nowhere to be found. The young count had clearly thought better of his agreement to fight his burly stepson. In the heat of the moment and smarting from the insult of an accusation of treason in open court, he had agreed to the combat to demonstrate that he had nothing to hide and thus nothing to fear from the duel. In the clear light of a new day he realised that fighting Walter was exactly what his enemies wanted and that he was unlikely to survive the contest. Perhaps also his wife Emelota and his cousin Queen Melisende implored him not to fight. Whatever his reasons, Hugh did not appear at the appointed time, which made him look guilty in the eyes of all around him. He was pronounced a traitor across Outremer.

Circumstances forced his hand and Hugh fled Jerusalem. In retaliation for Fulk's rather transparent attempt on his life, in the following months Hugh attempted to whip up a rebellion to challenge Fulk and throw him off the throne. It is likely that this storm had been brewing for some time, even before Walter's accusation, and that this farce had in fact been intended to neutralise Hugh's rebellious schemes before they could be enacted. Instead they served as the catalyst to set the wheels of his revolt in motion. As has previously been noted, Hugh's name is found among the witness lists of charters issued by Alice when she was in exile in Latakieh, so it is clear that Hugh had been in league with anti-Fulk sympathisers for some time. Similarly, the name of Romanus of Le Puy, a baron who had previously had his own lands in Transjordan confiscated for treason, appears in the witness lists for Hugh's own charters, indicating that he had, like Alice, become a figurehead for those resentful of Fulk's authority.

The ruling Lords of Outremer were splitting into two distinct camps. Those who supported the rights of the sisters Alice and Melisende over Fulk and his Angevin comrades, and those who supported Fulk's single rule and claims of suzerainty over the other Lordships of Outremer. Fulk had been trying to deprive Melisende of her power as queen and exclude her from affairs of state. Hugh, both as her friend and the loyal vassal of her father, was outraged by this and sought to promote Melisende's interests against the egotism of her husband. This was the real cause of Fulk's hatred of Hugh, and it was fear of Hugh's faction gaining support that may have caused Fulk to push Hugh into open rebellion by an accusation of treason. In organising the stunt with Walter of Caesarea's accusation, he would have simultaneously discredited his wife and defeated Hugh, the greatest threat to his kingship since Alice's last rebellion.

When he was found guilty of treason, Hugh would have known that the next phase of Fulk's plan would be to deprive him of the County of Jaffa. Understandably, he panicked. He fell into the same trap that Alice had when she appealed to Zengi for aid against her father. While Hugh originally had the support of his vassals against Fulk, he lost all their sympathies when he made the error of calling for aid from the Egyptians of Ascalon. They were Muslims, and thus the sworn enemies of the Franks in Outremer, while temporary alliances were sometimes made, as has been seen with Alice it was always taboo to ally with Muslims against the King of Jerusalem. They marched with Hugh into Outremer and proceeded to raid the Christian territories, ostensibly to help Hugh defend Jaffa against Fulk, but really with greed and self-interest as motivation.

On hearing of this invasion, Fulk marched Jerusalem's armies south. Thus far Hugh had enjoyed the loyalty of key vassals of his County. However, they were uncomfortable with his foolhardy alliance with the Egyptians and his plan to try and hold Jaffa against the king – a futile enterprise. They tried to persuade him away from this rash course of action, but could make no headway with the furious and determined count. Hugh was still smarting from the numerous insults and accusations levelled against him, and the humiliation of being blindsided by an accusation of treason from his stepson in open court. When Hugh's vassals saw that their attempts to reason with their lord fell on deaf ears, they abandoned him and went to join Fulk.

As the army of Jerusalem approached and the Ascalonites saw that

Hugh's own people were turning against him, they too left his side as quickly as they had come. Hugh was left alone and without allies, and Jaffa capitulated to the king without a struggle. Hugh was powerless, disgraced and at Fulk's mercy.

However, Queen Melisende was on his side, and the church was on Queen Melisende's side. She had already established herself as a patron of the church and a devoutly Christian queen, and the church clearly believed the side of the story that hinged not on her infidelity but on Hugh fighting for her rights and the rights of the local nobility against Fulk. The Patriarch of Jerusalem, a Flemish priest named William of Malines, intervened to soothe Fulk's rage and promote Hugh and Melisende's interests. The fact that he did this demonstrates clearly both the influence of Melisende and the fact that justice was on Hugh's side. He had acted foolishly in joining forces with the Egyptians, and for this he must be publicly punished, but it seems the sympathies of enough people were with his cause that a harsh punishment would have been impolitic.

Melisende and Patriarch William's entreaties were effective, and perhaps Fulk had been shaken by the extent of the opposition against him, for he ostensibly agreed to patch things up with Hugh with a lenient sentence. Instead of being deprived of his lands, like his unlucky ally Romanus of Le Puy, or subjected to disgrace and indefinite banishment like Alice, Hugh was given only a three-year sentence of exile. During this time King Fulk could claim the revenue from his lands, but when the sentence of exile had been served, Hugh would be fully reinstated as Count of Jaffa. This was lenient indeed. Had it not been for the intervention of Melisende and the clergy, Hugh would have faced at best the loss of his lands forever, or at worst a death sentence.

The fact that Hugh was so openly against Fulk before his accusation of treason and was not charged with any crime, suggests that his resistance to Fulk had legal basis, or at least that his actions had the approval of the nobles of the land. This in turn shows that Fulk was acting illegally, or at the very least impolitically. This adds weight to the argument that Fulk was attempting to deprive Melisende of her political power, and that Hugh was fighting to preserve it.

Following the negotiations regarding Hugh's punishment, the count made plans to return to Italy to serve out his exile in Apulia, the land in which he had been raised. As he awaited a ship to convey him there, he idled away his days in Jerusalem. One evening, he was playing dice on a table outside the shop of a local merchant in the Street of the Furriers. Hugh's guard was down, as the rebellion had been resolved and he had no reason to fear for his safety. The street was full, bustling with the usual traffic of traders, pilgrims and crusaders. Suddenly, out of the midst of the crowds an armed Frankish knight wielding a naked sword leapt forward. He stabbed the unsuspecting Hugh repeatedly, wounding him grievously in broad daylight and in full view of the stunned crowd, before making his escape.

Hugh's wounds did not at first glance seem to be fatal, but they were still extensive, and in the medieval world, before the advent of modern medicine and antibacterials, a wound that didn't kill by blood loss would frequently fester and kill by infection. The city was shocked by this act of barbarity committed in a civilian setting and upon a high-ranking nobleman.

Given the widely publicised enmity between Fulk and Hugh, it is unsurprising that soon tongues were wagging and all fingers were pointing to the king. The attack *had* to be a premeditated assassination attempt. It was too much of a coincidence that Hugh should be attacked by chance by a motiveless knight in the aftermath of his infamous conflict with the king. The knight who had carried out the attack, swiftly caught, was a nobody from Brittany. He had to be acting on the orders of someone else. Who that someone else was, was an open secret: nobody had more reason to want Hugh dead than King Fulk. He had already declared war on him, had him accused of treason, and it was widely believed that Hugh had been sleeping with his wife.

This was a public relations disaster for Fulk, unpopular as he was already. Public opinion sided with Hugh and with Melisende. They rallied to Hugh, who was now indisputably the injured party and the underdog in this bitter feud. Fulk went to great lengths to try and establish his innocence. Even though medieval crusader culture had a reputation for bloodlust, it was not a culture of literal backstabbing and covert assassination. This type of underhanded skulduggery still drew public outcry, and this cowardly, sly and not to mention failed attempt on Hugh's life only served to make the king look weak and desperate, and undermine his case against Hugh. Chivalry was the lynchpin of medieval ideals of knighthood, and assassination was unchivalrous in the extreme.

Fulk did the only thing he could do – he distanced himself from the attack. He sent a clear message that he was as outraged by it as the rest of the public were, and had the knight arrested and forced to stand a public trial. Witnesses abounded, and the man's guilt was assured, but it was his motive that the people wanted established. Fulk wanted both to make an example of the would-be assassin, and demonstrate to both his wife and the people of Jerusalem that he had not given the orders for the attack.

The unfortunate attacker was sentenced to suffer the most draconian of punishments: the 'mutilation of his members'. Fulk stipulated that everything that could be sliced off would be sliced off, all except his tongue, which was to be left intact so as not to suggest Fulk was trying to silence him. With his intact tongue the man was challenged under torture to tell why he had committed the crime. Dutiful until the end, he proclaimed that he had acted without the King's knowledge, and not on the King's orders, but that he had hoped to gain favour with Fulk because he knew of his hatred for Hugh, and thought to win his notice by getting rid of his most hated adversary.

Fulk's reputation was to some degree salvaged by this, but the prognosis was still far from good. The credibility of such a story was dubious. It was a high-risk strategy to decide to independently attempt to murder one of the most well-known figures in the land on the off chance of winning royal favour as a result. Even if the story were true, it was still Fulk's hatred and jealousy of Hugh that had caused him to be stabbed in this crude fashion, and the Count's life still hung in the balance.

Hugh stayed in Outremer long enough to recover his health and prepare for his journey, but once in Apulia, he fell into a deep pit of depression, despite the warm welcome he received from the king of that land. He still felt the injuries not just of the attack in the streets of Jerusalem, but of the attack on his honour and pride from Fulk and Walter of Caesarea's accusations, and doubtless too he was despairing of his separation from Melisende, who if not his lover, was his queen and close confidante. It seemed he never recovered to full health following this unhappy episode and separation, and died shortly after arriving in Italy. This sudden death of this young and handsome count, so shortly after the scandal of his accusation and attempted murder, rekindled public anger in Jerusalem.

It was not only the public that was furious.

THE QUEEN'S FURY

Melisende was incandescent with rage at Hugh's death and the whole debacle. Demonstrating remarkable self-restraint, so far her anger at her exclusion from rule had been contained, and she had been content to allow Hugh to fight her corner. With Hugh's death, this restraint dramatically ended. A great and public chasm erupted between the king and queen, and many courtiers were in danger of being dragged into it.

Thus far Queen Melisende had been a relatively quiet wife, despite the injustices perpetrated by her husband. While she must have been aware of and involved in Hugh's rebellion, she had never openly abandoned Fulk. Nor had she ever strongly campaigned on her own behalf for the co-rulership to which she was entitled, and had endeavoured, despite difficult circumstances, to at least keep up the pretence of being a good wife and mother and pious queen. Now, however, Melisende's fury against her husband knew no bounds.

William of Tyre writes: 'her heart was wrung with deep sorrow for the exiled count, and her own good fame was besmirched by the infamous accusation.' The men who had supported Fulk against Hugh now ran from her in fear of their lives. Melisende was furious both for the death of Hugh but also for the vicious insults made against her honour and good name in the public scandal around her alleged affair with him. Fulk's jealousy had been egged on by his supporters, in particular Rohard of Nablus, and she persecuted him to a greater extent than the others. She drove these men from the court and they shied away from public gatherings where assassination attempts like that carried out against Hugh might be staged. Even Fulk himself was terrified for his life, and studiously avoided situations where he was alone or unarmed among the followers of the queen. William of Tyre wrote of Melisende's wrath:

> From that time, all who had informed against the count and thereby incited the king to wrath fell under the displeasure of Queen Melisende and were forced to take diligent measures for their safety [. . .] it was not safe for these informers to come into her presence; in fact, they deemed it prudent to keep away from public gatherings. Even the king found that no place was entirely safe among the kindred and partisans of the queen.

Melisende's exact involvement in Hugh's rebellion is hard to glean. William of Tyre, the only chronicler to write an in-depth account of this episode, does not explicitly link her to Hugh's seditious actions, but merely repeats the rumours that the pair were 'too familiar'. However, it must be assumed that while Hugh was in Jerusalem at least, the queen was involved. If the pair were close enough to incite gossip, and Hugh was campaigning for her rights and the rights of the local nobility, and what's more, was visiting her rebellious sister in Antioch, then Melisende must have been aware of Hugh's plans. It is clear that there was a bitter rivalry between Fulk and Hugh, and whether this rivalry was political or romantic, Melisende was at its centre.

Fulk represented newcomers from the West, eager to adapt Outremer to suit their own tastes and ambitions, at the expense of the native nobility. It is clear that the vast retinue Fulk brought with him caused anger and dissent among the local nobility, of whom Melisende and Hugh were the most prominent. As Fulk attempted to exclude Melisende from rule, she became the natural symbol of the dispossessed nobility, and in standing up for her Hugh was challenging the entire regime that Fulk had attempted to introduce.

Orderic Vitalis, an Anglo-Norman monk writing almost contemporaneously, and indeed much closer to the events than William of Tyre, who was very young at the time of this incident, wrote a perhaps more accurate account of the reasons behind Hugh's rebellion:

> To begin with he [Fulk] acted without the foresight and shrewdness he should have shown, and changed governors and other dignitaries too quickly and thoughtlessly. As a new ruler he banished from his councils the leading magnates who from the first had fought resolutely against the Turks [. . .] and replaced them with Angevin strangers and other raw newcomers to whom he gave his ear; turning out the veteran defenders, he gave the chief places in the councils of the realm and the castellanships of castles to new flatterers. Consequently great disaffection spread, and the stubbornness of the magnates was damnably roused against the man who changed officials so gauchely. For a long time, under the influences of the powers of evil, they turned their warlike skills, which they should have united to exercise against the heathen, to rend themselves. They even allied [. . .] with the pagans against each other.

Although Melisende is not mentioned by name here, she was the epitome of the idea of veteran defenders displaced by Angevin interlopers. Orderic Vitalis makes a slight error in his presentation of these events, as by the time of Fulk's reign the truly veteran defenders who had helped Godfrey suppress the Muslims were more or less all dead. It was their sons and daughters, their inheriting successors, many of whom had been born in Outremer, whom Fulk was depriving of power and influence. He was attempting to consolidate his power in much the same way as Baldwin II had done, by giving gifts to men he trusted and thus securing their loyalty, and not listening to his wife. However, Fulk's error lay in failing to realise that such a scheme would not work against the established Christian nobility, and that his claim to power existed only through Melisende who was the bloodline linking him to the first crusaders who had captured Jerusalem.

The full extent of Melisende's feelings on the situation were masked by Hugh's actions. He championed her cause and drew the heat away from her and onto himself. When he died, her fury was beyond compare and her true attitude and involvement were revealed in her reaction. She drove her husband out of court, and it was only by the desperate mediations of Patriarch William and those close to her, frantic to preserve the Kingdom from further fracture, that her 'wrath was appeased' and a reconciliation was brought about between the king and queen. Melisende certainly had grounds for fury. During her father's reign, a number of laws were made specifically to punish adulterous women. At the council of Nablus in 1120, it was decided that in the Kingdom of Jerusalem a woman caught in adultery was liable to undergo rhinotomy, a barbaric practice in which either the nostrils are slit or the nose completely removed. In accusing her of adultery, Fulk had not only threatened Melisende's political status but had also placed her in serious danger.

Fulk now grovelled before his wife, chastened and terrified by the awfulness of her rage, and realising perhaps for the first time what sort of formidable woman he was married to. From that day forward, Melisende was the senior partner in their relationship, and Fulk became completely uxorious towards her. He never dared go against his wife's will publicly or act in any way in the Kingdom of Jerusalem that would cause her displeasure. Hugh's rebellion may have failed and ended in the Count's exile and death, but it achieved its goal: Melisende reclaimed her right to rule, and the status of the local nobility was preserved. Following the rebellion, Melisende's name appears on virtually every charter issued by Fulk in the Kingdom of Jerusalem, giving her consent and demonstrating her increasing power.

However, out of the ashes of this abject marital and political disaster, a closer relationship began to blossom between Fulk and Melisende. William of Tyre relates how 'through the mediation of certain intimate friends [. . .] the king finally, after persistent efforts, succeeded in gaining a pardon.' Two pieces of evidence exist to show Fulk's efforts to make amends to his wife, and his success in this field. The first is the exquisitely wrought psalter described above, that Fulk presented to Melisende as a peace offering. And the second is the birth of their second child, Amalric, some years after the revolt.

ZUMURRUD OF DAMASCUS

Melisende was not the only strong woman defying male rulers and making waves in the Middle East during the 1130s. A noblewoman of similar pedigree to Melisende was puppeteering the politics at the court of Damascus. Besides Jerusalem and Constantinople, Damascus was the third shining jewel in the Levant at this time, and the Damascene court was the Muslim counterpart to the Christian court of Jerusalem, bursting with intrigues, tensions and sinister mischief. Standing at its heart was a strong queen as fierce and headstrong as Melisende herself.

Khatun Safwat al-Mulk Zumurrud was the daughter of the prominent Muslim Amir Jawali. Her given name, Zumurrud, was Arabic for 'Emerald'. Through her mother, Zumurrud was half-sister to Duqaq of Damascus, a Muslim leader who had fought against the leaders of the First Crusade as they made their way eastwards. Her older brother had clashed time and time again with Melisende's father, and Zumurrud's own husband, the Damascene Atabeg Buri, fought against Melisende's father Baldwin II. Indeed, Zumurrud found herself besieged by both Melisende's father and husband together in the Damascene crusade of 1129.

Zumurrud was the widow of Buri, the last Lord of Damascus. Her son Isma'il had seized power on his father's death. He was a young and volatile character. Barely twenty years old when he claimed the throne in 1133, he swiftly developed a reputation for greed and cruelty. Among his retinue was an adviser inherited from his father's reign, Yusuf ibn Firuz, who remained close to the reigning family. In time, Zumurrud would be accused of an extramarital affair with this man, and a scandal would erupt in the Damascene court that would shape the face of politics and dynasties in the world of Muslim Syria.

Thus while Hugh of Jaffa was dodging metaphorical and physical blows in Jerusalem, a similar sequence of injustices was unfolding on the other side of the Golan Heights.

Zumurrud's husband had come up against one of the most simultaneously secretive and famous of Muslim sects, the order of the Nizari Ismailis, more commonly known as the Assassins. He was attacked by two slaves in his retinue who were secretly members of the Assassins, and although he recovered from his injuries, he rushed his convalescence and attempted to ride too soon, which reopened the wound, and he died in June 1132. His son Isma'il succeeded him as ruler of Damascus. Zumurrud ostensibly entered a period of mourning and withdrew from public life as the widowed queen mother. Her first act following the death of her husband was to order the building of a great madrasa. The Madrasa Khatuniyya *extra-muros*, as it came to be known, was only the fifth madrasa to be founded in Damascus, and would influence the construction of Nur ad-Din's colossal mausoleum–mosque–madrasa complex some thirty years later. It was located on the upper *sharaf*, west of the walled city, and preceded Queen Melisende's own architectural projects in Jerusalem.

Isma'il's reign had started well, with him reclaiming the fortress of Banyas from the Franks, and thus demonstrating to King Fulk that he was a new rival for prominence in the East. Zengi, the Lord of Aleppo, also took note of Isma'il's military vigour. However, Isma'il was a poor diplomat and highly paranoid. He alienated those close to him through unfair taxation and by fits of passionate rage, and as a result feared that he was in constant danger of assassination. He cannot have been a son of whom Zumurrud would have been proud. Ibn al-Athir reports that he 'used extreme tortures to extract money and manifested excessive greed and meanness of spirit . . . his family, his followers and his subjects loathed him.'

Matters came to a head when a slave in Isma'il's household did indeed attempt to murder the unpopular atabeg. On his capture, the slave proclaimed that he had acted to win God's favour by ridding the world of Isma'il's reign of terror, and under questioning he named others supposedly complicit in the scheme. Without any trial or further investigation, these suspects were tortured and executed. Among them was Isma'il's own half-brother, whom Isma'il had walled up alive and left to die of starvation. This unfortunate brother was not Zumurrud's own son – he was the child of one of Buri's other wives – but while she may not have felt personal grief, she was doubtless shocked by the barbarity of her own son's actions.

Isma'il compounded the ill feeling towards him by his extreme (but retrospectively justified) paranoia, believing he was no longer safe at the court of Damascus. He began to shift his fortune and possessions south to the city of Sarkhad. He then wrote to Zengi, the Atabeg of Aleppo, outlining his intention to abandon Damascus, telling Zengi that if he did not come and claim it, it would fall into the hands of the Franks.

The Damascenes, however, had no intention of simply giving their beloved capital to the Atabeg of Aleppo, and instead rushed to Zumurrud to beg her to intervene with her son and put a stop to his insanity.

Zumurrud was 'vexed and alarmed' at the reports of Isma'il's actions, and promised to resolve the situation. In addition, rumours not unlike those surrounding Melisende and Hugh of Jaffa had been circulating for some time about Zumurrud's relationship with her late husband's chief advisor, Yusuf ibn Firuz. Zumurrud caught wind that these rumours were public, and more than this, that the news had reached her son and he intended to kill Yusuf. This put Zumurrud in a difficult position. In the end, it was also astonishingly easy to resolve. Her son was on the rampage, haphazardly murdering courtiers and abandoning crucial territory. The life of a man to whom she was close was under threat. If Isma'il decided she was guilty of having an affair with his dead father's closest advisor, she herself was not safe. Yusuf ibn Firuz fled Damascus and went into hiding in Palmyra, and Zumurrud summoned her son before her. After remonstrating with Isma'il and upbraiding him severely for his decisions and his reprehensible behaviour, she became convinced that he was beyond the influence of words.

Circumstances may have forced her hand, yet Zumurrud acted with remarkable sang-froid. The dowager queen quietly but determinedly arranged the assassination of her son, to protect her realm, her lover and her own life. She persuaded Isma'il's slaves – with gold or without is unknown – to turn against their master. Given the young man's temperament, it is unlikely much arm-twisting was required. Zumurrud gave instructions that when an opportunity arose when the slaves were alone with him, then they should quickly murder him, and this they did. Isma'il was only twenty-one years old at the time of his death. When the slaves sent word to Zumurrud that the deed was done, she went a step further and ordered that his corpse be dragged to some public place, that the people might learn of his death and rejoice. Ibn al-Qalanisi wrote that she showed 'neither mercy nor sorrow for his loss, because of his evil actions, the corruption of his mind, his vile conduct and blame-worthy behaviour.'

Zumurrud's next step was to install her second son, Mahmud, as Lord of Damascus. Shortly after the conclusion of this scandal, Atabeg Zengi arrived at the gates of Damascus in response to the late Isma'il's summons, only to be politely but firmly informed that Damascus had decided against surrendering to his rule. Zengi retired, but already his mind was working to find other ways in which he could add Damascus to his empire without bloodshed, and his thoughts began to linger on the beautiful widowed Zumurrud, whom he clearly saw as the power behind the throne. Following brief negotiations, the pair were married, and Zumurrud brought Homs as her dowry. Through his marriage to Zumurrud, Zengi had hoped to rule Damascus, but this plan never came to fruition.

Not long after their wedding, Zumurrud's second son, Mahmud, was also assassinated, in June 1139. His mother, in contrast to her reaction to her first son's death, was 'troubled and distressed' and 'grieved at his loss'. She wrote to her husband at Mosul, 'spurring him on to march without delay and take vengeance'. The object of his vengeance was none other than Zumurrud's third son, who had installed himself as Lord of Damascus following the death of his brother. This man died of disease before Zengi had succeeded in taking the city, and troublesome as the assault was proving to be, he abandoned it following the death of its lord.

Zumurrud was probably at least seven years older than Melisende, given that she bore a son in 1113, meaning that she herself must have been born by 1100 at the latest. It is more likely she was born between 1095 and 1100. However, the two women are eminently comparable as queens. While Melisende ruled in Jerusalem, Zumurrud wielded power in Damascus. She was never formally recognised as heir or queen in the way that Melisende was, but the fact that despairing politicians came to her to intervene with the lord of the city demonstrates the respect she commanded and the power she wielded within the court of Damascus. They were both politically astute and determined noblewomen, and patrons of art and architecture. While Melisende certainly never arranged the murder of her son, she was fiercely protective of Hugh of Jaffa, and when she believed Fulk had had a hand in an attempt on his life, she railed at him in fury. Similarly, when in the later years of her reign she perceived her son to be challenging her authority, she did not hesitate to act against him.

Both women were tireless patrons of their respective faiths, with Melisende undertaking the great expansion of the Church of the Holy Sepulchre, and Zumurrud building the Madrasa Khatuniyya in Damascus, an impressive domed building standing to this day. It was the last major female contribution to the religious topography of Damascus until the time of the supremacy of Saladin.

RECONCILIATION

Following Melisende and Fulk's reconciliation, a rare period of calm descended over Outremer, and during this time Melisende's patronage of art and architecture flourished. Among other religious works and donations, the opportunity had presented itself for Melisende to do something for her youngest sister, Yvette, who had had the misfortune to be held hostage by the Muslim ruler Timurtash for a year during her infancy. Yvette's future seemed to be the most complicated of Melisende's three sisters, but in many ways it would prove to be the simplest. Melisende had done her best to ameliorate the lot of Alice, but she had brought about her own ruin and died young. Melisende had then arranged a grand marriage for her sister Hodierna to Count Raymond of Tripoli, securing her position as one of the foremost ladies in Outremer. But Melisende could find no suitor for Yvette. Indeed, there is no evidence to suggest that she even tried. She knew as well as anybody that a woman who had lived among the enemy was unlikely to make a good marriage.

Whether or not she had been abused in captivity, the experience had still tainted Yvette's reputation. The only respectable path for an unmarriageable girl of noble rank was to enter a nunnery, and thus Yvette entered the Convent of St Anne at a young age. This was the same convent that Baldwin I's second wife Arete had so detested, and Melisende decided that a lifetime spent quietly treading the cloisters of St Anne's under the supervision of an abbess of inferior birth and lineage was not quite good enough for her youngest sister.

Instead, when the politics of the Kingdom allowed her, she conceived the plan to found a new religious establishment over which her sister could eventually preside. In some ways, giving Yvette control of a wealthy religious order would make her more powerful than many secular male lords. The church had its own laws, hierarchy and property and was not subject to the same bonds of vassalage and suzerainty as the secular world. As the abbess of an order of nuns, Yvette could be sure of a meaningful and respected life as one of the most powerful women in Outremer, as befitted her royal status as the fourth daughter of Morphia and Baldwin II.

Queen Melisende personally took charge of the creation of this convent for her sister. She surveyed suitable sites, and after considering several options among the plentiful religious sites available in the Holy Land, she carefully chose the village of Bethany. This village lies about three kilometres from the Old City of Jerusalem, and thus was a place where Melisende would be able to visit her sister with relative ease. The village was also significant from a religious perspective as it was the biblical home of Lazarus, whom Jesus raised from the dead, and his two sisters who nursed him, Mary and Martha. A piece of land so important to two female biblical figures was a fitting place for Melisende to found a community of sisters. Once she had settled upon this particular village, which was owned by the Church of the Holy Sepulchre, she traded lands in the vicinity of Hebron for ownership of Bethany.

Melisende then began a programme of construction. She built both a convent of suitable grandeur, and also a fortified watchtower to provide protection for the nuns. She endowed the convent with wealth and lands, with the aim of making her sister's new home wealthier than any other monastery, convent or church. To avoid the rather obvious suggestions of nepotism, Melisende did not immediately install Yvette as abbess. Instead she chose a venerable woman who was well into old age and in ill-health. This lady conveniently did the royal sisters the service of dying shortly after her appointment. The remaining nuns dutifully elected Yvette as the new abbess, and Yvette ruled over the Convent of Bethany for the rest of her days. Within the sheltered cloisters, she outlived all of her sisters. She remained close and devoted to her elder sister the queen, who continued to be her and the convent's primary benefactress for many years. When Melisende became seriously ill nearly twenty years later, Yvette would rush to her sister's side and personally nurse her.

On Yvette's succession as abbess, Melisende donated further wealth to the convent. She went so far as to donate the entirety of Jericho and its surrounding lands, which made Bethany one of the wealthiest religious houses in Outremer. It also provided the convent with ongoing revenues, which would ensure its survival even if subsequent rulers of Jerusalem took little interest in supporting the convent. Melisende also presented to the convent 'a large number of sacred vessels of gold and silver adorned with gems. She likewise gave it silken stuffs for the adornment of the house of God and vestments of every description, both priestly and Levitical, as ecclesiastical rule required.'

Perhaps Melisende, like her father, was concerned with her legacy and her immortal soul. The church had cleverly engineered the belief that donations to religious orders stood one's soul in good stead in the afterlife, and perhaps this influenced Melisende's decision to give so lavishly to this new religious order. Perhaps too she was concerned with leaving lasting monuments to her own achievements and reign. If she hoped the Convent of Bethany would survive down the ages, she was sadly mistaken, as it was vandalised by Mamluks less than a century later.

In her charter, which donated money to the leper hospital of St Lazarus – and indeed, before too long leprosy would become a disease with which her lineage would be intimately acquainted – Queen Melisende acknowledged some of her reasons for her extensive patronage of religious organisations and monuments: 'It is the custom of wise men to record in writing their [. . .] works so that it is impossible to erase them from memory [. . .] and thus their successors may imitate what their ancestors have done.' It is interesting that the queen does not refer to women in this charter, demonstrating that in her acts and deeds she wished to be a queen equated with princes and kings, not princesses and wives.

In addition to her work on Bethany, Melisende also undertook with her husband an ambitious project to improve the Church of the Holy Sepulchre. Together they had promoted this church, over the Church of the Nativity in Bethlehem, as the state church of the Kingdom of Jerusalem, as demonstrated by their novel choice to hold their coronation there, breaking with tradition. In the twelfth century the church would undergo a major effort of construction and restoration, and this project was begun under the joint rule of Fulk and Melisende.

From a perusal of this flowering of patronage under their joint rule in the latter portion of their reign, it is evident that Fulk and Melisende's marriage recovered enough for them to have a second child, and for the Kingdom to prosper under their joint rulership. The clearest sign of a fractured government is the inability to get things done and apparent stagnation, and nothing was less evident during the joint reign of Melisende and Fulk. The Kingdom's borders were well defended, and as we have seen, art and architecture flourished under their patronage. No new scandals rocked the Kingdom during this time, and it seemed that the king and queen, once pitted so bitterly against each other, began to develop a genuine mutual affection. Their relationship, which had started so unequally and under the strain of the gulf between their ages and Fulk's personal ambition, tempered into something very much resembling love.

The pair gradually began to keep court together once again, and as we have seen, they wrote letters and released charters under their joint names and authority, a formal model of marital unity. However, the wedded bliss, so hard won, was not to last. At the close of autumn, on 7 November 1143, the royal couple were staying at Acre in the north of the Kingdom, situated amid beautiful hills and on the coast, near the border with modern-day Lebanon. Perhaps wishing to make the most of the late-autumn light and bored within the high walls of the city, Melisende decided to go out riding, wishing for a change of scene and to view the springs in the countryside surrounding the fortified city.

Medieval cities were not fragrant places and Acre was less pleasant than most, given its prominence as a major trading port. It was overcrowded and bustling with trade and activity, and so excursions like this into the hills in search of fresh air were a matter of routine. Fulk offered to escort the queen, and the pair rode out together, flanked by a small retinue.

As the party rode along, a hare was disturbed in a trench and took off across the countryside. The king gave immediate chase, riding at full pelt over the uneven ground and brandishing his lance, eager to impress his wife with his hunting prowess and horsemanship. Under the intensity of Fulk's urgings, the panicked destrier stumbled, the break in pace flinging Fulk off its back and head first onto the rocky terrain. He was knocked senseless by the fall, and seconds after he had hit the ground, his heavy saddle became dislodged too, falling after him and striking him hard on the head. The extent of his injuries was apparent immediately, as blood and brain matter began to gush from his nose and mouth. His attendants soon caught up with him and gathered around, clamouring to help and be of service, but the king was by this point unconscious and unresponsive.

It was at this point that Melisende arrived. She was distraught at the sight of Fulk; hysterical, she tore at her hair and threw herself on the ground beside him. She embraced him, weeping furiously and unable to speak for choked sobs. She was not alone in her tears; her grief was infectious and a tragic spectacle in its own right; soon the household attendants too were weeping over the unconscious and injured Fulk. In Outremer in the Middle Ages, an injury of this severity was usually tantamount to a death sentence.

News of the accident soon spread to the city, and crowds of townspeople and nobles quickly flocked to the scene of Melisende's grief, where presumably the retainers were still trying to gather their wits and stop the bleeding. With the aid of the crowd of onlookers, Fulk's senseless yet still living body was conveyed with tenderness and speed to the city, where he was carefully nursed. He lived without waking for three days, before eventually succumbing to his injuries on 10 November.

He had reigned in Outremer for twelve years, and had been Melisende's husband for fourteen. Although both his reign and their marriage had been rocky at the outset, they had settled into a state of stability and prosperity that the Kingdom and the queen mourned to lose.

Fulk's body was borne to Jerusalem with much ceremony, and the entire city, both clergy and lay people, gathered in the streets to meet his body and form a funeral procession. He was laid to rest alongside his father-in-law and other predecessors as the King of Jerusalem at the holiest site of Christendom, at the foot of Mount Calvary in the Chapel of Adam in the Church of the Holy Sepulchre. Patriarch William of Jerusalem led the funeral mass. The royal tombs of Jerusalem have long since been lost, vandalised by the Turks in later centuries, but the place where Fulk was interred can still be visited under the steps of Calvary amid the throngs of pilgrims.

Fulk's family mourned him. He left behind Melisende, now aged thirty-eight, and their two sons, Baldwin, aged thirteen, and Amalric, aged seven.

4

THE SECOND REIGN OF QUEEN MELISENDE

Baldwin, king of Jerusalem, a youth of great promise, and his mother, a wise and circumspect woman, strong of heart and not inferior in wisdom to any prince whatsoever . . .

William of Tyre

With the death of Fulk, Melisende lost her partner of fourteen years. She also gained the opportunity to rule the Kingdom of Jerusalem. While it appears that she mourned her husband sincerely, his death presented her with a golden opportunity: to have unchallenged primacy in the holiest city of Christendom. This was an ambition held by many and fulfilled by very few. For an educated and ambitious woman, the chance to step out of the shadows cast by men was fortuitous indeed and made her the envy of royal women of both East and West.

Melisende had fulfilled her role as queen admirably thus far, providing two healthy male heirs for the Kingdom. However, both Baldwin and Amalric were still minors at the time of their father's death. Melisende had been a voice of authority within the Kingdom since the death of Hugh of Jaffa, and by this point she commanded great loyalty, not least from her old ally Patriarch William, and as such wielded tangible power. The result of these fortuitously aligned factors was that there were few barriers or rivals to prevent Melisende becoming co-ruler of the Kingdom of Jerusalem with her young son Baldwin.

This was in direct contrast to the circumstances of her unfortunate sister Alice when she had tried to capitalise on the death of Bohemond II and take power in Antioch. Melisende was in a far stronger position than her sister had been. She had succeeded during her husband's lifetime in achieving equal status with him as co-ruler. Beyond this, she had a claim to the throne and regency of Jerusalem by hereditary right, whereas Alice had only been Princess of Antioch through a very brief marriage to a now-dead husband.

Despite the fact that Melisende had already been crowned and anointed queen in 1131, she was re-crowned as co-ruler with her eldest son, Baldwin III, on Christmas Day 1143. Although they were crowned together, given Baldwin's youth and the strength of Melisende's influence in the Kingdom, William of Tyre asserts that 'the royal power passed to the Lady Melisend, a queen beloved of God, to whom it belonged by hereditary right.' It was clear from the earliest moments that Melisende alone now held the reins of power in the Kingdom of Jerusalem.

Shortly after her accession to the throne Melisende received a letter of support from an unexpected source: Bernard, Abbot of Clairvaux. He had risen to become one of the most prominent and influential men in Europe, with arguably more influence over the monastic orders of Europe than the Pope himself. He wrote the following letter to Melisende in the aftermath of Fulk's death:

> With the king your husband dead and the young king not yet ready to bear the business of the kingdom and to carry out the office of king, the eyes of all look to you and on you alone the whole weight of the kingdom falls. You must put your hand to strong things and show a man in a woman, doing what is to be done in the spirit of counsel and fortitude. You must dispose all things so prudently and moderately that all who see them will think you a king rather than a queen from your acts, lest perhaps the people might say, 'Where is the king of Jerusalem?' 'But I am not,' you say, 'capable of this. These are great things, beyond my strength and my knowledge. These are the deeds of men, while I am a woman, weak of body, unstable of heart, not prudent of counsel, not accustomed to affairs.' I know, daughter, I know these are great things, but I also know this, that the swellings of the sea are wondrous, and the Lord is wondrous on high. These are great, but our Lord is great and his power is great.

While to a modern reader this letter appears a little condescending, to a medieval audience it was remarkably open-minded and forward-thinking. This letter constitutes a unique document, in which one of the most powerful figures in the Catholic church warmly encourages a woman to rule a Christian kingdom in her own right. He advised her to follow her own instincts and make her own decisions. While Bernard was careful to apportion any success Melisende might have as a queen to God's greatness rather than any personal talent or acumen on her own part, he asserted that she was equal to the challenges of rulership that would face her. His letter implicitly acknowledged that Queen Melisende was more capable of ruling than a male child – something that was not always taken as a given in medieval Europe. He did not advise her to marry again swiftly so as to install a male ruler in Christ's Kingdom, or to defer to the judgement of better or wiser male advisors, but rather to arm herself with prayer and confidence to take on the challenges of rule. This is remarkable, in the context of the patriarchal structures that existed across Europe and Outremer at this time. Even England's Elizabeth I, the most famous unmarried queen of all time, and ruling four centuries later than Melisende, still found herself pressured from many angles to marry and defer to the advice of men.

Bernard of Clairvaux, the author of this exceptional letter, would become an important figure in Melisende's life beyond being an encouraging, albeit condescending, correspondent. He was to become the man responsible for preaching the Second Crusade, which would bring a wave of European royalty to Melisende's shores.

It is a mark of Queen Melisende's personal force of will that she managed to remain a widow for the rest of her days. However, some years after Fulk's death there were rumours of a lover on the scene, which earned the queen a second letter from Bernard of Clairvaux, chastising her for rumours of her not being 'a good widow':

> To his beloved daughter in Christ, Melisende, queen of Jerusalem:
> We have heard, I confess, I know not what treacherous things which, although we do not believe them for certain, we grieve that whether by truth or falsehood they stain your reputation [. . .] the queen, whose acts, worthy or unworthy, cannot be hidden under a bushel. They are above the candlestick so they are seen by all. Remember the widow, who is no longer concerned with what pleases a man so she can please God alone. You are blessed, if you make the Saviour a wall to protect your conscience and an outer wall to repel infamy. Blessed, I say, if as forsaken and widowed, you commit yourself to be ruled completely by God. You cannot otherwise rule well, if you are not ruled well. [. . .] Therefore when you think of your high position, attend to the widowhood since, if I may offer you purely what I feel, you could not be a good queen if you were not a good widow.

This letter is less remarkable than Bernard's previous missive, preaching as it does. It seems clear that rumours had reached Bernard of Melisende having an affair, but whether or not she really was, and if so with whom, has been lost to history. What it does, however, confirm is that Melisende was certainly ruling in her own right at the time when the letter was written, and with a certain degree of personal freedom.

Unlike most royal princesses of the age, Melisende's father, and perhaps also her mother Morphia, had prepared her well for rulership and given her the tools and experience she needed to rule the Kingdom. Had Baldwin II not taken special care to educate his daughter beyond the expected standards of the age, and gone so far as to include her in council meetings and recognise her as his heir from a young age, then she would not have found it so easy to step into his and her late husband's shoes and receive the crown.

THE LOSS OF EDESSA, AND THE SECOND CRUSADE

For all the comparative ease of Melisende's accession, her reign would prove to be exceptionally rocky.

In 1144, just one year after Fulk's untimely death, a calamity shook Outremer. Edessa, the easternmost state of Outremer, was captured by the forces of the Atabeg Zengi, Lord of Mosul and Aleppo.

Zengi's conquest of Edessa was brutal and shocking. The ruling family, the Courtenays, escaped, and their story and in particular that of their eldest daughter Agnes will be related later. However, the same was not true for the majority of the population. The massacre of the Latin inhabitants resembled that inflicted upon the population of Jerusalem by the conquering crusaders in 1099.

The city of Edessa had special significance for Queen Melisende, as it had been her father's original lordship and the place of her own birth and early childhood. That said, it had very limited defences at the time of Zengi's attack. Its lord, Joscelin II of Courtenay, was absent. It was one of the oldest Christian cities, and its population were mainly Armenian and Chaldean traders and craftsmen rather than soldiers. Edessa had always stood as a point of weakness for the crusader states, and at this time its defences were left mainly in the care of mercenary soldiers hired by the clergy, and not the best-motivated mercenaries either, as their wages were often left unpaid. When Zengi's assault was launched the people of Edessa were woefully ill-equipped to repel him.

Melisende was equal to her father in many respects but she failed to live up to his example in the early part of her reign in one key way. Since the death of her father and the unpopular rule of Fulk, the control that the Kingdom of Jerusalem exerted over the rulers of Tripoli, Antioch and Edessa had been waning. At the time of Melisende's accession the matter of suzerainty in the crusader states hung in a delicate balance, and the lord–vassal relationships between rulers of Outremer were essentially renegotiated with each new ruler.

Following the death of Fulk and Melisende's elevation to sole ruler, she did not take the necessary steps to assert the authority of Jerusalem over the barons of Outremer. Perhaps this was due to the limits of queenship as opposed to kingship, but the historical record does not suggest that she tried particularly hard to bring the Prince of Antioch and the Counts of Tripoli and Edessa to heel; perhaps she knew it would be a fruitless quest. Although Melisende did arrange a marriage between her sister Hodierna and the Count of Tripoli in the early years of her reign, this marriage was not successful, and she never attempted to use martial strength to secure loyalty and cooperation. Melisende's reticence in asserting her suzerainty over Antioch, Tripoli and Edessa may also have been because so much ground had been lost under Fulk's rulership that the feudal bonds enforced by Baldwin II seemed to be irrevocably lost. Indeed, it is possible that the only reason the Lords of Tripoli, Antioch and Edessa were so willing to accept her as Queen of Jerusalem was because they anticipated less meddling from a queen than a king.

The decline of centrality in this period had dire consequences for all of Outremer, and Edessa and Antioch in particular. A bitter enmity had been brewing between Raymond of Antioch and Joscelin II of Edessa, which would prove to be Edessa's undoing. William of Tyre states bluntly that by the time of Fulk's death this conflict between Raymond and Joscelin had reached the stage of 'open hatred [. . .] each rejoiced in the distress of the other'. In the days of Baldwin II, the King might have had no difficulty in forcibly brokering a peace between the two feuding barons, but Melisende did not ride north to address the disunity. As a result a great disaster would befall her Kingdom, less than one year after she assumed governorship.

The Atabeg Zengi had mustered a mighty army of cavalry, foot soldiers and specialised siege equipment, and swiftly took advantage of Lord Joscelin's absence and his enmity with Raymond of Antioch to besiege and blockade Edessa. The city was ill-prepared to receive this attack.

Zengi cut off all exit and entry points to the city, meaning that no one could escape, nor could food pass into the city. William of Tyre writes euphemistically that the population trapped inside were forced to 'extremes' to avoid starvation. It was whispered in the more explicit sources that when pushed to extremes during siege warfare, soldiers would turn to eating everything – from their horses, to trees, to men.

When word reached Lord Joscelin of Zengi's attack he immediately sent urgent missives to Jerusalem and Antioch requesting aid, and while Melisende convened a council and dispatched an army under the command of her trusted Constable, a man named Manasses of Hierges, Raymond was unmoved by Joscelin's entreaties. The desperation of the situation was not enough to override the enmity between them. Despite its prime position to offer assistance, Antioch sent no troops to relieve the Siege of Edessa. Just as disunity between the Muslim factions had allowed the crusaders to advance and conquer Muslim territory in the eleventh century, so disunity between the crusader factions allowed the Muslims to reclaim what they had lost in the twelfth.

Zengi's assault was relentless. In addition to sending storms of arrows, stones and missiles over the walls to strike the population, he sent tunnellers to undermine the walls. After four weeks of persistent siege, a tower collapsed, breaching the wall, providing a gap in the fortifications through which Zengi's soldiers flooded the city on Christmas Eve 1144. On Christmas Day, the Christian inhabitants were massacred. The Latin Christians were slaughtered indiscriminately, but the native Armenian and Chaldean Christians were granted reprieve.

In a desperate bid to save themselves, the citizens converged upon the fortified citadel in the city's centre. The imposing fortress and the unclimbable walls against which they were crushed still stand today. Finding the doors closed against them by the Archbishop, their panic rose to a furore, and many were trampled to death in the stampede. Among those crushed in the mob was the Archbishop of Edessa, the very man who had closed the citadel against his people. It seemed he had ventured out into the throng in an attempt to calm the populace, but when trapped between scimitars and stone walls, the terrified Christians were disinclined to respond to remonstrations for calm. Hugh's death was not mourned, as there were many who held him accountable for the city's fall: he had much wealth and had neglected to use it to protect his flock by employing more soldiers.

The aid Melisende sent and the relief force assembled by Count Joscelin proved to be too little too late. Joscelin had awaited reinforcements at Turbessel to the west of Edessa, seeking to mount a united relief force with the armies of Jerusalem and Antioch combined, and expecting the city's high walls to hold out longer than they did. Towers, moats and fortifications were all very well, but quite useless without a trained and motivated body of soldiers to man them. This, while not directly Melisende's fault, must still be seen as a military and political failing on her part. What monarch could leave such a significant part of Christian territory undefended and open to such an attack?

This episode was a great blow to Melisende's reign and reputation as a ruler, but it did serve to demonstrate that it was she and not her son running the Kingdom. It was not the young Baldwin III who convened the council of nobles and dispatched an army, but Melisende. It seems the queen was taking active steps to hold her son back from military involvement. She did not allow him to march with or command the army that went to challenge Zengi at Edessa. On a simple level, this may have been typical maternal concern for his welfare, and the welfare of the heir to the Kingdom, but it may also have had political motivations. The one aspect of medieval rulership that Melisende was excluded from on the basis of her sex was that of military action and leading the army. While queens could defend cities in sieges, and plan military action, they did not lead troops in the field. If her son gained too great a reputation as a soldier, he would be in a much stronger position to challenge her authority. Signs were already appearing that Melisende mistrusted her eldest son, and feared that he would attempt to supplant her. These fears, which may have appeared groundless at first, in time would prove to be astute.

In response to the loss of Edessa, Melisende then sent envoys to Antioch to discuss how best to proceed. Edessa was her birthplace and the setting of her childhood, and she must have felt great pain at its loss and been anxious to retake it. She was certainly moved by the plight of the citizens of her native city. While bloodshed and atrocity may have been comparatively more common in the Middle Ages than now, the news of the massacre at Edessa reverberated across Christendom and wrung the hearts of monarchs in Europe and the East alike. Of the survivors of the massacre, who were few, many were captured and enslaved, and many others were tortured and tormented to death. The scale of this horror is attested by the many and varied accounts of the siege and slaughter that abounded in the Middle Ages. Indeed, graphic depictions of this disaster are to be found in Arabic, Latin, Greek, French and Armenian sources alike. Melisende's sympathy for those refugees that escaped is demonstrated by the provision she made for them when they reached

Jerusalem. A stone-carved plaque commemorating her aid survives to this day, as does a passage in a Syrian lectionary which includes a prayer for the queen, because of her work in aiding the Syrian and Armenian refugees.

It was quickly decided that it was beyond Outremer's scope to reconquer the city. If they mustered all their soldiers across their lands, it might well be possible to retake it, but such an act would leave their remaining territories unacceptably vulnerable to attacks from other quarters. What Melisende needed was reinforcements from Europe, and with this in mind she determined to send an embassy to Rome, to entreat the Pope for his support in calling on the lords of Europe to send assistance to the East. The result of this embassy in 1145 was the greatest Christian call to arms seen since 1095, and it was personally backed by the two most powerful Christians in Europe, Pope Eugenius III and Melisende's earlier correspondent, the influential Bernard of Clairvaux.

On 1 December 1145 the Pope issued a papal bull to the kings and nobles of France, commanding them to 'gird themselves to oppose the multitudes of the infidels'. Bernard 'zealously and indefatigably' preached the crusade across Europe, painting vivid pictures of the plight of the Latins and Eastern Christians of Outremer. He described how the holiest cities of Christianity were suffering in dire servitude to Muslim overlords, and how faithful men and women lay bound with chains and shackles, consumed by hunger, confined in horrendous prisons, living in filth and squalor. So compelling was Bernard's case that the two most powerful secular lords of Europe – King Louis VII of France and King Conrad III of Germany – were moved by his entreaties. This venture, in later years called the Second Crusade, will be the subject of the next chapter.

While Europe rallied its forces to come and answer the call from the East, the struggle for Edessa continued in Outremer. Count Joscelin of Edessa, anxious to regain the seat of his lordship, had not given up hope of retaking the city.

Not long after his capture of the city, Zengi's history of brutality caught up with him. He was assassinated by a Frankish slave in his retinue, a man who had clearly been pushed too far. Zengi's end was bloody and undignified, and Christendom breathed a sigh of relief at the news. Nur ad-Din, Zengi's 28-year-old son and successor to his Syrian lands, rather than mourning his tyrannical father, prised Zengi's signet ring from his cold dead hand and set about securing his inheritance in Syria.

This dramatic and sudden transition of power drew attention away from Edessa. The Christian citizens who had survived the massacre and had been allowed to stay in the city sent word of its vulnerable state to the exiled Count Joscelin, who wasted no time in assembling his army and marching on the city.

Undefended as it was, Joscelin quickly succeeded in breaching the outer defences and gaining entry to the city. Despite this initial success, he could not take the citadel. In his haste to strike, he had neglected to bring with him appropriate siege equipment and could find no materials to make any. Moreover, Joscelin had not taken into account the might of Nur ad-Din, who would in time garner a reputation for harrying the Christians that would rival his father's, and indeed would not be eclipsed by any other commander until the rise of Saladin himself.

Nur ad-Din responded with record speed to Joscelin's attack. He marched on the city, so that Joscelin and the Christian inhabitants of the city quickly found themselves trapped between the Muslim-held citadel and Nur ad-Din's army surrounding the walls. As he could not hope to take the citadel, Joscelin's only viable strategy for escape was to attempt to break out of the city, and cut a path through the Muslim army. This plan was all very well for armed soldiers, but made no provision for the wounded and unarmed. The native Christian citizens who had survived the original slaughter when Zengi captured the city were in a difficult position. They had been well treated following the conquest, allowed to worship and live as before with a certain degree of autonomy, but they could not expect such mild treatment a second time, especially when they had so flagrantly co-operated with Joscelin and returned the city to him while Nur ad-Din's attention was elsewhere. William of Tyre describes what happened when Joscelin's soldiers forced their way through the Muslim ranks:

> A passage was opened by the sword [. . .] A helpless throng of unwarlike citizens, old men, and sick people, matrons and tender maidens, aged women and little ones, even babes at the breast, all crowded together in that narrow gateway. Some were trodden under the feet of the horses; others, crushed by the on-pressing multitude, were stifled to death, while still others fell under the merciless sword of the Turks. The greater part of the citizens, both men and women, who had elected to follow the departing army perished miserably at that time.

Not only the civilians suffered; the battle was bloody for the soldiers as well, and Count Joscelin was lucky to escape with his life. Nur ad-Din pursued and harried the retreating army along the banks of the Euphrates and all order broke down, with Christians fleeing in all directions.

Joscelin's comrade in arms and co-commander Baldwin of Marash was not so lucky as his lord, and he was killed alongside the unnamed multitude of soldiers and citizens. William of Tyre, in an uncharacteristic burst of emotion, exclaims: 'Many other excellent men perished also at this time who were well worthy of remembrance . . . Their names are forgotten but are surely written in heaven.'

A MURDER MYSTERY IN CAESAREA

Hodierna, Melisende's younger sister and the third daughter of Baldwin II and Morphia of Melitene, had made a good marriage with Raymond II, the Count of Tripoli, around 1135. This marriage had no doubt been organised by the queen, who had taken a close interest in securing the futures of her younger sisters.

Raymond had been a good match for Hodierna. He was the son of Pons of Tripoli and Cecile of France, the half-sister of King Fulk and the widow of Tancred of Hauteville. Raymond was a passionate, quick-tempered man who had made a name for himself with the swift and bloody vengeance he wreaked upon the people who had killed his father. No sooner did he hear of his father's death than he took an army up Mount Lebanon to find the culprits. He captured the men, along with their wives and children, before torturing and killing them all. Extreme and chilling as these actions might seem, they earned him wide renown in Outremer as a man not to be trifled with, and who was ready to back up his words with decisive blows. This reputation, and the County of Tripoli that he inherited from his father, earned Raymond the hand of Princess Hodierna. Through this marriage she became Countess of Tripoli.

During the time of the Second Crusade, brought about by the fall of Edessa, this title came under threat. With the kings of France and Germany who arrived in the East came another nobleman from France, Alphonse Jourdain, the Count of Toulouse, and his son Bertrand. Alphonse was the son of the original conqueror of Tripoli, Raymond of Saint-Gilles, the unofficial leader of the First Crusade. Alphonse had been born in Outremer, to Raymond's lawful wife Elvira, before being taken back to Toulouse to be raised and govern there. Elvira had been Raymond's third wife; this was the only marriage for which he was not excommunicated for marrying too close a relation. His first marriage, to his cousin, had produced a son, Bertrand, the grandfather of Hodierna's husband Raymond II. Bertrand had succeeded his father as Count of Tripoli, and was the first count to rule from the city itself. He was, however, illegitimate – made such following the dissolution of his parents' controversial marriage. Consequently Alphonse Jourdain had a stronger claim to be Count of Tripoli than Raymond II did, given that he had been born legitimately in a Tripolitan fortress in Outremer.

Alphonse also had the weight of the strange concept of porphyrogeniture – a system of inheritance favoured at the Byzantine court – on his side. Porphyrogeniture refers to those 'born in the purple' – that is to say, born to reigning monarchs. As Alphonse was born after his father had become the Count of Tripoli, he had better claim to Tripoli than the descendants of a man born before his father held that title.

His arrival in the East was bad news for Raymond II, and for Hodierna as well. If Alphonse succeeded in dispossessing her husband of his lands, then she, a princess of the blood, would find herself stripped of her title of countess and stuck married to the landless descendant of a bastard.

This scenario could not be tolerated, but fortunately for Hodierna and unfortunately for Alphonse, it never had to be. He arrived in Acre in 1148, and clearly intended to visit Jerusalem and fulfil his vows before turning his attention to laying claim to Tripoli. He broke his journey from Acre in the maritime city of Caesarea. Here, just weeks into his trip to the East and aged forty-five, Alphonse died suddenly and without any probable cause. There were swiftly rumours that this was poison: an assassination organised either by Raymond and Hodierna, or by Queen Melisende herself on behalf of her sister. William of Nangis, a thirteenth-century French chronicler, specifically lays the blame at the door of the Queen of Jerusalem.

It is impossible to ascertain if there is any truth to these rumours, but it is unlikely that the previously active and healthy count dropped dead all of a sudden, from an illness that affected no one else. It is likely that he was assassinated, and the people with the most to gain from his death were Hodierna and her husband. What was to prove still more shocking was that a year after his own death, Alphonse Jourdain's son Bertrand would likewise fall victim to foul play in Outremer.

Bertrand seemed keen to press his advantage in the County of Tripoli, despite his father's unexpected death. Indeed, a desire to avenge his father's murder may have made him even more determined to claim what he may have believed to be his rightful inheritance. In 1149 he marched into the County of Tripoli and took control of the fortress of Areimeh, which today lies on the Syrian side of the Syrian–Lebanese border, roughly forty miles north of Tripoli. Raymond and Hodierna viewed this as a direct threat to their governance in the county of Tripoli. According to two Muslim chroniclers, Ibn al-Athir and Kemal ad-din, Raymond sent an urgent letter to Nur ad-Din asking for aid to retake Areimeh. Bertrand had clearly reckoned on Raymond II not having the resources to oust him from Areimeh and thus considered himself safe. What he had not considered is that Raymond II and Hodierna would reach out to their enemies for assistance.

According to Ibn al-Athir, by happy chance, when Nur ad-Din received Raymond II's letter he was at Baalbek in the company of Mu'in ad-Din, Lord of Damascus. He was only too pleased to acquiesce to Raymond's request. Together with the Lord of Damascus and Sayf ad-Din, whom he had summoned to join him, Nur ad-Din marched through the County of Tripoli with his army, unhindered by Raymond II and Hodierna's armies, and besieged Bertrand in Areimeh.

Despite Bertrand mounting a robust defence, Nur ad-Din succeeded in taking the city, and captured Bertrand and his mother. Bertrand would not be ransomed until 1158, spending almost a decade in captivity. Raymond II and Hodierna had traded an important fortress for their security in Tripoli, presumably because they believed that if they did not, they stood to lose control of the entire County. Ibn al-Athir wrote sardonically about Bertrand's ambition in attempting to take Areimeh and Tripoli: 'The ostrich went out, seeking two horns and returned minus both ears.' Bertrand had gambled, and he had lost.

THE RESTORATION OF THE HOLY SEPULCHRE

While the embarrassment of the Second Crusade was ingloriously unfolding outside the walls of Jerusalem and scandal after scandal was rocking the County of Tripoli, Melisende was meeting with more success closer to home: her restoration and renovation of the Church of the Holy Sepulchre, the holiest site in Christianity and the spiritual heart of Jerusalem.

It was during the years of Melisende's primacy that an ambitious programme of artistic restoration took place in the church. Beyond its religious significance, this place had great personal meaning for Melisende too. It was there that she had been married, twice crowned, and her father and husband were buried there. As a blessed distraction from the failure of the Second Crusade, the church was symbolically rededicated following extensive renovation on 15 July 1149, fifty years after its capture by the triumphant leaders of the First Crusade.

By the time Melisende assumed the rule of the Kingdom and began to direct the renovation works, the Church of the Holy Sepulchre had already stood for eight centuries. It had been built following the conversion of the Roman Emperor Constantine to Christianity, and with him the Roman Empire. His mother, St Helena, had come to Jerusalem and purportedly discovered the True Cross lying in a cave near the site of Christ's tomb and crucifixion. Mother and son had commanded that a church, with a great dome and rotunda, should be built on the site, and it was consecrated in AD 335.

Since then, it had been damaged and rebuilt on multiple occasions before Melisende set to work to restore it. The first major blow befell the great domed church of Constantine in 614, when the Sassanid Persian Khusraw II captured Jerusalem, seized the True Cross and burned the church. The Byzantine Emperor Heraclius had leapt to action to retake the city, and had succeeded within two decades. He rebuilt the church, and despite the city falling into Muslim hands in the wake of the Arab conquests in the mid seventh century, it remained intact and functional as a place of Christian worship for centuries to follow.

However, despite this leniency on the part of the Muslim governors of the city, the site was struck by a series of earthquakes and fires during the eighth, ninth and tenth centuries. Following a devastating defeat of Muslim armies in 966, a riot broke out amid the usually tolerant population, and the church was intentionally burned, and the Patriarch was murdered. Despite these many assaults, the greater part of Constantine's original structure still stood.

In 1009 the church would endure a vicious assault designed to obliterate it forever, by a man named Abu Ali Mansur, or better remembered as Al-Hakim bi-Amr Allah, the 'Mad Caliph'. This Fatimid leader launched a general campaign against Christianity and ordered the complete destruction of the church. The demolition was systematic and devastating. Dedicated wrecking crews worked with pick-axes and fire, smashing what remained of the walls and the dome and digging into the rock tomb itself, stopping only when debris so covered the site that they could make no further progress, at which point they built a great fire over it and burned what remained.

For all this tenacity with which they set about their destruction they were not successful in the complete eradication of the site. A few pieces of Constantine's structure from six centuries earlier survived including parts of the rotunda and walls and, most importantly, the rock tomb of Christ was not destroyed. This thorough attack upon the most holy site in Christianity shocked Christians across Europe, and may have planted one of the earliest seeds of the crusades in the minds of the Byzantine Empire and the papacy.

Nineteen years later, after the death of the Mad Caliph and following hard-wrung negotiations between the Byzantine Empire and the Fatimids, the extensive reconstruction of the church was permitted at the expense of Byzantium, in exchange for the reopening of a mosque in Constantinople. Even with this show of magnanimity, it was still not possible to construct, in such a hostile setting, anything like the great structures of the Hagia Sophia in Constantinople or the grandest European cathedrals, as might have been expected.

While the church was rebuilt, it was a relatively modest building, and by the time Melisende and Fulk had been jointly crowned in its great nave, it was still relatively humble compared to what one might expect of the holiest site of Christianity. This doubtless played a part in inspiring Melisende to begin such an extensive and impressive programme of construction. It should be remembered that Melisende, for all her Frankish heritage and cosmopolitanism, never set foot beyond the boundaries of Outremer. She had never seen the great architectural triumphs of Christianity, and thus her vision must have been guided by well-travelled Europeans, including her late husband King Fulk of Jerusalem, her old ally Patriarch William and William's successor Patriarch Fulk.

Under Melisende the holy sites within the complex of the church, including the hill of Calvary, the place where St Helena had found the True Cross, and the rock-cut tomb where Christ was laid to rest, were to be united as a single architectural complex. A new plan was introduced to incorporate the surviving elements of the rotunda of Constantine with the other places, creating a building in the style of the Romanesque cathedrals of Europe. The new vision of the church had not one great dome but two, in addition to a bell tower and a magnificent new double-doored, southern entrance through which the hordes of Christian pilgrims that visited each year could pass. This double doored entryway, with its intricately carved façade, stands to this day, and although one of the doors was walled up by Saladin, today's throngs of pilgrims still flood through the same arched entrance that thousands of medieval pilgrims once passed.

The interior also underwent renovation and decoration, with a fusion of Western and Eastern styles incorporated in carved decorations on capitals and lintels. This fusion can still be clearly seen in the church today, in particular in the carved façade to the church, and in the twelfth-century capitals in what is now the Armenian chapel. A profusion of coloured and glowing golden mosaics spread across the domed and vaulted ceilings. Only one image of Christ survives from this period, alongside the poorly preserved frescoes of the cave chapel of St Helena.

Above the new entrance a delicate set of stone relief carvings were installed, the western lintel depicting scenes from Christ's entrance to Jerusalem, and the eastern showing mythological beasts tangled in spiralling branches. These friezes survived down the centuries, until they were removed ostensibly for their protection and restoration, and now the space above the great doors lies bare. The original carvings can be viewed in the Rockefeller Museum just outside the walls of the Old City of Jerusalem.

Melisende's architectural patronage of the city of Jerusalem extended beyond merely religious buildings and saw a revamping and enlarging of the central souk of the city. The labyrinthine marketplace of Jerusalem stands to this day. Her renovations included the Rue de Malquisinat (Street of Bad Cooking), which is essentially a street-long food hawkers' market for pilgrims. The pilgrim trade was the medieval equivalent of today's tourist trade (pilgrims were spiritual tourists), and just like today, fast-food outlets were in high demand around the holy places.

An idea of what medieval Jerusalem was like following Melisende's extensive building works can be gleaned through the words of an anonymous French pilgrim, who wrote an early thirteenth-century equivalent of a *Lonely Planet* guide to holy places in the Kingdom of Jerusalem, entitled *La Citez de Jherusalem*. The mysterious author of this travel guide visited the city when it was held by Muslims and heavy restrictions were imposed upon Christian tourists. Nevertheless, through his descriptions of the covered herb markets, hospitals, crowded guesthouses, alleyways and churches, modern readers can catch a glimpse of Melisende's Jerusalem. Of Melisende's new and improved covered markets, the author gives us this evocative description:

When you come to the exchange where David Street ends there is a street called Mount Sion Street, for it goes straight to Mount Sion [. . .] And on the left of the Exchange is a covered street, vaulted over, called the Street of Herbs, where they sell all the herbs, all the fruits of the city, and spices. At the top of the street there is a place where they sell fish . . .

His words give a sense of the hustle and bustle, the sights and smells of medieval Jerusalem.

It is unclear how long Melisende's renovations of the Holy Sepulchre and the surrounding area of the city took, but testimony of the Muslim geographer Muhammed al-Idrisi in 1154 demonstrates that the Holy Sepulchre's bell-tower at least was finished by this point, as he includes a description of it in his chronicle. This indicates that the bulk of the construction was carried out during the period of Melisende's primacy in the Kingdom of Jerusalem. Given her other demonstrated interest in ecclesiastical patronage, it is certain that she played a large part in arranging and commissioning this renovation, in co-operation with the Patriarch of Jerusalem.

Moreover, Melisende's personal involvement with the improvements to the Holy Sepulchre is further demonstrated in the stylistic similarities between the Church of the Holy Sepulchre and the Church of St Anne, which had long been associated with the women in Melisende's family. Eminent crusades historian Hans Eberhard Mayer has suggested further that Melisende's support of the renovation of the Church of the Holy Sepulchre went further than a display of her personal piety and patronage, but rather was a bid to consolidate her political position by winning the support of the church as her son grew older. The importance of this would be demonstrated in the coming years. A storm was brewing that would fracture the relationship between mother and son.

WAR BETWEEN MOTHER AND SON

While Melisende had enjoyed command of the Kingdom virtually unchallenged since the death of her husband, with the co-operation of her sons, as Baldwin began to grow older and reach the age of majority, he became restless with the imbalance of power within the Kingdom.

Melisende had a strained relationship with her eldest son. She favoured her second child Amalric, who remained her staunch supporter all of his life. Melisende must have always regarded Baldwin III with unease. Given the laws of succession, he was always going to be the one to supplant her, and she must have lived with the fear that he too might try to exclude her from rule, just as Fulk had tried to. Moreover, Baldwin III was more than an heir or rival: he was an anointed co-ruler, and queenship was less secure than kingship. Just as Matilda's claims to the English throne had been shunted aside by an opportunistic cousin, Melisende lived with the fear that her son would grow into a man who would attempt to squeeze her out of rulership. Some kings had the luxury of enjoying their relationships with their sons, who would only succeed them when they died, and would carry on their legacy and bloodline, but Melisende enjoyed no such security. As her son's majority crept near, her grip on power loosened.

In contrast, Amalric posed no threat to his mother, and she was able to lavish the affection and support on him that she withheld from her eldest. In time she would come to use him as a pawn in her bitter struggle with his elder brother, raising him to be Count of Jaffa and setting him up as a powerful opponent to his brother, just as her cousin Hugh of Jaffa had once been to Fulk. In spite of this, or perhaps in gratitude for it, Amalric remained invariably sympathetic to his mother's cause, and it is perhaps this devotion that we see reflected in William of Tyre's admiring descriptions of the queen. William was Amalric's court historian, and he doubtless emphasised the qualities of Melisende out of deference to her son.

As Baldwin III grew he began to resent his mother's monopoly on the power that was meant to be shared between them. They had been crowned together, and while he was a young child it had been appropriate for her to assume the duties and the power of a sole ruler, but as he approached manhood it began to look more and more strange that a middle-aged widow was ruling the Kingdom, when there was a grown man with proven military ability waiting in the wings. Furthermore, Baldwin III was a perfectly fitting candidate to rule. Even William of Tyre, a staunch supporter of Queen Melisende, sings the young King's praises in his chronicle. He relates that the young man was 'superior to all in vivacity of mind and brilliancy of speech', and that 'he had an unnaturally keen intellect and was gifted by nature with the rare advantage of eloquent speech', and he even went so far as to say that he was far better educated than his brother Amalric.

Meanwhile Melisende was proving as shrewd as she was dedicated to holding on to power. Since the early years of her reign, even when the threat of her son taking power from her was still years away, she had begun readying herself for a struggle by consolidating her power and influence in Outremer. It is easy to be tempted to view Melisende in much the same way that William of Tyre viewed her sister Alice, as power hungry and unmaternal, but her wider position must be considered. Women who did not speak up and hustle for power received none and were traded like chattels in the marriage market. Those who voiced reasonable and proportional complaints were silenced and received less than their fair share. Melisende may never have intended to keep control of the whole Kingdom, but it is likely that she knew that she had to play for all in order to receive a sliver.

Whatever her motivations, Melisende did not take chances with securing allegiance, and set about appeasing the people of Jerusalem alongside winning over the church and chosen nobles. She was as successful in excluding her son from the business of the Kingdom as her husband had been in excluding her during the first part of her reign. It should therefore have come as no surprise to her that her own flesh and blood would rebel against this exclusion as forcefully as she herself had done.

William of Tyre, in his admiration for Melisende, was uncomfortable attributing the responsibility for the ensuing conflict at the Queen's door. Instead, he suggested the blame lay with the hubris of her most trusted deputy, Manasses of Hierges.

One of Melisende's first acts as queen following Fulk's death had been to promote Manasses to the position of Constable of Jerusalem, one of the most important and influential offices in the Kingdom. He was to command the Queen's army, a role that sapped potential power from Baldwin, who might have sought to be in charge of martial matters while his mother administered political ones. William records that power went to Manasses' head, and through his smug and snide behaviour he began to anger the nobility of the Kingdom. Melisende had made a mistake similar to Fulk's: promoting a newcomer from France to one of the most exalted positions in the land, over the heads of more established and better qualified local candidates. In addition to promoting him to the position of Constable, Melisende also gave him Helvis of Ramla to be his wife. This woman was the widow of Balian of Ibelin, and through her he acquired the important fortresses of Ramla and Mirabel, thus backing up his new symbolic rank with tangible power, land and wealth. William of Tyre writes:

> he assumed an insolent attitude of superiority towards the elders of the realm and refused to show them proper respect [. . .] The King was foremost, both in feeling and act, among those who hated Manasses and claimed that the man was alienating his mother's good will from him.

Those slighted by Manasses rallied round the king, reminding him that he had rights to rule the Kingdom, and telling him that now he was a man, it was not 'fitting' that he should be ruled by his mother. When Fulk died, Baldwin III was just thirteen years old, but by 1152 he was twenty-two and had been of ruling age for seven years. The only surprise was that he had not fought for his mother to cede power sooner.

The young King's first attempt to snatch the reins of power out of his mother's hands was purely symbolic. Perhaps he was optimistic enough to think that the change could be made without open conflict, and that his mother would cede to his authority gracefully. It is unknown whether he approached her in private or not, but what is known is that in the lead-up to Easter 1152 he approached Patriarch Fulk of Jerusalem with an odd but deeply meaningful request. He asked that Fulk symbolically re-crown him in the Church of the Holy Sepulchre during the Easter Mass, which would be attended by a multitude of witnesses. He further asked that his mother be excluded from the occasion.

Had Fulk agreed to Baldwin's request, the act would have been politically charged and profoundly symbolic. For Baldwin III to be crowned without his mother, even though it would not invalidate Melisende's previous coronation, would nevertheless send a clear message to the subjects of the Kingdom that he was now the sole ruler. Mother and son had been crowned together in 1143 but Baldwin's actual power had been extremely curtailed since then, despite his coming of age. He now wished to assert his maturity and dominance. Patriarch Fulk was all too aware of the implications of the young King's request, and following Melisende's long period of governance and her support of the church, he was unwilling to agree. If he had crowned her son without her, and without her knowledge or consent, it would have appeared a base betrayal of one who had so diligently co-operated and collaborated with him, supporting the church and its institutions tirelessly.

Baldwin had put Patriarch Fulk in a very difficult position in asking him to scheme against the queen in this way. While he could not outright refuse to crown the king at Easter, which was customary, he urged the young monarch to allow his mother to participate in the glory of the occasion and be crowned alongside him. To share the re-coronation with his mother would of course entirely defeat the purpose of the young King's planned political manoeuvre, and so he sulkily declined this offer.

The Easter festivities took place as planned, but no monarch was crowned in the Holy Sepulchre that day. Patriarch Fulk doubtless breathed a sigh of relief, believing a great and public rift between the two rulers had been avoided. He had known Melisende long enough to know that she would not take kindly to such a public subversion of her power in the very centre of her domain. The city of Jerusalem was, of course, where she had built her strongest network of allies, and the Church of the Holy Sepulchre was both the heart of the city and the heart of her personal projects of improvement, patronage and restoration.

The next day, 31 March 1152, Baldwin appeared outside the church sporting a new piece of intriguing headgear: not a crown, but a Roman Emperor-style laurel wreath. This was no official re-coronation – Patriarch Fulk had known nothing of this and had certainly not anointed the king nor set the wreath upon his head, but the symbolism of Baldwin's appearance at the church was obvious and definite. He was taking matters into his own hands and was preparing to assert himself both symbolically and practically as the sole ruler of the Kingdom of Jerusalem. With this act, he incontestably challenged his mother's regime.

The nobles of the region were shocked, and the Haute Cour was convened to debate the event and what it meant. Both King Baldwin III and Queen Melisende were present, and their rights to the throne of the Kingdom of Jerusalem were to be debated. Baldwin bluntly demanded that he be given his share of his inheritance. He wished for the Kingdom to be divided in two, so that he could rule part of it completely free from his mother's interference. The council debated, and this was agreed. They had no legal grounds to refuse. The will of Baldwin II, which had favoured Melisende thus far, now began to work against her. Power had been left equally to her, her husband and her son, and now that her husband was dead and her son was of age, there were no grounds for denying him equal co-rulership.

Ostensibly, the council allowed Baldwin to decide which areas of the Kingdom he would like, but really he had no choice. Melisende's political hold over Jerusalem and nearby Nablus was ironclad, and no ruling of the Haute Cour could dislodge her influence in these regions.

Thus Baldwin contented himself to 'choose' the coastal cities of Acre and Tyre, where he himself was more established. In reality, this division of the Kingdom had occurred in practice, if not in name, two years previously. Melisende had set up her own personal scriptorium and enjoyed near-complete influence in Jerusalem and Nablus, while Baldwin had been steadily building his power base and sphere of influence in the north. The division of the Kingdom was therefore merely a formal confirmation of what had already been policy in practice since 1150. This, however, was in violation of the intent of Baldwin II's will. The old king would doubtless have been appalled to learn of the division of his Kingdom because of his heirs' mutual thirst for power.

Queen Melisende agreed to this decision, but was clear that she was acquiescing to something unreasonable rather than being forced to give up territory fairly. She was careful to assert that although she would part with control of half the Kingdom, it all belonged to her as her inheritance. Melisende must have known that this was not the case. Her father, who had safeguarded her interests and rights, had never intended for her to hold power for her lifetime without a husband, at the expense of her son.

We look at these events with the benefit of hindsight, but at the time all Melisende saw was her eldest son aggressively attempting to supplant her. She compromised as best she could and accepted the division of the Kingdom, but it swiftly became apparent that the division was just the first part of Baldwin's plan of attack on Melisende's rule. He intended to chip away at her power bit by bit and claim the rest of her possessions for himself as well. This became clear all too quickly, as the king began to take steps that demonstrated that he wished to seize Nablus and Jerusalem and fully exclude his mother, in spite of their agreements.

When Melisende learned of her son's plan she was understandably furious. She sprang into action. She had been holding court at Nablus, a prosperous but unfortified city north of Jerusalem. She could not make her stand in a city without walls, and so went at once with her loyal vassals to Jerusalem, which was both a strongly fortified city and the symbolic heart of the Kingdom. As she did this, her son was taking steps to destabilise her position. He marched with his army to Mirabel and besieged his mother's trusted yet troublesome supporter, Manasses of Hierges. It did not take Baldwin long to seize the city, and Manasses was exiled in ignominy. Deprived of his lands, he was dispatched on a ship to Europe and forbidden to set foot ever again in Outremer. Thus one of Melisende's strongest advocates was removed, and she lost a crucial foothold in the Kingdom.

Following his success there, Baldwin moved once again against his mother, marching to Nablus and swiftly succeeding in occupying it, given its lack of fortifications. This proved to be the turn of the tide, and any vassals who had professed loyalty to Melisende on the basis of convenience or location rather than personal loyalty, swiftly switched sides to support the king. In any conflict there is always a portion of bel-ligerents who jump ship to the winning side at the right moment, and the occupation of Nablus proved to be that point in this conflict, which had by this time escalated from a political dispute between members of the ruling family to fully fledged civil war in the Kingdom of Jerusalem.

Despite abandonment by some of her Lords, Melisende still retained some staunchly loyal and powerful allies. These included her younger son, Count Amalric of Jaffa, Philip of Nablus (now dispossessed of his territory) and Rohard the Elder.

Without further ado, the young king marched against his mother in Jerusalem. Unsurprisingly, he found the gates of the city barred against him and the walls defended, so mother and son both began prepara-tions for a siege. A Christian son besieging his Christian mother in the holiest city of Christianity must have been a sight to behold, and demonstrated the depth of the fractures in the ruling elite of the King-dom of Jerusalem.

Baldwin's excuse for trying to deprive his mother of the land that he and the Haute Cour had agreed for her to retain was that now he was confirmed as king, he needed access to the full resources of the Kingdom in order to carry out his defensive duties. Holding the cities was not simply a matter of making political decisions but also one of collecting the revenues and taxes from these lands. Melisende holding the cities of Jerusalem and Nablus and the lands between and around, including Samaria and Judea, meant a significant dent in the income at Baldwin's disposal. However, it was an exaggeration to suggest that the revenues from Baldwin's lands at Tyre and Acre were not sufficient, as these were certainly two of the richest and most commercially pros-perous cities in the Kingdom. Alongside Jaffa, they were the two most significant trading ports in Outremer. It was an excuse to give him moral justification for flagrantly disregarding the compromise reached in the Haute Cour, demonstrating perhaps that Melisende was right to have never trusted her eldest son.

When Melisende learned that Baldwin was preparing his army to besiege her, she withdrew to the citadel, the Tower of David beside the Jaffa gate, and fortified her position as best she could. She would not take her son's betrayal lying down. Patriarch Fulk, who had pre-viously attempted to walk the tightrope between the two camps of mother and son, and not openly come out in support of one party or another, now publicly threw his full support and that of the church behind Queen Melisende, their great benefactor. With the clergy now choosing sides, and what's more choosing to side against the king, the civil war took on a graver dimension. However Fulk, as Patriarch of the city, saw his duty first and foremost as protector and peace-maker, and to this end he rode out to negotiate with the headstrong royal antagonist.

Headstrong, royal and an antagonist Baldwin proved to be indeed. He refused to be swayed by Fulk's entreaties, listening stony-faced as the Patriarch gushed and extolled reconciliation and compromise. Fulk had brought with him a posse of churchmen, and perhaps his tone was too chastising and sanctimonious as he admonished the king for his actions and charged him to desist at once and abide by the former agreement.

Baldwin, as he had defiantly shown, was tired of being pushed around and governed by pious and middle-aged nobility of the previous generation. The Patriarch had revealed himself to be completely his mother's creature, and he would be damned if he would throw away political and military advantage at the request of this man, only to find himself on a short leash once again. Autonomy and rulership of the Kingdom of Jerusalem were within his sights, and he would not be swayed by the cajoling of this old churchman.

In truth, he would have been foolish to listen. The queen had no remaining cards to play: Baldwin had her surrounded and she could not indefinitely withstand a siege. No forces would come to relieve her. Baldwin, if he pressed on, would certainly achieve a complete victory eventually.

Frustrated and insulted by Baldwin's refusal to listen to his entreaties, Fulk returned furiously to the city, pronouncing that Baldwin was ill-advised and a borderline criminal. These bitter snarlings, public as they were, were more significant than simply the ranting of an angry priest. Rather, they implied that Baldwin would not have the support of the church should he triumph and become sole ruler. This did not seem to concern the citizens, who were keen for peace. They saw that the fastest way of achieving this goal was to aid Baldwin to victory so that the conflict could be over and done with as quickly and smoothly as possible. To this end, they defied their queen and benefactor and threw open Jerusalem's gates to Baldwin's army.

The king had come prepared for his mother's resistance, and had no qualms about besieging his own capital. He had brought with him 'ballistae, bows and hurling machines', the full roster of medieval siege equipment, and began to set up and settle in for a furious and relentless assault on King David's tower, the citadel in which Melisende had barricaded herself. He commenced the siege with all the ferocity he would have used against a Saracen fortress:

> so incessant were the attacks that the besieged were denied any chance
> to rest. They, on their part, resisted with all their might and strove to
> repel force by force. Using the same methods employed by the besieg-
> ing force outside, they hesitated not to hurl back injuries upon their
> enemies and to work equal destruction upon them.

It seems Melisende gave as good as she got, but the odds and resources were stacked against her, and after three days of bitter war she capitulated. The conditions within the citadel must have been desperate by this stage. Sleep-deprived, injured and battered from relentless bombardment, Melisende and the besieged must have been at the end of their tethers to agree to a surrender.

This was no small event, despite the few lines devoted to this episode in most histories of the crusades. The Tower of David was a citadel, and siege equipment must have been raised within the walls of the Old City itself. Christians were slaying Christians in the Holy City. This was unprecedented in the history of crusader Jerusalem.

More than this, the small size of the citadel meant that wherever Melisende positioned herself, she would have been in the thick of it, in constant danger from falling rubble and arrows. She had never been besieged before, and it must have been a shocking experience for the middle-aged queen. It is remarkable she held out against the hopeless odds for as long as she did, and demonstrates true strength of resolve, an unshakeable faith in her own birthright and a certain measure of obstinacy.

A decision was taken by someone in the queen's company, perhaps even Melisende herself, that although the king was making little progress against them, it would be a fruitless endeavour to resist indefinitely. This would simply culminate in Melisende's eventual defeat and the destruction of one of the capital's key defensive structures. In the name of peace, a messenger came forward to negotiate terms with the king. Melisende was persuaded to surrender Jerusalem to her son, on the solemn condition that she would retain Nablus 'in perpetuity' and that the king would never seek to challenge this or deprive her of these lands. A fragile peace was somehow brokered between the mother and son. Perhaps they were simply both relieved that it was over.

Melisende was defeated, but this did not diminish the significance of her reign and her resistance to relinquishing power, which was a rare example of the mettle of medieval queens.

COUNTESS HODIERNA AND AN ASSASSINATION IN TRIPOLI

The fortress of Tripoli, northern Lebanon

Following her fall from power, Queen Melisende maintained her household in Nablus, and remained a powerful figure in the female spheres of politics. While Baldwin III had clearly made an effort to exclude his mother from matters of military strategy, he still allowed her to hold sway in the arena of family politics and match-making, and kept her close as an advisor. Melisende took an active role in the lives of her nieces Constance of Antioch and Melisende of Tripoli, and indeed in the lives of her sisters, Hodierna and Yvette. Her influence over the church remained profound, and in 1157 she, together with her sister Hodierna and stepdaughter Sibylla of Flanders, successfully rigged the patriarchal election of Jerusalem, securing the position for her own personal chaplain, Amalric of Nesle.

Despite the sudden death of Alphonse Jourdain during the Second Crusade, which left their claims to Tripoli unchallenged, Hodierna and Raymond II of Tripoli were unhappy together. From a practical perspective their marriage was successful, producing an able-minded and able-bodied male heir, Raymond III of Tripoli, and a beautiful daughter, named Melisende of Tripoli after her aunt. However, it seemed the pair were ill-suited in temperament and inclination. There was a disparity in age between the couple, and there were rumours that Hodierna was unfaithful to her husband. Moreover, other tensions must have simmered between them, perhaps rooted in Hodierna's superior rank. As a daughter of Baldwin II, sister of Queen Melisende and aunt of Baldwin III, she was of higher social status than her husband, who was only descended illegitimately from Raymond of Toulouse. Hodierna had retained close links with her family in the Kingdom of Jerusalem, and there is evidence that she made visits to her sister's court without her husband.

Matters came to a head in 1152, when a feud erupted between the couple of such intensity that Melisende saw fit, during a visit to Tripoli, to mediate between them and effect some kind of reconciliation. The dispute centred on 'an enmity that sprang from matrimonial jealousy'. The queen's efforts were unsuccessful and she resolved instead to separate the couple and bring Hodierna back with her to Jerusalem, either taking the view that some time apart might remedy their marriage, or to effect a lasting separation. It does not seem that Hodierna's two children accompanied her out of Tripoli.

Count Raymond II escorted his wife and sister-in-law with their party out of the city. Once he had seen them safely on the road to Jerusalem, he bid the royal sisters farewell and turned back towards Tripoli. As he approached the gates of his city he was ambushed and fatally stabbed by a group of men. These were no common murderers or brigands, but agents of the infamous Nizari Ismaili sect. This sect has since become known by another name: the *Hashashins* or Assassins.

The Assassins were a religio-political group who used this type of targeted and high-profile murder as a political tool, to make up for what they lacked in armies. The name *Hashashin* became corrupted in medieval French and Latin into the word *assassin*, which still exists today in modern English. The name originated from stories of the killers' custom of smoking hashish before carrying out their grisly work, which for them was a religious and vocational act rather than a sin. Their sect was shrouded in mystery, compounded by the sudden and shocking nature of their killings, and the fact that they based themselves in imposing fortresses high in the mountains and away from communities.

They were not the hired hands that most modern readers might assume. The word 'assassin' has become synonymous with 'hitman'. Instead, they had their own political ideology and goals, which was to establish an Ismaili rule over Islam, and an Islamic rule over the East. Their unpredictable and undetectable manoeuvres meant that they were greatly feared in the twelfth and thirteenth centuries, and an aura of terror and mystique surrounded their activities.

Raymond's murder – targeted and sudden and of a high-status victim – was a typical operation by this Islamic sect, yet a Christian target was unusual. Raymond II was the first recorded non-Muslim victim of the sect, and the ramifications of his murder were extensive. In the immediate aftermath, the Latin Christians of Tripoli rose up and massacred the native inhabitants of the city – Christians, Jews and Muslims alike – in a manner no less brutal than the Muslim massacre of Christians at Edessa. It was a race riot of unprecedented proportions in a peaceful crusader city. William of Tyre writes with perhaps a subtle indication of shame:

> At the news of the Count's murder, the whole city was roused. The people flew to arms and without discrimination put to the sword all those who were found to differ either in language or dress from the Latins. In this way it was hoped that the perpetrators of the foul deed might be found.

The fact that William felt the need to add the final sentence explaining the massacre betrays the indiscriminate futility of the slaughter.

This horror meant new and unexpected power for Hodierna. With the death of her husband, leaving her with her two children as heirs, she found herself in a similar position to that of Melisende when Fulk died. Her twelve-year-old son was the undisputed heir to the County, and now she could enjoy three years at least of regency until he came of age. Thus, the County of Tripoli found itself ruled by a female countess. Nothing is known of why the Assassins, if it even was the Assassins, chose to kill Count Raymond II.

On learning of Raymond II's death, Baldwin III immediately sent word to his mother and his aunt to turn their horses around and return at once to Tripoli, where he was taking charge of the situation. Once Hodierna arrived, he created a triumvirate of rulership not dissimilar to that which his own grandfather Baldwin II had created on his deathbed. He commanded all the nobility of Tripoli to swear an oath of fealty to Hodierna, her twelve-year-old son Raymond III and her still younger daughter, Lady Melisende of Tripoli. It seems the nobles did this without demur, and there is no record of another suitor being considered for Hodierna's hand, indicating that Baldwin III accepted that Hodierna would rule Tripoli without a husband. This meant that to all intents and purposes, Hodierna was ruler of the city until her son came of age. This type of decision was not uncommon either in Europe or Outremer, but that Baldwin III gave his blessing to such a scenario stands in stark contrast to his father's and his grandfather's treatment of the Antiochene Princess Alice. Hodierna's older sister Alice had been denied exactly this power at Antioch.

Baldwin III clearly had faith that, like his mother, Hodierna would be a competent ruler, and thus he was content to leave the County of Tripoli in her hands until her son came of age. Hodierna was a powerful, headstrong woman as independently minded as any of her sisters. However, she is not remembered by history for this trait, but rather gained a legendary status in the thirteenth century and later as the sexual fantasy and involuntary muse of the famous troubadour Jaufre Rudel. He was a nobleman of middling rank, hailing from Blaye in southwestern France, who pioneered the motif of *l'amour de loin* ('love from afar') in the emerging genre of Occitan romance literature. He produced hundreds of lines of besotted lyrics about a distant princess in a faraway land with whom he was in love. His errant biographer, writing some fifty years later, asserted that the lady who was the subject of these songs was not an allegory at all, but in fact the very real Hodierna, Countess of Tripoli. The biography claims that Jaufre's love grew from hearing tales of Hodierna's beauty from pilgrims returning to France from Antioch, and that throwing caution to the wind for the chance to see his love, Jaufre leapt aboard a ship bound for Outremer. However, his planned adoration did not go as he might have hoped: by the time he reached the shores of Tripoli, this legendary lover had already contracted a disease on the ship and was at death's door. Hodierna, hearing of his devotion and plight, graciously descended from her tower in the citadel of Tripoli to nurse the dying man, and held him in her arms as he expired.

This tale is almost certainly fiction, although it is possible that elements could have the ring of truth. It is plausible that Jaufre went to the East with the Second Crusade, landed in Tripoli and died there, and it is possible that he adored Hodierna and that she tended to him in his final moments. However, there is little evidence to support this beyond the account given by the dubious thirteenth-century biographer. What this story can give to historians is a glimpse of the glamour and romance attributed to the ladies of Outremer in Europe, and a taste of the growing romance genre that would influence much of the historiography surrounding many medieval queens.

THEODORA – A NEW QUEEN FOR JERUSALEM AND A BYZANTINE ALLIANCE

Once the Haute Cour had recovered from the shock of Raymond II's assassination and the conclusion of the civil war, attention was turned to the marriage of the king. Baldwin III was now confirmed in his supremacy in Jerusalem, the influence of his mother had been satisfactorily curtailed, and now it was time for a marriage to be arranged for him so that he could set about producing an heir to secure the succession. Baldwin III himself had been in no rush, as it seems he had plenty of premarital affairs and had his whole life ahead of him to father legitimate children. In 1157 the Council, in debating the matter, decided that the best course of action was to solidify and renew the Frankish alliance with the Emperor of Byzantium. The current incumbent of the imperial office was Emperor Manuel Komnenos, the same man whom Princess Alice of Antioch had flirted with previously as a husband for Princess Constance.

An embassy was dispatched to the court of Constantinople in the hope of securing a Byzantine bride and a sizeable dowry. After many months of negotiations a bride was selected and a marriage contract brokered. The new Queen Consort of Jerusalem would be Manuel's niece, the 'illustrious maiden', twelve-year-old Princess Theodora. She would bring with her a dowry of 100,000 gold *hyperpyra* (the new Byzantine equivalent of a dinar, bezant or solidus), and 10,000 more to pay for the most magnificent wedding ever hosted in Jerusalem.

William of Tyre was rarely moved by female beauty, but he was moved by Theodora's. He wrote that she was a 'maiden of unusual beauty, both of form and feature, whose entire appearance favourably impressed all who saw her.' The clothes and personal effects she brought with her were splendid too – silken clothes richly embroidered with pearls and gems, as well as tapestries of immeasurable value and precious drinking vessels and the like. William estimated that the combined value of her baggage was close to a further 14,000 gold *hyperpyra*.

The marriage was an excellent one for King Baldwin, who was looking for heirs, a cash injection and beauty. Theodora arrived by ship in Tyre in September 1158, accompanied by an entourage of some of the highest-born Greeks of the Byzantine court and a vast display of its wealth. The party continued to Jerusalem, where her marriage to Baldwin III was solemnised by the Patriarch of Antioch and she was anointed and crowned Queen of Jerusalem.

Her effect on her husband was dramatic. From the day of their marriage he was reported to have given up entirely his previous philandering and to have been utterly devoted to his new wife, loving and cherishing her and becoming completely reformed as both a man and a king.

Despite this adoration, it seems Theodora, perhaps given her youth and carefully guarded upbringing in the court of Constantinople, took next to no part in the governance of the realm. She accepted her role of consort without protest, and Melisende still lived and wielded influence from Nablus. Baldwin III was an active and healthy ruler who chose not to delegate responsibility to his child bride. He may also have been wary of sharing power unnecessarily with a woman, given his history of conflict with his mother.

MELISENDE OF TRIPOLI, MARIA OF ANTIOCH AND A NEW EMPRESS FOR BYZANTIUM

The Byzantine alliance was further strengthened when, the following year, Manuel's wife died, and he decided to seek a new empress from among the ruling families of Outremer.

Following the assassination of their father Raymond II of Tripoli, Queen Melisende took an active interest in the future of her now father-less niece and nephew. In 1160, eight years after the death of Raymond, the Emperor Manuel let it be known in Outremer that he was looking for a wife. He paid Baldwin III the seemingly great compliment of placing him in charge of selecting a bride from among his royal relatives.

'Melisende, a sister of the Count of Tripoli, a maiden of fine character and ability' and first cousin of Baldwin III, was chosen by the king to be the Frankish candidate to marry the Emperor Manuel. Her aunt and namesake Queen Melisende was at this point approaching old age and had begun to experience ill-health. She had largely withdrawn from politics, but despite this, still played an active role in the more traditionally female aspects of diplomacy, such as marriage.

Queen Melisende clearly greatly approved of this proposed match, for she set herself to its execution with energy. The dowry that she and her sister Hodierna together assembled was clearly designed to reflect the magnificence of the trousseau that the young and lovely Theodora had brought with her:

> an enormous array of ornaments, surpassing those of royalty itself, was prepared at infinite expense of the mother and aunt of the maiden destined for this exalted position, and by her brother and her many friends as well: bracelets, earrings, pins for her head-dress, anklets, rings, necklaces, and tiaras of purest gold. Silver utensils of such weight and size were prepared . . . bridles and saddles . . . all these things were prepared with great zeal . . . [surpassing] the luxury of kings . . .

This treasure trove was put on twelve mighty galleys and sent to Constantinople.

This description of the young Melisende's dowry, as well as showing us the care that Queen Melisende took in promoting the interests of her female relatives, also gives us a rare glimpse into the world of fashion at the royal court of Jerusalem. More was more. Tiaras, veils, anklets, everything that could be adorned with jewels would be adorned with jewels. It also shows that demonstrating the wealth of the Kingdom of Jerusalem and the County of Tripoli to the Byzantine Emperor was a state priority. Marriage between the two royal houses amounted to much more than a political alliance based on love and good faith. If anything, it was closer to an exchange of hostages. In the sending of a princess to the court of Constantinople, the two royal houses were blending, but more than that, a high-status member of the royal house of Jerusalem would be absorbed by the Komnenoi dynasty. Intermarriage with lesser Christian kingdoms was a key element of late Byzantine foreign policy.

Yet for all the extravagance of Melisende's trousseau and dowry, the marriage never took place. Despite Baldwin III's recommendation and the lavishness of the dowry, Manuel's ambassadors still seemed suspicious of the suitability of the match. While ostensibly agreeing to the marriage and allowing the royalty of Outremer to go to vast expense in preparation, the envoys from Constantinople dithered and delayed. They made impertinent inquiries as to the young Lady Melisende's character and conduct, and also demanded examination of her 'most secret physical parts' in order to ascertain if she and her family were being truthful about her virginity. Such an examination would have proved humiliating for the young girl, and was certainly not part of normal marriage negotiations. The very suggestion of this was a great insult to the ruling family of Tripoli.

Months glided by, and all the while Lady Melisende's brother Count Raymond III of Tripoli was entertaining all the nobility of the region in his capital at vast expense. They had assembled to see the maiden off on her voyage to become Empress of Byzantium, and Raymond III had planned to accompany her himself on the crossing. The count and his guests were highly indignant at the continued delay, demanding to know whether or not the marriage would indeed take place. William of Tyre records that, even after a public interrogation and being presented with this ultimatum, the envoys answered only vaguely, attempting to prevaricate still further. In frustration Raymond III dispatched his own envoy to Constantinople, and after a bitter exchange of words and various insults, it swiftly became apparent that the marriage between the Lady Melisende and the Emperor Manuel would not go ahead, even after a year of anticipation and negotiation. Count Raymond III, King Baldwin III and the rest of the nobility of Tripoli and Jerusalem were still none the wiser as to why the emperor had so swiftly changed his mind and insulted them in this grave manner. Lady Melisende took the termination of her engagement particularly hard. She had already begun styling herself in official documents as the future Empress of Constantinople. This rejection was abject humiliation for the young girl.

Meanwhile conversations were taking place further north in Antioch that might shed light on the Emperor's and his envoys' change of heart. After fleeing Tripoli in disfavour, it seems the evasive envoys of the emperor had not sailed for Constantinople, as previously thought, but instead had taken their boat to Antioch. There they had entered into earnest negotiations with the Princess Constance for the hand of her daughter, Maria of Antioch, Queen Melisende's great niece. Perhaps Maria was simply prettier, or perhaps rumours of Hodierna of Tripoli's infidelity had called into question the legitimacy of her daughter Lady Melisende. Whatever the case, Melisende of Tripoli had been jilted. So mortified, she died shortly after the ordeal. Her brother Raymond was furious, and in retaliation set about repurposing the galleys he had built to convey his sister to Constantinople, to become pirate ships to harass the Byzantine coast.

The Byzantine chroniclers offer a different version of events to this cold-hearted jilting of Melisende of Tripoli. John Kinnamos records that all was set to go ahead, and Melisende was preparing to board a ship to Constantinople, when she fell desperately ill:

> Severe illnesses beset the girl [. . .] The radiance of her appearance, which previously gleamed beautifully, was shortly altered and darkened. Seeing her, one was filled with tears at such a meadow withered untimely. Thus the maiden was in a bad state [. . .] she caught still greater diseases which did not at all abandon her. As this happened repeatedly, it led [the ambassadors] to endless reconsiderations.

The ambassadors prayed for guidance and received a sign that Melisende of Tripoli was not the one for the Emperor Manuel. Kinnamos continues that this, coupled with the fact that the ambassadors had already been devastated to hear a rumour 'that the girl was not born of lawful wedlock', caused them to abandon the match. Following this, the envoys considered as well the two daughters of Raymond of Antioch, who were of outstanding beauty. They had been born to him by Constance, Princess of Antioch, the girl who was married at eight to the conqueror of her mother. Maria was chosen as the bride of the emperor, and Kinnamos wrote: 'Our era has never yet been acquainted with such beauty.'

This account of Melisende of Tripoli's illness and the rumours surrounding her paternity, while certainly a convenient excuse for the Byzantines for some shoddy double dealing, does potentially have a glimmer of truth to it. John Kinnamos was a famously unreliable chronicler, but the marriage of Lady Melisende's parents was famously unhappy, and the girl did die not long after the failed marriage negotiations. However, it is more likely that the emperor changed his mind as a result of rumours of her illegitimacy rather than of some mysterious illness: there would have been far less frustration and consternation among the Franks, had Lady Melisende genuinely been at death's door and unfit for marriage.

Still more surprising than the rejection of Baldwin III's chosen candidate and the wasting of Queen Melisende's efforts to raise a royal dowry, is the behaviour of Princess Constance of Antioch in going behind her cousin's back, subverting the efforts of Jerusalem and supplanting her own cousin Lady Melisende of Tripoli with her daughter Maria. Constance's life and reign in Antioch are the subject of a later chapter, but this event reveals real political agency on her part, and a rebellious, ambitious and calculating nature reminiscent of her mother, Princess Alice.

THE DEATH OF THE QUEEN

This episode would prove to be the last political scandal of Queen Melisende of Jerusalem's long and colourful life. The month that Maria of Antioch set sail to Constantinople was the month Melisende died. She had fallen victim to a sudden illness in early 1161, which left her bed-bound and deprived of many of her previous abilities. She was tenderly cared for by her two sisters. William of Tyre wrote:

> During this time Queen Melisend, a woman of unusual wisdom and discretion, fell ill of an incurable disease for which there was no help except death. Her two sisters, the Countess of Tripoli and the Abbess of St Lazarus of Bethany, watched over her with unremitting care; the most skilful physicians to be found were summoned, and such remedies as were judged best assiduously applied. For thirty years and more, during the lifetime of her husband as well as afterwards in the reign

of her son, Melisend had governed the kingdoms with strength surpassing that of most women. Her rule had been wise and judicious. Now, wasted in body and somewhat impaired in memory, she had lain on her bed for a long time as if dead, and very few were allowed to see her.

Finally, in September 1161, after many months of struggling, she succumbed to her illness:

> ... his pious mother, wasted by the constant suffering attendant on a lingering illness, went the way of all flesh. Her death occurred on the eleventh day of September. When the king received the news, he gave himself up to grief and by the depth of his emotion clearly showed how sincerely he had loved her; in fact, for many days thereafter he was inconsolable.

Mourned sincerely by her son the king, Melisende was buried beside her mother Morphia in the church of St Mary in the valley of Jehoshaphat, near the shrine of the Virgin.

That same year Zumurrud of Damascus also died. Following the death of Zengi in 1146, Zumurrud had retired to the holy city of Medina, extricating herself from the bloody politics of Damascus and living in pious isolation.

5

ELEANOR OF AQUITAINE

Eleanor is the eagle, for she spreads her wings over two nations, England and Aquitaine; also, by reason of her *excessive beauty*, she destroyed or injured nations.

Matthew Paris

With the death of Melisende, a period of strength in Outremer ended. Her sons would govern well, but the crusader states were beginning to unravel. The wheels of this decline had been set in motion more than a decade prior to Melisende's illness and death. The demise of the Kingdom of Jerusalem had been heralded clearly by the first great disaster of her reign: the loss of Edessa and the failure of the Second Crusade.

The exact cause of this failure has been the subject of intense and somewhat weary debate among historians for centuries. Poor organisation, shortages of food and water, inexperienced troops, poor discipline and the presence of women with the army have all been blamed.

Historians writing in the decades following the disaster were keen to assert that it was the sinfulness of the army, exacerbated by their consorting with women, that caused the hosts of France and Germany to lose the favour of God and their right to victory. The most significant woman riding with the army was Eleanor of Aquitaine, Queen of France, and the first queen to go on crusade.

Eleanor's story and entanglement with Outremer began not in the fortified citadels of Edessa, Antioch, Tripoli or Jerusalem, but several thousand miles west amid the vasty fields of France, in the sprawling Duchy of Aquitaine.

Eleanor's experience as a crusader queen was fundamentally different from that of her counterparts ruling in Outremer. She was a queen who went on crusade, sharing in the hardship and adventure on the journey across Europe, rather than a queen born in the crusader states.

Eleanor must have been just as much an object of fascination and just as exotic for the ladies of Outremer as they were to her. She was the most well-travelled of the crusader Queens discussed in this book. Even though they were dynamic and fiery, none of Morphia's daughters or granddaughters ever ventured further than Constantinople. Most never left Outremer.

How did Eleanor come to make this journey, which would lead her to meet Melisende of Jerusalem and Constance of Antioch? In 1147, ostensibly in answer to the call for aid to liberate Edessa, the Kings of France and Germany assembled their armies and marched eastwards on crusade. Louis VII of France, either because he could not bear to be without her, wanted to conceive more children or doubted her fidelity, decided to bring his wife on crusade with him. That wife was Eleanor of Aquitaine.

Little is known for sure about Eleanor's appearance, except that she was remarkably beautiful, and this no doubt played a part in Louis's decision to bring her with him. Her funeral effigy in the Abbey of Fontevraud presents her with blonde hair, and a mural that likely depicts Eleanor with her husband and sons in Chinon, a beautiful medieval town and fortress situated in the Loire Valley, shows her with red hair. One contemporary chronicler wrote that she was 'more than beautiful', and the troubadour Bernard of Ventadour, writing of her in her early thirties, wrote that she was 'gracious, lovely, the embodiment of charm'. Indeed, the Queen's beauty and personal attributes are constantly alluded to throughout the chronicles, Richard of Devizes famously describing her as 'an incomparable woman'. All of this feeds into the myth of Eleanor that has proliferated down the ages. In reality little is known of the real Eleanor, but the following pages attempt to piece together what is known, and construct a narrative of her experiences on crusade and her impact as a crusader queen.

ELEANOR'S EARLY LIFE

She was born in early 1124 into a family notorious for sensuality and scandal. In time she would prove herself able to live up to her dynasty's salacious reputation. Her grandfather William IX, who was still alive when Eleanor was born, had been a famous poet and seducer, and also a crusader, having gone east in 1101 following the success of the First

Crusade. William's career as a crusader was not distinguished, but his work as a troubadour was. The lyrics he composed are one of the few surviving examples of twelfth-century songwriting and are widely praised as both accomplished and influential. One must wonder if Eleanor was exposed to his work as a child, and whether the emerging genre of medieval romance influenced her life as an adult.

Eleanor's grandmother, Philippa of Toulouse, made the judicious decision to leave her husband once she had completed her heir-providing duties and retired to the Abbey of Fontevraud, where Eleanor herself would eventually be laid to rest. William IX wasted no time in appointing a replacement: his mistress Dangereuse, the wife of a neighbouring lord, was brought to live with him. Regardless of what family news was censored from the nursery, the young Eleanor could hardly have failed to notice the departure of her grandmother and the arrival of this new woman. Doubtless the scandals surrounding her grandfather's legacy have contributed to the rumours swirling around Eleanor's own.

She scarcely knew her grandfather; he died just three years after her birth. That said, his legacy must have loomed large as he was a far more colourful and domineering character than his son, Duke William X, Eleanor's father, proved to be. Following an ill-fated pilgrimage, William X died at Santiago de Compostela in 1137, and as his wife Aénor had predeceased him, this left the two surviving female children as heirs to the richest province of Europe. Eleanor and Petronilla were suddenly orphans, but orphans of great wealth. Eleanor was thirteen at this time – of marriageable age, should the right candidate be found.

Aquitaine and the adjacent territories under its control comprised the richest region of France, larger than the northern duchies of Normandy and Anjou combined, with territory far more significant than the French King's land surrounding the Île-de-France. Stretching over the sunny and fertile south-west corner of the country, including Gascony and Poitou and bordering the County of Toulouse to the east and Anjou to the north, it was nominally held in fief from the King of France. However, in practice the Capetian Kings of France never ventured into Aquitanian territory, let alone managed to control it. The Duchy was independent in language, culture and heritage and the French of Aquitaine had little in common with the French of Paris. They spoke Occitan, a dialect still spoken but endangered in South West France.

Aquitaine was important not only for its vast tracts of land but also for its exports and trade: salt was produced along the region's wide Atlantic coasts, and wine was made in the vineyards of Gascony and Bordeaux, as they still are today. These industries made Aquitaine rich. The abbot of Lobbes wrote of Aquitaine in the eleventh century: 'Opulent Aquitaine, sweet as nectar thanks to its vineyards dotted about with forests, over-flowing with fruit of every kind, and endowed with a superabundance of pastureland.' The ruler of these lands was fortunate indeed.

No sooner was her father interred and the news of his passing had reached the old French king, 'Louis the Fat', than he determined that Eleanor should be married to his son with all haste, in order to bring Aquitaine under his control in deed as well as name. The King of France had a relationship with the Duke of Aquitaine similar to that between the King of Jerusalem and the Prince of Antioch; that is, the status of each and the hierarchy of the relationship depended on the person. If there was a weak Duke in Aquitaine, the King of France might be able to assert his technical authority over him and foist his influence on the south, but if there was a strong ruler in Aquitaine, the chances of the king asserting any real power in Aquitainian lands were minimal. King Louis must have been gleeful to learn that the control of this most pivot-al region now lay in the hands of an unmarried orphan girl of thirteen. If his eldest son (also a Louis) could marry her and manage her, this would bring control of Aquitaine at last into the hands of the Capetian dynasty, an ambition that had been continuously sought after, but bun-gled, down the generations.

Eleanor, it seems, had little choice in this matter, but furthermore she would have been foolish to object. On a political level, the match was excellent, and marrying a man of a similar age to herself who had the power of the Capetians behind him might prevent her from being deprived of her rights of inheritance. It remained to be seen what auton-omy she would manage to retain after her marriage. Once again, the practicality of power depended on personality. Some wives managed to command the loyalty of their vassals and retain this after marriage; others became silent and passive.

Thus, just three months after her father's death, the fourteen-year-old Eleanor found herself standing in the great Cathedral of Bordeaux, the medieval nave of which still stands in the centre of this vibrant French city. In reciting marriage vows to the young Prince Louis, Eleanor became the future Queen of France and secured her own inheritance as Duchess of Aquitaine.

It was significant and indicative of the shifting power dynamics in France that the young prince travelled to Bordeaux, south of Poitiers, to meet and marry Eleanor. Never before had a Capetian king travelled so far into Aquitanian territory. The fact that he undertook this journey and the risks associated with it spoke volumes about Eleanor's value and the significance of the match.

QUEEN OF FRANCE

Shortly after their vows were solemnised in Bordeaux's vaulted cathedral, Eleanor's new father-in-law died suddenly. The newly-weds were propelled to the most exalted position in the land, becoming the King and Queen of France, in addition to Duke and Duchess of Aquitaine. Together they now stood at the head of an extensive and formidable territory.

This new honour involved a change of location. Eleanor bade goodbye to Bordeaux and Poitiers and the rolling hills of her childhood, and journeyed north to Paris and the Île-de-France, the heart of her husband's kingdom. When Eleanor had first married Louis, she might have hoped and expected that they would live their married life for some years in Aquitaine, holding court at Bordeaux and Poitiers, as her father had done. Before the death of Louis's father, their primary position was to govern Aquitaine as Duke and Duchess. In contrast, the King of France traditionally resided in Paris. So, like many royal brides before her, Eleanor was parcelled up and sent off to a new land where she had no friends and where the language was different. She was lucky in that her younger sister, Petronilla, was permitted to accompany her north. It seems the girls were close, and Eleanor's championing of her sister's interests was soon to land both her and her husband in hot water.

The journey from Poitiers to Paris was certainly not the longest journey made by a royal bride in the Middle Ages, but it was equally isolating. Eleanor might have been lucky to stay within the boundaries of France, but the language and customs of the north were still entirely foreign to a girl born and bred in the south. Moreover, as the heir to her father's Duchy, Eleanor had enjoyed high status within her household, whereas now, although technically as Queen of France she had risen in the aristocratic hierarchy, she was the wife of the King of France, and as such had significantly less freedom than she would have enjoyed in her own lands. For Eleanor, Paris did not prove to be the stuff of dreams or a city of love, but rather a cold, dirty city in which she was married to a feeble man of monkish temperament.

The advent of the Second Crusade would permanently fracture the monotony of Eleanor's existence in Paris.

THE ROAD TO HELL

The groundwork for Eleanor's voyage east had been laid long before news reached the Pope of the massacre at Edessa, or St Bernard had preached the crusade to Louis. It did, however, start with a massacre of Christians, but this was one carried out much closer to home, and at her husband's instigation.

In 1142 Eleanor's sister Petronilla had rushed into a marriage with the King's cousin Raoul. The match seemed perfect in every way, except for one slight hiccup: Raoul was already married. The existence of his hale, hearty and nobly born wife, Eleanor of Champagne, was a serious obstacle. Unjust pretexts were conjured to annul the marriage and shunt this woman to one side, to clear the way for Petronilla to step into Raoul's bed.

This plan was simple enough for Louis to execute, given the ready availability of corrupt and biddable bishops, but it had far-reaching ramifications. While the bishops might be willing to turn a blind eye to the flagrant disregard of canon law, Eleanor of Champagne's family were not prepared to overlook such shabby treatment of their kinswoman, and nor it seems was the Pope.

Petronilla and Raoul were promptly excommunicated, and the royal family became embroiled in a bitter conflict with the jilted duchess's brother, Theobald of Champagne. Theobald was not willing to stand by and see his sister's happiness and his family's reputation reduced to tatters on the whim of the young queen and her sister, and ostensibly to allow the King's cousin to jump into bed with a teenage bride.

This conflict, beginning with the royal invasion of Champagne, burning of towns and general terrorising of the citizens, culminated in what has become known as the holocaust of Vitry. King Louis's troops careened into a small and relatively undefended town in Theobald's lands east of Paris, Vitry-le-François. The residents, fleeing the lances and swords of the King's horsemen, took refuge in the town's church, believing that in that holy place they would be safe. The walls were torched, and they were burned alive inside. It is unknown whether this was an accident, or wilful slaughter by soldiers carried away by the red mist of battle. In any case, possibly as many as 1,000 innocent Christians died a horrific death in the burning church, and this atrocity and the symbolism it embodied would remain a blot on Louis VII's reign, not only during his lifetime but throughout history.

Louis was extremely penitent in the aftermath of the disaster, and it is small wonder that when the opportunity presented itself for the pious king to atone for his sins by going on crusade, he leapt at the chance. Eleanor too may have felt pangs of guilt for the murdered citizens of Vitry. Icy-hearted as many believed her to be, it would be difficult to remain unmoved by news of such an appalling tragedy, and she herself had certainly had a hand in it, given that it was her influence that had led to the repudiation of Eleanor of Champagne in the first place.

Following the Vitry campaign, the royal couple of France became the objects of censure and horror throughout Christendom, and no one was more forthright or damning in his condemnation than the fierce Bernard of Clairvaux, the same man who had written repeatedly to Queen Melisende, variously to praise and chastise her. Bernard certainly saw it as his role in life to castigate Christian royalty when he believed them to be slacking.

Bernard pulled no punches when it came to admonishing recalcitrant royalty. He unleashed the full force of his wrathful judgement on the already contrite Louis. There can be no doubt that the spartan Bernard had little time for the decadent Eleanor, a woman who in due course would prove her disdain for canon law time and time again. However, for the moment, despite their manifold differences, the two must have eyed one another with wary respect. They were both figures on whom providence had bestowed great influence over the king.

On 11 June 1144, Louis and Eleanor met with Bernard at the newly reconsecrated Cathedral of St Denis, on the outskirts of Paris. While Louis certainly still had the screams of the victims of Vitry ringing in his ears, Eleanor's most pressing concerns were of a more personal and intimate nature. Louis was not the most amorous or energetic of husbands, prompting Eleanor to compare him to a monk instead of a monarch. Despite being married for seven years by 1144, and being of healthy childbearing age, the couple had as yet failed to produce a healthy child. Eleanor's later career in childbearing (giving birth to at least ten healthy children, including Richard the Lionheart) proved that the problem lay not with her but with the timid and pious Louis.

In the Middle Ages blame for such matters was always attributed to the woman, and no doubt Eleanor was anxious and afraid about the potential ramifications for a woman who could not fulfil her most important duty as queen and wife. She had seen at first hand that faithful wives could be repudiated for lesser things than infertility. If Eleanor failed to produce an heir, it was very likely that her husband would seek to divorce her, and she might fail to gain another husband. Similarly, while she would never lack for wealth, given her inheritance and patrimony, if she was repudiated or heirless, then her family's lands would be absorbed into those of another dynasty. Time was of the essence in proving her fertility and securing her position.

Thus it seems that when Eleanor met with Bernard of Clairvaux, a man with whom she had little in common except fearlessness, charisma and willingness to speak bluntly, the pair made a deal. Bernard would pray for Eleanor to bear a healthy child, and she would do her best to use her influence with her devoted but hapless husband to bring his domestic and foreign policies more in line with the teachings of the church.

Both parties were as good as their word, and perhaps due to renewed optimism or divine intervention, Eleanor gave birth to a daughter named Marie in 1145, just over nine months after Bernard offered up his prayers. The birth of a girl, healthy as she might be, did not solidify Eleanor's position entirely. A girl was, after all, not a son and heir, but it did demonstrate that she was not barren and bought her some time.

Shortly after the birth of Marie, the news of the massacre at Edessa reached French shores, and Bernard began his campaign preaching a call for crusade throughout Europe. As we have seen, he met with great success, and not only noblemen but royalty signed up for the adventure.

It was not only the eloquence of Bernard and his own personal guilt that led Louis to commit to the crusade. The ruling couple of France had strong familial connections to the states of Outremer. Eleanor's uncle was that same Raymond of Poitiers who had serendipitously arrived at Antioch during Alice's final rebellion, and used his silver tongue to wed Princess Constance and drive out Princess Alice. Louis also had a connection to Antioch: his aunt Constance of France had been the first Princess of Antioch and was the grandmother of the current Princess Constance, wife of Raymond. Raymond had sent envoys with rich gifts to his niece Eleanor and her husband King Louis, entreating them to ride to the relief of Antioch. Queen Melisende had also written to Pope Eugenius, resulting in the publication of a Papal Bull, urging the King of France and all faithful Christians within the vast country to take up arms to save Outremer from the infidel.

Bernard had framed the loss of Edessa as a punishment from God for the sins of man, but the crusade was the lifeline God had thrown to mankind – the chance to redeem itself, expunge its sins and retake the land conquered by the Muslims. It seemed like the golden ticket for pious Louis to atone for the disaster at Vitry, and to have a taste of adventure. The young king was twenty-seven years old, and had scarcely travelled beyond France. Moreover, his greatest move towards augmenting the lands of his realm had been through his marriage to Eleanor, rather than on the battlefield, so it is possible that he also thought the crusade would give him a chance to prove himself militarily. He had been raised on the legends of the success of the First Crusaders. His own aunt Constance had married Bohemond of Taranto and become the Princess of Antioch, and doubtless he thought he would be blessed with similar glory in the East.

Whatever the case, he was sadly mistaken. The crusade would cement his reputation as a useless soldier and a still more useless husband. Beyond this, the events that transpired in Antioch also laid the groundwork for his loss of Aquitaine, the greatest territorial gain made by his family in a century.

Despite his failure to produce a male heir with Eleanor, the sources agree that Louis was devoted to her, and guarded her jealously. Scholars generally offer three reasons as to why the decision was taken for Eleanor to accompany her husband on crusade. The first, that he adored her and wanted her company; the second, that he was anxious that if he left her to her own devices in France, she would be unfaithful; and the third, simply that she wanted to come and would brook no opposition. In all likelihood it was a combination of the three. What Louis did not realise was that in taking her away from the rigid environment of the court, he was not removing all threats to her fidelity, but rather taking his marriage out of the frying pan and thrusting it into the fire. William of Newburgh wrote of Louis's motivations and their consequences:

> [Eleanor] had, at first, so completely bewitched the young man's affections, by the beauty of her person, that when, on the eve of setting out on that famous crusade, he felt himself so strongly attached to his youthful bride, he resolved not to leave her behind, but to take her with him to the Holy War. Many nobles, following his example, also took their wives with them; who, unable to exist without female attendants, introduced a multitude of women into those Christian camps, which ought to have been chaste, but which became a scandal to our army.

William's response and hostility to the notion of Eleanor and her ladies joining the campaign was far from unusual or unexpected. Wives were not often brought on crusade. Baldwin I had brought his first wife, Godehilde, on crusade, and she had first been taken hostage and then died before completing the journey from Asia Minor. None of the other leaders had brought their noble Frankish wives with them. Another noblewoman who had travelled east in 1101 was rumoured to have been taken captive following a crusader routing, and had become a sex slave to a Turkish warlord, before becoming the mythologised mother of Zengi. The journey was perilous enough for armed knights, let alone for groups of ladies, and more than this, the presence of high-value noblewomen with the army could prove to be a liability. For an army focused on pilgrimage as much as war, the presence of a beautiful French queen and her attendant ladies would almost certainly be a distraction. Yet Eleanor came.

THE ROAD TO HEAVEN

At the Christmas court of 1145, Louis 'disclosed the secret of his heart' and he and Eleanor announced their intentions to respond to the call for aid sent by the nobles of Outremer. It would be three months more before they formally pledged their support and that of their vassals to the crusade. This august ceremony took place in the town of Vézelay, a place of religious significance and geographical convenience. Lying between Paris and some of the great monastic houses of France, and located at the start of one of the roads to the central site of Christian pilgrimage in Europe, Santiago de Compostela, it was as convenient a location as one could find to preach a crusade in the Middle Ages. Today it is anything but conveniently located. Nestling in a picturesque spot atop a hill in the heart of the Burgundy region, it retains some of the atmosphere that must have been felt by the medieval attendees of this council. The central point of the town is the basilica on the hilltop, containing the shrine and relics of Mary Magdalene. For modern visitors, it is certainly worth the climb for the impressive views of the Burgundy region commanded by the ancient church, and the great sense of tranquillity.

This tranquillity was probably elusive for the French nobility who turned out to hear Bernard preach the crusade. The sermon was spectacular, and has gone down in history as one of the great oratorical events of the Middle Ages. The number of people who came to see Bernard preach the new crusade far exceeded the capacity of any of the great structures of the town, and thus a platform was erected for Bernard to preach from in a field. It must have been a sight to behold: a middle-aged abbot, dressed in his humble monk's garb, made frail from a self-inflicted life of privation, moved by passion to deliver one of the most rousing speeches of history, and captivating a military audience with such skill that the bulk of the crowd agreed on the spot to sign on for an expedition that would march them thousands of miles into the unknown, and many of them to certain death.

Following this rousing sermon, Louis and Eleanor knelt before the preacher, and displayed the fabric crosses sent by the Pope, prominently stitched onto their robes, which they wore proudly on their shoulders. There was a great clamour for more of these crosses to be distributed to the avidly listening congregation, and rumour has it that when the supply ran out Bernard tore cloth from his own robes to make more and satisfy the demand. A new fever for crusading had been ignited within Europe.

Gervase of Canterbury, a twelfth-century English chronicler, asserts that following this ceremony, Eleanor and the other ladies who had joined her in pledging themselves to the crusade dressed themselves as Amazons mounted on white horses and galloped around the town gathering support. This story is more or less certain to be false, created out of the legends of Eleanor and other crusaders at a later date. Gervase was writing some twenty to thirty years after the event, but his fictionalised depiction of Eleanor reveals how the queen and her participation in the crusade was perceived during her own lifetime. Perhaps those contemporary chroniclers who did not hate her as a meddlesome 'destroyer of nations' saw her as an energetic champion leading by marvellous example.

Following the spectacle of Vézelay, one final example of medieval pageantry marked the official beginning of the Second Crusade. In June 1147, Eleanor, Louis, his mother Adelaide, Abbot Suger and the Pope himself celebrated the Lendit Fair in the Cathedral of St Denis in the Île-de-France. There in the church the king prayed to relics of the Holy Martyrs. Then, in front of the great altar, Abbot Suger ceremonially bestowed upon Louis the *Oriflamme* or *Vexillum*, the ceremonial standard of the County of the Vexin, the standard that the kings of France carried to war. This banner had much mythology associated with it, having been mentioned in the *Song of Roland*, and purportedly carried to war in the Holy Land by Charlemagne himself. Legend had it that from the tip of the banner flames would spring to drive out the Saracens. When Louis received this banner, the Second Crusade had begun.

There have long been myths, spurred on in no small part by Katharine Hepburn's portrayal of Eleanor in the 1968 film *The Lion in Winter*, that Eleanor dressed her women as Amazons and 'rode bare-breasted halfway to Damascus'. These rumours have been definitively debunked by modern historians. Eleanor certainly did not ride bare-breasted anywhere. If she had, it would certainly have made it into at least one of the chronicles of the time. However, William of Tyre does refer to up to '70,000' women with breastplates in the army, in addition to women and children travelling with the army. This is unlikely to be accurate, but it does suggest that *perhaps* some armoured women rode with the army. Niketas Choniates and Gervase of Canterbury both assert that women in the European army dressed as Amazons. Niketas had been present at the court of Constantinople when the Frankish army arrived with all its pomp, and he would have seen Eleanor, and Gervase knew Eleanor personally during the later years of her reign. Niketas writes of the approaching German army:

> Females were numbered among them, riding horseback in the manner of men, not on coverlets or sidesaddle but unashamedly astride, and bearing lances and weapons as men do; dressed in masculine garb, they conveyed a wholly martial appearance, more mannish than the Amazons. One stood out from the rest as another Penthisilea and from the embroidered gold which ran around the hem and fringes of her garment was called 'Goldfoot'.

Niketas had a traditional Greek disdain of Western Europeans, and called the French everything from Germans to Italians. It is perfectly possible therefore that this martial company of females were in fact seen among the French forces rather than the German. There is no mention of a similar posse with the army of Conrad, whereas it is the second contemporary reference to a noblewoman dressed extravagantly and riding astride in the French army.

For all the pageantry and glory of their departures, the armies of Louis and Conrad were decisively routed in Asia Minor. The French contingent had journeyed overland from Metz, where the army was rallied, to the splendid court of Manuel Komnenos in Constantinople, where they arrived on 4 October 1147. This would have been Eleanor's first real glimpse of the splendours of the Orient: she must have been fascinated by what she saw. The extravagance and pomp of Constantinople could not have been further from the austere courts of Paris which had so dismayed her at the time of her early marriage. In the descriptions of Louis's stay in Constantinople we find no mention of Eleanor, suggesting that perhaps she was separated from him during his public excursions and entertained privately by the women of the Greek court, led by Manuel Komnenos's first wife, Empress Irene.

It is unlikely that Eleanor would have had much in common with the devout Empress Irene. A German by birth, she was better suited to a marriage with Louis than the decadent and profligate Emperor Manuel. Niketas Choniates described the empress as 'not so much concerned with physical beauty as with her inner beauty and the condition of her soul. Disdaining face powder, eye liner, and eye shadow underneath the eye, and rouge instead of nature's flush, and ascribing such aids to silly women.' He goes on to relate that 'in matters of the bed, however, she was wronged [. . .] For Manuel, being young and passionate [indulged] in sexual intercourse without restraint and [copulated] undetected with many female partners.'

Eleanor, with her taste for extravagance and finery, was likely one of the 'silly women' disliked by the empress. Nevertheless, the nobles leading the French army made themselves at home. After slightly overstaying their welcome in Constantinople, where it seems Eleanor relished the hospitality and different company, she and Louis marched on with their armies into Anatolia. The landscape that lay between Constantinople and Antioch was varied and extreme. To avoid the breathtaking but inconvenient topography of the central Anatolian plateau and to mini-mise skirmishes with the Seljuk Turks, the French army took a longer, more indirect route that kept them firmly in Byzantine territory as much as possible. To march as the crow flies would have exposed their armies to unnecessary dangers, whereas to take the safest option and hug the coast would have simply taken too long. The route they eventually chose represented a compromise between risk management and efficiency.

Conrad and the German host had departed before Louis and Eleanor, and on the word of the Emperor Manuel, Louis expected that when he caught up with Conrad he would find the German ruler had been met with a series of victories in his march against the Turks. This could not have been further from the truth. During their march to Antioch the French army chanced upon a band of wounded and half-starving German stragglers, who lamented that they were all that was left of Conrad's army. They related to the appalled Louis that their army had suffered a terrible defeat at the hands of the Seljuk Turks in the second Battle of Dorylaeum.*

Conrad had ordered a slow retreat to Constantinople, but found his army continuously ambushed and harassed by the victorious and pur-suing Muslims. When he was met by Louis and Eleanor at Lopadion he had personally sustained such a gory head wound that the sight of it made Louis weep. The French were 'stupefied with grief' at the news of

---

* The first, and arguably more famous, Battle of Dorylaeum had taken place during the First Crusade and had been a great victory for the Franks.

the German defeat, and perhaps for the first time, the very bloody reality and danger of crusading began to sink in.

Hitherto, they had ridden a wave of enthusiasm and zealotry, bolstered no doubt by a belief in their invincibility based on the tales told of the glory and success of the First Crusade. The difference here was that the leaders of the First Crusade took nothing for granted, and none of them were green youths. Among them were some experienced warlords such as Bohemond of Taranto and Raymond of Toulouse, both seasoned soldiers. The callow French king was the opposite of this. His most ambitious military undertaking thus far had been the appallingly mismanaged campaign which had resulted in the Vitry holocaust. Louis had not been raised to warfare, and prior to his older brother's death had been destined for the priesthood.

The Germans had been the victims of misinformation and poor preparation. They had been underprovisioned for their journey, and expected less competent resistance than they had in reality encountered. Their fate should have served as a warning to the French contingent, for they too were destined to be routed. Depleted, the German army joined forces with the French. The remnants of Conrad's army, together with Louis and Eleanor's, made for Ephesus, arriving there in December 1147. While Conrad and his army licked their wounds, Louis and Eleanor were anxious to press on. Conrad sailed for Constantinople, while Louis and Eleanor led the French army onwards towards Antioch, where the fortunate ones would arrive after a gruelling journey in March 1148.

During their three-month march from Dorylaeum, despite never being directly alluded to by the sources, Eleanor proved she was made of sterner stuff and more resolute than one might expect the richest princess in medieval Europe to be. The march was anything but uneventful, and as they pressed on Eleanor and her entourage soon found themselves marching past the unburied corpses of the unfortunate German army that had passed that way before them. A sense of foreboding and the smell of death were thick in the air. As they neared the coast close to modern-day Antalya, the French army were presented with a very serious obstacle by the name of Mount Cadmus. This mountain could not be circumvented and thus it had to be scaled. With its steep ascent and narrow, treacherous paths, it seemed like it would take the baggage-laden army the best part of the day to do this. In order to make the crossing, the army separated into three discrete sections. The first was an armed vanguard led by experienced nobles – Geoffrey de Rancon, a vassal of Eleanor's, and the King's uncle, the Count de Maurienne. These two men were accompanied by the majority of the army's fighting men and would lead the way and scout for danger. Immediately behind them followed the slower-moving baggage section, including pack animals and wagons laden with provisions and camping equipment, and unarmed pilgrims marching on foot. Behind this section marched the rearguard led by King Louis, consisting of forty mounted noblemen.

Many historians, particularly popular ones, have accepted a colourful but unsubstantiated claim, made by the nineteenth-century historian Alfred Richard, that Eleanor and her ladies rode with the vanguard of the army. While this is possible, it is highly unlikely, and there is no contemporary source material to suggest that this was the case. Despite any Amazonian costumes Eleanor may or may not have favoured, she was a non-combatant and had no business marching with the vanguard. She and her ladies constituted a vulnerable and valuable part of the army, and it is therefore very likely that she travelled mostly, particularly in hazardous regions, with the section of the army that should have been best protected. This was certainly the middle section, which had the protection of armed units both in front and behind. It was here in the middle that Odo of Deuil, the King's chaplain and chronicler, travelled as well.

The mountain had seemed such a great obstacle that it had caused much debate among the French about how best to tackle it, and eventually it was agreed that an entire day would be spent traversing it. In reality it presented less of a challenge, topographically at least, than expected. The vanguard had climbed the mountain with unexpected ease, and thus had seen fit to ignore the carefully worked-out plan. Instead of waiting for the rest of the army at a previously agreed meeting point near the summit, they marched ahead and made camp in the plain on the other side. This manoeuvre was short sighted and naïve, as it left the rest of the army unprotected. The only reason the vanguard's ascent had been so quick was because they had been allowed to pass unmolested by the Turks, and because they were unhampered by the cumbersome baggage train, which would have a good deal more difficulty negotiating slippery and steep mountain paths than an agile group of soldiers. The rest of the army was less fortunate.

The baggage train was left to cross the mountain slowly and completely undefended. The crossing itself was perilous, with sheer drops and narrow paths. The Turks, closely monitoring the army's progress and waiting for a moment of weakness within which to strike, saw this division as the moment they had been waiting for and let loose a rain of arrows and a vicious attack upon an exposed section of the army – that surrounding the baggage train. The result was pandemonium and must have resembled a scene out of hell: the men and women of the exposed baggage train were trapped between a sudden onslaught of hostile swords and arrows raining from the sky, and a sheer drop to certain death.

The main chronicler of the Second Crusade, King Louis's chaplain Odo of Deuil (incidentally, a man who hated Eleanor) was himself travelling with the attacked section, as indeed the queen must have been. In the midst of the Turkish attack, in which many men were either killed by steel or plummeted to their deaths, Odo himself hurried back to where the king waited with the rearguard to cross the mountain. Louis hurried to the rescue, and the Turks were driven off, but not before they had caused significant damage to this valuable and vulnerable part of the convoy.

There had been heavy losses, both to the foot soldiers and nobility. When writing to his ministers back in France to inform them of the disaster, Louis wrote that he would furnish them with a complete list of casualties at a later date, implying that the deaths of noblemen had been too numerous to list in a hurried letter from an army camp.

When all three sections of the army met up with the prodigal vanguard and regrouped, relief that Louis had survived and mourning the dead were mixed with fury that such a disaster could have been allowed to happen at all. Not only had the vanguard ignored their orders, but they had failed to send a messenger either to the baggage train or the rearguard to inform them of the steps they had taken. There was a strong sentiment that Geoffrey de Rancon, a Poitevin vassal of Eleanor's and leader of the vanguard, should be hanged.

Eleanor seems to have taken this skirmish in her stride. Like anyone else, she must have been shaken by the episode. Caught in the middle of a Turkish ambush with panic, slaughter and sheer drops all around her, the attack must have been terrifying for her. It would have been her first taste of true danger on the journey, but there is nothing to suggest that she lost her nerve or taste for the crusade.

The rest of the journey to Antioch, while not marked by more military defeats, was still far from smooth for the crusaders. The topography of Asia Minor is not forgiving to a marching army, and two rivers still needed to be forded. Moreover, with the loss of much of their baggage, the French crusaders soon fell victim to the same scourge as the Germans before them: food shortages.

In January the army at last made it to the seaport of Adalia, and following debate it was concluded that Louis and Eleanor and a portion of their retinue would proceed to Antioch by sea, abandoning their infantry to the more hazardous land route. The king and queen arrived with their entourage at the walls of that fabled city on 19 March 1148.

ELEANOR IN ANTIOCH

Prince Raymond of Antioch, Eleanor's uncle and the husband of Princess Constance, was anxious to make a favourable impression upon his exalted guests. Constance was likely either pregnant or recovering from childbirth at the time of the royal couple's arrival, but her husband welcomed them with all the extravagance that the Principality could muster, and lavished the splendour of oriental hospitality on his road-weary guests. Antioch must have seemed to Eleanor and Louis an oasis in the desert. A rich oriental Principality, ruled by a Poitevin lord, it must have been something close to paradise for Eleanor, combining flavours of the exotic East with the comforting familiarity of her own mother-tongue and the customs of southern France.

We have no reliable images or descriptions of the dwellings of the ruling family of Antioch. However, we do have a lavish near-contemporary description of the palace of John of Ibelin, son of a Queen of Jerusalem and Lord of Tripoli, and it is likely that the Princes of Antioch inhabited a palace of similar if not surpassing grandeur. John's palace was ornate, and created by Syrian, Greek and Muslim craftsmen. His hall had a marble pool at its centre with marble flowers and sculptures of animals and birds. The walls were inlaid with marble, and perforated by windows on every side. The ceiling was decorated with frescoes of scudding clouds, and the marble floor was designed to suggest a sandy beach and moving water. The Queens of Jerusalem doubtless inhabited quarters of similar splendour, that likewise fused aspects of Eastern and Western design, and it is known that in Tripoli Countess Hodierna personally owned an ornamental garden known as 'La Gloriete'.

Beyond the ties of kinship, Prince Raymond had every reason to roll out the red carpet for his royal guests. Despite their trials on Mount Cadmus, the royal couple still brought with them a considerable army and valuable resources. It was Raymond's fervent hope that they could be persuaded to turn their attention from the recapture of Edessa to the conquest of Aleppo.

Aleppo was Antioch's enemy to the east and a constant thorn in Raymond's side. Edessa, following the failed attempt to recapture it by Joscelin II de Courtenay and the massacre and flight of the Christian army, no longer stood as a realistic goal for the crusaders; but if Aleppo could be captured from Nur ad-Din, then the Principality of Antioch and the northern borders of Outremer would be far more secure.

Despite the logical sense of this scheme, Louis's mind was, as ever, on the celestial rather than the practical and, thoroughly shaken by his harrowing journey across Anatolia, he was in no hurry to rush to war against an all-too-real enemy to the east. Instead, he announced his intention to march peacefully to Jerusalem in order to fulfil his vows and pray at the Church of the Holy Sepulchre. On learning this, Prince Raymond became mutinous.

United by their common blood, tongue and contempt for Louis, Eleanor and her uncle began to form a particularly close bond. They would meet privately and discuss tactics, strategies and politics. Raymond, who would only have met his niece in her early teens, was soon favourably impressed by her mind as well as her beauty, and could clearly see that she was wasted on King Louis.

In contrast to the ineffectual Louis, Raymond was an impressive and attractive man with far more worldly and military experience. By this point in the crusade, the never-steamy marriage of Eleanor and Louis was under strain. They did not travel together and were spending less and less time in each other's company.

Rumours began to spread that a sexual affair was taking place between Eleanor and Raymond, despite the distance in their ages and the closeness of their blood. The truth of this story is one of the most hotly contested mysteries of the medieval world. Many contemporaries certainly believed it, and while many modern historians have been quick to dismiss it as ill-founded gossip, readers of this book are invited to make up their own minds. The story of what happened and the evidence is related below.

Prince Raymond was the Poitevin lord who had arrived secretly in Antioch, duped Princess Alice and wed her young daughter, thus securing himself the rule of the Principality. He was described by William of Tyre as 'handsome far beyond all the kings and princes of the world' and 'affable and agreeable in conversation'. While William of Tyre is often effusive in his praise of aristocratic male beauty, this is certainly one of his more lavish descriptions. Eleanor arrived in Antioch eleven years after Raymond's hasty marriage to Constance, and his good looks had not yet left him.

We have, then, a handsome man with a probably heavily pregnant and indisposed wife, and a beautiful woman unhappy in her marriage and all but separated from her husband. They had much in common, and spent more time together. Two of the most level-headed chroniclers of the Middle Ages, William of Tyre and John of Salisbury, both suggest that infidelity took place. William writes:

> Raymond had conceived the idea that by [Louis's] aid he might be able to enlarge the principality of Antioch . . . When Raymond found that he could not induce the king to join him, his attitude changed. Frustrated in his ambitious designs, he began to hate the king's ways; he openly plotted against him and took means to do him injury. He resolved also to deprive him of his wife, either by force or by secret intrigue. The queen readily assented to this design, for she was a foolish woman. Her conduct before and after this time showed her to be, as we have said, far from circumspect. Contrary to her royal dignity, she disregarded her marriage vows and was unfaithful to her husband.

John of Salisbury gives a slightly differing account:

> . . . the most Christian king of the Franks reached Antioch, after the destruction of his armies of the East, and was nobly entertained there by Prince Raymond, brother of the late William, Count of Poitiers. He was as it happened the queen's uncle, and owed the king loyalty, affection and respect for many reasons. But whilst they remained there . . . the attentions paid by the prince to the queen, and his constant, indeed almost continuous conversations with her, aroused the king's suspicions. These were greatly strengthened when the queen wished to remain behind, although the king was preparing to leave, and the prince made every effort to keep her, if the king would give his consent. And when the king made haste to tear her away, she mentioned their kinship, saying it was not lawful for them to remain together as man and wife, since they were related in the fourth and fifth degrees. At this the king was deeply moved [. . .] he loved the queen almost beyond reason. [. . .] There was one knight amongst the king's secretaries, called Thierry Galeran [. . .] He boldly persuaded the king not to suffer her to dally any longer at Antioch, both because 'guilt under kinship's guise could lie concealed', and because it would be a lasting shame to the kingdom of the Franks if in addition to all the other disasters it was reported that the king had been deserted by his wife, or robbed of her.

While they disagree as to the motive, instigator and impetus behind the affair, they both agree that some kind of treachery was hatched between Eleanor and Raymond. While neither is explicit that there was sexual infidelity, both strongly imply it. John of Salisbury makes an ominous reference to a famous poem by Ovid, in which Phaedra, a married older woman, writes a passionate letter to her stepson and attempts to seduce him. The incestuous parallel drawn between Phaedra's love for Hippolytus and Eleanor's alleged love for Raymond is obvious. Furthermore, William of Tyre and John of Salisbury both agree that when Louis attempted to interfere by separating his wife from her uncle, she threatened him with the most powerful weapon she could wield over her pious and devoted husband: divorce.

Perhaps the most telling piece of evidence is a letter sent from Louis's chief minister, Abbot Suger. In his letter, the minister mentions the scandal surrounding Eleanor, and instead of dismissing the rumours, counsels the king against anger and congratulates him on not overreacting in the East. This suggests that he had received reliable intelligence of Eleanor's infidelity and/or threat of divorce, as he is clearly aware of the issue. Had he merely heard it from scurrilous mouths, he would have dismissed it out of hand. Instead of warning the king to keep his temper, he would have told him not to heed idle gossip. Abbot Suger writes:

Concerning the Queen, your wife, we venture to congratulate you, if we may, upon the extent to which you suppress your anger, if there be anger, until with God's will you return to your own kingdom.

As if to compound the allegations, William of Tyre wrote about Raymond:

He was not provident and was far too fond of vicious games of dice and chance. He had, among other defects of character, a rash disposition, a habit of acting on hasty impulse, and he frequently gave way to anger without restraint or reason.

In addition to painting a portrait of a man given to profligate living and risk taking, this description also tallies with the idea that when Louis rejected Raymond's request for assistance against Aleppo, Raymond became furious and vengeful. The French king had, after all, accepted his lavish hospitality and gifts, and now appeared to throw his generosity back in his face. Beyond this, it was clear that Louis was no match for Eleanor, and Raymond, perhaps stirred by familial affection and loyalty, wanted to help his unhappy niece get rid of her inadequate husband. This would tie in with William's assertion that Raymond sought to separate the couple in retaliation for Louis's refusal of aid, and John of Salisbury's suggestion that Eleanor wished to stay at Antioch and obtain a divorce. This move need not have been motivated by sexual attraction to her uncle. Raymond may have suggested to her the way by which she could be rid of Louis, and having made up her mind to divorce him, it was natural that Eleanor would have wished to be separated and remain with her kin in the comfortable and celebrated city of Antioch.

Gervase of Canterbury, who has previously been mentioned for describing Eleanor charging around on a white war-horse at Vézelay, also hints at her alleged infidelity in his chronicle, alluding to significant tensions between the royal couple on their return from the East concerning events that had transpired on crusade, that he would prefer not to give details of. Similarly, Eleanor's usually supportive chronicler Richard of Devizes suggests that whatever happened at Antioch was Europe's worst-kept secret: 'Many know what I would none of us knew. This same queen, during the time of her first husband, was at Jerusalem. Let no one say anymore about it.'

Perhaps the strongest piece of evidence that the affair did take place – or even if it didn't, that Louis was jealous of Eleanor's relationship with her uncle and the marriage was breaking down – was that when Louis demanded that they leave Antioch, Eleanor refused and declared that she would stay. Louis's reaction to this was to drag her away by force in the dead of night, and take her to Jerusalem. One chronicler writes: 'His coming [to Antioch] had been attended with pomp and glory; but fortune is fickle, and his departure was ignominious.'

ELEANOR IN JERUSALEM

Louis and Eleanor travelled through Tripoli to Jerusalem. When they and their train arrived, the entire court, including Queen Melisende, turned out to greet the royal couple. A great procession was mounted in their honour, with all the clergy and nobles awaiting their arrival, and the people of the city lining the streets. Hymns and chants were performed as Louis and Eleanor processed with their retinue to the Church of the Holy Sepulchre to pray at Jesus' tomb.

Once Eleanor, Louis and their nobles had had their fill of the holy places, a council was convened in the north near Acre to decide what the strategy would be for the armies in the East. The Haute Cour of Jerusalem met with the leading nobles of the German and French armies on 24 June 1148.

William of Tyre lists the names of forty of the officials present at the council, and also makes it clear that Melisende was there with the reference, 'Baldwin, king of Jerusalem, a youth of great promise, and his mother, a wise and circumspect woman, strong of heart and not inferior in wisdom to any prince whatsoever.' He does not mention Eleanor, which doubtless he would have done had she been there, given that he created such a meticulous list. It seems Eleanor, despite being a leader of vassals in her own right, was excluded from this council, suggesting that she was in disgrace. More than this, she would certainly have felt slighted and infuriated by this deliberate exclusion: she saw the Queen of Jerusalem partaking in affairs of state, and yet she herself, as Queen of France, was excluded. Their situations were not directly comparable; Melisende was, after all, queen regnant, whereas Eleanor was only queen consort. However, it must still have rankled, as she was Duchess of Aquitaine in her own right. Incidents such as this and her forced removal from Antioch must have made her all the more determined to separate from her husband and achieve some degree of personal autonomy.

In Eleanor's absence, it was decided at this council that instead of marching to take Aleppo, as Raymond of Antioch had wanted, they would march on and besiege Damascus. It was certainly the greater prize, but it was also far less attainable. Had the armies joined with Raymond's, they might have been successful in dealing a decisive blow to Nur ad-Din's power in the East.

The armies marched on Damascus. Despite the fanfare of trumpets, prayers and the general excitement of the armies, the result was abject failure. They did not succeed in taking the city and the army was humiliated.

Limping and castigated, the armies of the European kings trailed back to Europe. The Second Crusade had been an unmitigated failure for Louis. Not only had the military venture been scuppered with heavy losses to his army and a huge amount of gold wasted, but his marriage and international reputation lay in tatters. He remained in Jerusalem until late spring 1149, during which time he borrowed money and gave generously to subsidise Jerusalem's defences. After this, he and his armies departed.

THE ROAD HOME

Seething, Louis and Eleanor boarded separate ships to make the journey back to Europe, unable to stomach the prospect of a long journey confined in each other's company. Whether it was Eleanor or Louis who demanded this separation, or if it was mutual, is unclear, but it adds to the mounting body of evidence that strife had erupted between the King and Queen of France.

While the King's ships were met with fair winds, the journey was not smooth for the queen. The French convoy was harassed by Byzantine ships, and Eleanor's vessel was captured and detained before she was grudgingly allowed to continue her voyage. By the time she reached Palermo in July, after months at sea, many believed that her ship had been lost. It was here in Palermo that she learned grave news regarding the fate of her uncle, and perhaps lover, Raymond: the Prince of Antioch had been killed in battle.

The Battle of Inab had taken place in May 1149 and was a decisive moment in cementing Nur ad-Din's reputation as a formidable military commander. His forces had marched against the Frankish-held fortress and besieged it. Raymond had brought a relief force from Antioch.

The Franks made their familiar charge of heavy cavalry against their Muslim opponents, but Nur ad-Din's men feinted a retreat. They split their troops down the middle, inviting the enraged crusaders to charge into the gap, where they found themselves surrounded on both sides by the enemy. In the ensuing battle, the Antiochene army was vanquished and Raymond himself slaughtered amid his men. As was becoming a grisly tradition, the head of the Prince of Antioch was struck from his shoulders and sent in a silver box to the Caliph of Baghdad, along with his sword arm, no doubt to be set alongside that of his similarly unfortunate predecessor, Constance's father Bohemond II. Eleanor's face may well have grown ashen on hearing this news, for her failure to convince her husband to allow the Frankish army to stay in Antioch and march on Aleppo, instead of making their ill-conceived assault on Damascus, had undoubtedly paved the way for Raymond's defeat. His mutilated body was later found by a reconnaissance party sent by Antioch, and conveyed back to his wife for burial.

Eleanor met with her husband in Sicily, and instead of taking the direct route and sailing for France, they made a detour to Rome to visit Pope Eugenius, doubtless to address the issue of their marriage. Perhaps the emotions Eleanor felt on learning of her uncle's wasteful death made her more adamant than ever that she wished her marriage to Louis to be annulled – the very threat she had made in Antioch before he dragged her away. Whatever the case, Pope Eugenius would not entertain the notion of an annulment between the King and Queen of France, and vehemently objected to the idea. Instead he took steps to renew their marriage and clad the contract in iron before they departed. John of Salisbury writes:

> He reconciled the king and queen after hearing severally the accounts each gave of the estrangement begun at Antioch, and forbade any future mention of their consanguinity: confirming their marriage, both orally and in writing, he commanded under pain of anathema that no word should be spoken against it and that it should not be dissolved under any pretext whatever. This ruling plainly delighted the king for he loved the queen passionately, in an almost childish way. The Pope made them sleep in the same bed, which he had decked with priceless hangings of his own; and daily during their brief visit he strove by friendly converse to restore love between them.

John was well placed to write an accurate account of these events. As he was well acquainted with many of the key players in the Second Crusade, he likely had access to credible sources. Also his writing has the ring of balance and truth, in that he depicts Eleanor and Louis as having differing accounts of what happened.

Eleanor's journey home, then, was not a pleasant one: captured by the Byzantines and liberated by the Sicilians, grieving for her uncle and forced into a humiliating reconciliation with her husband at Rome.

Two years after this ordeal, Eleanor bore Louis their last child, a second daughter, named Alix. This further disappointment of a second female child finally earned Eleanor the divorce she craved. It was the last straw in the demise of the marriage. One chronicler wrote of Louis and Eleanor's marriage on their return:

> When the king had returned home, together with his wife, branded with the ignominy of not having accomplished his design, their former affection began, by degrees, to grow cold; and causes of dissension arose between them. The queen was highly offended at the behaviour of the king, and asserted that she had married a monk, and not a monarch.

Once the ink on the annulment was dry, Eleanor was again the most eligible woman in Europe, and many suitors vied for her attention. The newly liberated queen wasted no time. She knew the value of her youth, her fertility and the Duchy of Aquitaine. She also knew that while she remained unmarried with such value attached to her, she could be in danger of kidnap and forced marriage. Without delay she married the twenty-year-old Henry Plantagenet, future King of England, wedding him in the cathedral of her ancestral home, the city of Poitiers. Her career would go on to be tumultuous and glorious in equal measure. She bore Henry ten children, spent sixteen years as her husband's prisoner and lived to see her son, Richard the Lionheart, ascend to the throne of England and immortal glory. Of all the queens of the Middle Ages, Eleanor is the most scandalous, celebrated and revered in popular imagination. The fact that Henry Plantagenet lost no time in claiming Eleanor as his bride speaks volumes itself about her reputation among the social elite of her time: if Eleanor had indeed been widely believed to be a shameless adulteress then an English king desperate to continue his dynasty and enshrine the legitimacy of his heirs would certainly not have touched her. Even Aquitaine would not have seemed sufficient compensation for the threat of an unfaithful bride, but perhaps Henry simply believed that he would be better able to keep the unruly Eleanor in check than her previous husband. Indeed, he went to great lengths to do so, keeping her under house arrest for sixteen years in the later years of their marriage.

For all the reams written about Eleanor, she is also one of the most mysterious women of the medieval period. Even before her death, she was written into the narrative of medieval romance. She was mythologised and fictionalised to the extent that it has become very difficult to discern facts from fiction. The talk of her infidelity proved fertile fodder for the rumour mill, and soon stories were circulating in literature and by word of mouth that, beyond having an affair with her uncle, Eleanor had attempted to elope with Saladin himself and that she had been reclaimed by her husband with one foot on a Saracen ship, preparing to sail off into the sunset. It is worth noting that at the time of Eleanor's journey to the Holy Land, Saladin was not yet twelve years old.

The birth of the medieval romance genre, while a gift to students of literature and writers the world over, has been a thorn in the side of historians. In the Middle Ages there existed no real boundary between the genres of history and fiction: historians were also poets and tellers of tales. They were educated in classical epic, and allowed this to influence their work. It was the mark of a skilled writer and great scholar to include references and motifs from Virgil, Ovid, Homer and Horace in their histories, and thus history became blurred with myth.

Eleanor's legacy in particular has fallen victim to this trend. She has been portrayed as the archetypal hellcat, seductress and emasculator, from her portrayal in thirteenth-century songs to that in the twentieth century's *The Lion in Winter*. Matthew Paris wrote that her beauty led to the ruin of nations, and Shakespeare presented her as 'the monstrous injurer of heaven and earth'. Who she really was, and how she really thought, acted and felt, is far harder to discern. I have attempted to piece together the assertions of the most reliable and contemporary chronicles, but even these leave much room for interpretation.

Eleanor's true legacy is shrouded in mystery. She is a legend in herself. She has achieved more international and historic fame than the rest of the women in this book put together. In part, that is because she lived the longest, she had the most children and she wore two crowns in her lifetime. It is for this reason that films and plays have been written about her.

Even during her own lifetime she became a celebrity, the subject of ballads and troubadours' songs. However, this career in the limelight only began with her journey to the East. Had Eleanor not gone on crusade, perhaps she would have remained an unhappy Queen of France, producing daughters she did not want and stuck in draughty castles for all of her days. The freedom she learnt and the inspiration she received in the East proved to be the making of her. Her time in Constantinople, Antioch and Jerusalem breathed new life and will-power into her. It spurred her divorce from Louis, and in turn laid the groundwork for her marriage to Henry II of England. In time, she would give birth to Richard the Lionheart, whose obsession with crusading would make him famous. He was Eleanor's favourite child, and it must have been his mother and the stories she told him about her time in the East that instilled in him an obsession with the Orient and a thirst for adventure that would dominate his ten-year reign as King of England and Lord of the Angevin Empire.

6

CONSTANCE OF ANTIOCH

The princess, however, dreaded the yoke of marriage and preferred a free and independent life.

William of Tyre

Constance of Antioch was the much-neglected wife of Prince Raymond. When trying to ascertain the likelihood of the alleged affair between Eleanor and Raymond, most historians have focused on an analysis of the marital issues between Louis and Eleanor. Very little, if any, attention has been paid to the fact that Raymond also had a wife. She was the little Princess Constance, whom he had married by trickery when she was just eight years old, following her mother Alice's third and final rebellion in 1136. By the time of Eleanor's visit to Antioch in 1148, Constance was not so little any more: she was a grown woman of twenty, who had already given birth to two daughters and was most likely pregnant with, if not recovering from the birth of, their first son. These children were called Philippa, Maria and Bohemond III.

For most of her life Constance was relegated to the wings of the political arena, first by her husbands and then by her son. She was destined to meet with more success than her mother, adopting a policy of passive resistance rather than the active aggression her mother had opted for, and becoming one of the most subtly successful women ruling in Outremer in the twelfth century. During two periods of her life Constance managed to attain some real degree of power for herself, and these two periods of freedom and autonomy are the subject of this chapter.

From a medieval perspective, Constance's marriage with Raymond had been successful. They had none of the public marital issues of Hodierna and Raymond of Tripoli, they were blessed with children famed for their beauty and both parties commanded the respect of their compatriots and their opponents. Constance was attractive, and the frequency of her pregnancies shows that their marriage was certainly more amicable than that of Eleanor and Louis. Also, William of Tyre's description of Raymond includes the observation that he was faithful to his wife. This was not a detail William bandied about; indeed, he was more likely to accuse men of infidelity than to praise their restraint. Of Raymond he wrote: 'After his marriage, he was careful to observe and maintain faithfulness in the conjugal relation.'

For all this, it seems Constance was paid little attention during Eleanor's stay at the court of Antioch. She was outranked by the visiting Queen of France in her own city, both in status and in her husband's affections. None of the chroniclers tell us of Constance's reaction to Prince Raymond's closeness with his niece and their alleged adultery.

It is possible that Constance was absent from public life during the month or so that Louis and Eleanor passed in Antioch, as Eleanor's stay tallies with the approximate time of the birth of Constance's third child, Bohemond III. It was the custom for noblewomen in the later stages of pregnancies, and when they were recovering from childbirth, to be confined away from public life and even domestic life, to avert risk to the baby. Pregnancy and childbirth were more hazardous in the Middle Ages than now, given both the lack of modern medicine and the comparative youth of most mothers. As when menstruating, women were considered ritually unclean during pregnancy, breastfeeding and for forty days after childbirth. In this period of uncleanliness, sexual activity was prohibited, meaning that Raymond was likely barred from Constance's bed during this time.

The spring of 1148 must have been a time of great anxiety and emotional stress for Constance: she was either preparing for childbirth or recovering from it, Antioch was in a desperately precarious position since the fall of neighbouring Edessa and by all accounts her husband was spending more time than was usual with a beautiful and sophisticated other woman.

Furthermore, if there was talk of divorce flying around the city regarding the French king and queen, Constance would have been justified in fearing for her own marriage. There were grounds for its dissolution: she had been married when she was below the canonical age of maturity, and without the permission of either parent. As we shall see later in the case of one of Constance's cousins, this technicality could certainly be dredged up to dissolve a marriage if either party had a mind to take a new partner. The rigidity of law surrounding marriage vows was falling slack in Outremer, and wives had every reason to be afraid.

The situation was resolved with Louis's decision to remove Eleanor from Antioch and to essentially place her under house arrest. Antioch did not stabilise after the French Queen's departure, but remained vulnerable to raids from Aleppo. A little over a year after Eleanor left, Raymond died in the Battle of Inab. Just as King Fulk's death had provided her aunt Melisende with an opportunity to seize power, so Raymond's death gave Constance an opportunity to rule in her own right.

His death left her a widow in an unstable position but with everything to play for. While her position in Antioch was secure, given that she was the only adult descendant of the Principality's founder and she had given birth to healthy heirs, her future was far from certain.

She was unlikely to be allowed to stand as regent for her son, as Melisende had done for her son Baldwin III, and as her mother Alice had attempted to do for her. Since the loss of Edessa, Antioch had been a frontier state, and needed a strong military leader. Constance had the support and guidance of the Patriarch, but neither of them had the training to lead the army. Her cousin, King Baldwin III of Jerusalem, would doubtless wish to see her quickly remarried to an experienced but tame general who could defend Antioch against Aleppo for him.

As a new widow, Constance was a highly desirable bride, but for the time being at least, she decided to eschew marriage. This cannot be seen as a surprise, given that her first marriage had been forced on her as a young child and she had had little or no freedom so far in her life as a result. In addition to the inherent difficulties presented by Constance's marriage to Raymond at such a young age, the difference in age and experience between them meant that she had little hope of claiming status or equality in her marriage, as her husband would always have been the senior partner in their relationship. Raymond had been intentionally imported to wed her so that he could claim her patrimony and rule it on her behalf, rather than rule it with her. The actions of her mother Alice meant that there was little sympathy for the ambitions of Antiochene princesses. Constance's birth gave her the authority to be princess regnant during Raymond's reign, but in practice she had little power and fulfilled the role of consort only.

Constance was the rightful Princess of Antioch, the granddaughter of Bohemond I, daughter of Bohemond II, and mother of Bohemond III. This must have worked in her favour in securing loyalties within the Principality. However, it is debatable how much factional support and real political influence she enjoyed at the time of her husband's death. During his reign Raymond had afforded Constance little or no political status. Only approximately half of the charters surviving from his reign mention Constance, and none of them were issued with her specific consent, as had been the case during the joint rule of Melisende and Fulk. This demonstrates that while she may have been invested with authority, this did not translate to much in the way of power.

Raymond only acknowledged Constance's status as the rightful heir of Antioch when it suited him, and that seems to have been in only one missive issued in his reign. In 1137 he made an ill-advised deal with Emperor John Komnenos of Byzantium, which signed away his rights to much of the land of the Principality of Antioch. When John Komnenos sought to enforce this contract, Raymond declined to honour his side of the bargain, citing that as the lands were part of Constance's patrimony and not his own, he had not been legally at liberty to dispense with them: he declared the contract void.

This message to the emperor also ensured that he could not attempt to force Constance into signing away the lands, by asserting that the Princess of Antioch had no right to make gifts of her lands or trade them either, without the express consent of the nobility of the region. While this letter certainly asserts that Raymond was aware of Constance's legal standing, in reality it proves little about any status or power she actually held within the city. It was rather a convenient escape clause from some messy double-dealing.

When Raymond died, Constance lost both a husband and an oppressor. William of Tyre wrote that following Raymond's death the citizens of Antioch mourned him bitterly, and that Constance had been left 'in some charge of the state and the principality'. Baldwin III nominally took on the regency of Antioch, but in practice he had his hands full with responsibilities elsewhere in Outremer. The year following Raymond's death, the widowed Constance was styling herself 'Constance, by the grace of God Princess of Antioch, daughter of Bohemond the Younger'. In so doing she established herself clearly as ruler of the Principality and emphasised her heritage and rights to rule as the surviving heir of Bohemond. She also secured the rights of her children.

A Muslim chronicler recorded that during this period Antioch was ruled by a princess. It seems Constance had finally succeeded in becoming a princess regnant in Antioch. While it was certainly possible for her to issue charters and the like, it still remained beyond her scope to lead an army, and a military commander was something that Antioch in its newly fragile state desperately needed. As long as Constance was regent, the Principality was completely dependent on military aid from the Kingdom of Jerusalem. The issue of Constance's remarriage was therefore a pressing one.

Widows did not remain widows long in Outremer. Despite law dictating that a lord must wait a year before compelling a widow to remarry, this period of mourning was rarely observed. The examples of Constance's mother Princess Alice and her aunt Queen Melisende were exceptions, but they were exceptions that Constance wished to emulate. The most freedom a woman could ever hope to have was in widowhood, and thus it can be no surprise that Constance sought to remain in this state of happy limbo between male lords for as long as she could.

William of Tyre did not think much of Constance's rule in Antioch. He lamented that after the deaths of the lords of Antioch and Edessa, the territories were 'abandoned to feminine rule'. Speaking of Constance's period of regency at Antioch and comparing it to that of Beatrice of Edessa, the widow of Joscelin, he wrote: 'Therefore in recompense for our sins, both regions, bereft of better councillors, barely surviving by themselves, were ruled by the judgement of women.' In these instances at least, William saw female regency and the lack of male heirs not only as less than ideal politically, but rather as a punishment from God.

Despite such grumblings, Constance deftly managed to avoid remarriage for four years. During this time she was to all intents and purposes regent of Antioch and ruling in her own right. The Byzantine Emperor Manuel Komnenos recommended a candidate for her affections in 1152. The man in question was his son-in-law Caesar John Roger, a Byzantine aristocrat of Norman descent. He was of impressive ancestry and social status, and was a realistic enough candidate for Constance's second husband that he made the by no means easy journey from Constantinople to Antioch to vie for her hand. He was unsuccessful. While Constance had paid the Byzantine Emperor a compliment in asking for and considering his recommendation for a husband, she paid him a great insult in rejecting the man. Ostensibly she turned him down because of his age and personal unattractiveness. The Byzantine chronicler John Kinnamos writes:

> Caesar John went to Antioch, but achieved nothing of what he had come for (because he was aged, Constance regarded him with displeasure), and returned to Byzantion; when sickness beset him, he tonsured his locks and donned the black garb.

Constance was revealing herself to be a woman of steely disposition and determined resolve, like her mother and aunt.

Constance's cousin Baldwin III of Jerusalem, acting in his role as her closest male relative and perhaps also suzerain lord, exercised his right to offer her three candidates for marriage for her to choose from. This was one of the peculiarities of medieval marriage laws in Outremer. A widow could not refuse to remarry if pressed, but she had to be given a choice of three candidates (until the age of sixty, at which point her advanced age would get her off the hook). Baldwin III's offerings to Constance were Ives Count of Soissons, Walter of Falkenburg and Ralph of Merle. All were perceived to be attractive options for various reasons and quite capable of fulfilling the role of Prince of Antioch. Ives was a 'distinguished man, wise and discreet, of great influence'; Walter was 'a discreet man, very courteous, wise in counsel and valiant'; and Ralph was 'a nobleman of the highest rank, experienced in the practice of arms and noted for his good sense'. Despite their manifold qualities and suitability, Constance would have none of them, and this earned her much criticism. She was perceived as headstrong and selfish for delaying marriage, which many saw as wilfully jeopardising the stability of Antioch.

William of Tyre was simultaneously sympathetic and condemning about Constance's rejection of these suitors:

> The princess, however, dreaded the yoke of marriage and preferred a free and independent life. She paid little heed to the needs of her people and was far more interested in enjoying the pleasures of life.

This explanation of Constance's rejection shows an understanding of the predicament and oppression that the institution of marriage posed for medieval women. For them, it *was* a yoke. Women were subjugated, and they were property, and in this passage William shows some acknowledgement of this. At least once in his chronicle he quotes from Ovid's book *The Heroides*, which offers female perspectives on forced marriage, rape and war, so the idea of sympathising with a woman's lot cannot have been completely foreign to him.

He does, however, fall into the trap that so many chroniclers walk into: equating an independently minded woman with the unnatural and the whoreish. To his mind, Constance cannot have simply wished to live singly or on her own terms, but instead he paints her in much the same way as he depicted Arete, the second wife of Baldwin I, who, according to him, upon her divorce went to Constantinople and lived as something close to a prostitute. He attributes similar venal desire to the widowed Constance.

This kind of lambasting of rebellious women, particularly widows, was not uncommon. Widows were, after all, no longer virgins, and were therefore seen as sexually voracious manipulators. A woman without a man in control of her was a dangerous thing in the eyes of the medieval clergy. Besides, part of the duty of a female ruler was to remarry, and in remaining single for as long as she did, many perceived Constance to be neglecting her duty.

The result of Constance's recalcitrance was that a council was convened in Tripoli specifically with the purpose of arranging a marriage for her. It was attended by her two aunts, Queen Melisende (who by this point had been deposed from power) and Hodierna of Tripoli. William of Tyre writes:

> The king, well aware of [Constance's] predilection [for freedom], called a general council at Tripoli, consisting of the nobles of the kingdom and the principality [. . .] neither the king nor the count, her kinsmen, neither the queen nor the countess of Tripoli, her two aunts, was able to induce her to yield.

Indeed, it is likely that it was Melisende's downfall following her civil war with her son that induced Constance to even consider candidates for her hand. As long as Melisende was standing strong as a female ruler, Constance could aspire to the same status and freedom within her Principality. Her blood was as good as Melisende's. However, she lacked the training and factional support that Melisende commanded. Melisende had, from her childhood, been raised to rule, attending council meetings and witnessing charters as her father's heir. Constance, in contrast, had been hastily married to a powerful and domineering husband and had no first-hand experience of rulership.

However, the Patriarch of Antioch fought her corner. Aimery of Limoges, appointed by her late husband, argued vehemently against Constance's remarriage. This was either out of loyalty to his princess, or self-interest – perhaps he enjoyed being the highest-status male in the Principality. It was a tradition of the church to support widows, and Aimery made good on this. It is easy to see his point of view. Constance had already fulfilled her primary duty in providing male heirs for the Principality, and she and he together were managing the government more or less effectively. If a new prince came on the scene, not only Constance's power would be curtailed, but the Patriarch's as well.

Despite this support, Constance was single on borrowed time. While she clearly presented a formidable front at the council of Tripoli, which failed in its goal of foisting a husband on her, it would only be so long before a moment of calm would allow her cousin and other royal relatives to turn their full attention to the matter of her marriage once again. They might not be so easily defeated on the next occasion.

Doubtless realising this, Constance played a blinder: she beat her family to it and selected her own husband. The man in question was such a dark horse in the race for her hand that he had not even made it to the lists. He was a young knight from France who had come to the East with the Second Crusade and lingered there as a mercenary in the pay of the king. He had been a visitor to Antioch where, at some stage in the early 1150s, he made the acquaintance of the widowed Constance. Their meeting made a significant impression on the princess, and his relatively lowly status proved no barrier to her affection. He was a charismatic man with a forceful personality and a daring that variously impressed, terrified and frustrated those around him. His name was Reynald de Châtillon, and the reputation he forged for himself in Outremer has echoed down the ages. Justly or unjustly, he is one of the most reviled figures of the crusades.

History does not relate *how* Constance succeeded in gaining the King's approval for this match, but somehow she did. William of Tyre writes in consternation that the population of Antioch 'marvelled that a woman so eminent, so distinguished and so powerful [. . .] should stoop to marry so common a knight.' It is important to emphasise that Reynald de Châtillon was not a foot soldier; he was a knight of distinguished lineage. That said, he was not royal, he was not wealthy and he commanded no army. Therefore, while of the upper class and rubbing shoulders with the social elite, he was by no means on an economic or social level with Princess Constance. There was widespread shock at her choice of husband, perhaps all the more so because he was *her* choice rather than a candidate proposed by the Emperor of Byzantium or a male relative.

It is possible that Baldwin III only acquiesced to avoid scandal. There was clearly a love affair between the two. No other reason can be found to explain such a match, and if news of this was beginning to become gossip, then the most sensible course of action was to marry them quickly. William of Tyre makes clear the clandestine nature of their relationship:

The Lady Constance, widow of Prince Raymond of Antioch, who after the fashion of women had refused many distinguished nobles, secretly chose as her husband Renaud de Châtillon, a knight in the pay of the king.

The *Estoire d'Eracles* stresses the romantic nature of their courtship:

> Constance [. . .] gave her heart to a bachelor of France who was not a very rich man, but [. . .] a handsome bachelor and a fine knight. [. . .] Reynald returned to Antioch and immediately married the lady who greatly desired him. Many marvelled and gossip spread throughout the land, but no matter what people said, Reynald de Châtillon became Prince of Antioch.

Reynald and Constance's marriage is a story of romance and social mobility that would certainly have pleased the troubadours and romance writers of the age.

It is unclear how exactly Baldwin III was persuaded so readily to consent to such a match. He may simply have been glad that his cousin was consenting to wed at all, after the intractable position taken by her and the Patriarch at the council of Tripoli. Reynald, beyond social objections, was not a terrible candidate to be the protector of Antioch. Constance was noble enough for both of them, and Antioch was in sore need of a competent and experienced military leader, not a preening aristocratic fop. Reynald was a trained knight and a mercenary soldier, he had seen and learned from the failures of the Second Crusade, and any who met him would have been impressed by his dynamism. Imad ad-Din, a contemporary of Reynald who most likely met him when he was a prisoner of Saladin, described him in this way:

> Reynald was the most perfidious and wicked of Franks. He was the greediest, the most determined to destroy and do evil, to violate all agreements and solemn oaths, to break his promise and to lie.

So the new prince did not ingratiate himself to his Muslim foes, but that was obviously not his priority. To inspire such levels of hatred in his opponents stands as evidence that Reynald was a stick-at-nought thorn in the side of the Muslims of the Levant, and his military record certainly corroborates this. His abilities on the battlefield had been proven in front of King Baldwin III himself at the Siege of Ascalon, which had been one of the most important victories of Baldwin's reign. Ascalon had been held by the Fatimid Egyptians (the very same people that Hugh of Jaffa had allied with in his conflict with Fulk decades before) and had been used continually as a base for raids into Frankish territory. Baldwin assaulted the city in 1153 with the assembled might of many of the most notable lords of Outremer, attacking from both land and sea. The crusaders were eventually victorious, but it was a hard-won and protracted victory that took many months and claimed many lives. The chronicler Michael the Syrian asserts that throughout the assault, Reynald demonstrated commendable bravery, as does the Armenian chronicler Gregory the Priest.

It was while they were encamped before the walls of Ascalon that Reynald appealed to King Baldwin III for Constance's hand, flinging himself to the ground at Baldwin's feet and begging that he should not refuse him. He grovelled in the dirt, pleading his case and his love for Constance, and swore that with God's help he would defend Antioch and would be a loyal and obedient prince.

Reynald chose both his timing and his words well, for the king consented to the match. The timing was apt because Reynald had clearly demonstrated his martial ability. His words were persuasive, for in imploring the king in this manner, he was essentially acknowledging the king as suzerain lord of Antioch, a contentious issue that had been a great source of tension between the King of Jerusalem and the Prince of Antioch since the two states' inceptions. Baldwin III must have seen this as a choice between continuing conflict and dissension with his cousin and the Principality of Antioch, or an opportunity to place an able military commander in Antioch, mollify his intractable cousin, extinguish rumours of an extramarital affair and assert control over Antioch in one move. He quickly acquiesced to the marriage and dispatched Reynald to Antioch to make it official and salvage Constance's teetering reputation. Indeed, the loudest voice to speak out against the marriage was not Baldwin, but Patriarch Aimery of Antioch. He opposed the match and made no secret of it, despite his earlier support of Constance.

Why Constance chose Reynald can be attributed to two motivations. The first is love. That this relationship was a love match is evident both from the circumstances from which the match arose and the evidence in the chronicles. Constance was certainly drawn to Reynald, and chose him over the heads of better-qualified candidates. Whether Reynald loved Constance is harder to glean. He would not be the first man to seduce a wealthy heiress, feigning romance, but with his eyes always on the prize of her fortune. Constance's fortune was immense, and to a landless knight the widowed Princess of Antioch must have gleamed as one of the greatest potential brides in Christendom. It is also not too great a stretch of the imagination to believe that Constance, a young woman born into a famously charismatic family, was personally attractive.

Secondly, Constance too stood to gain personally from the status imbalance in her relationship with her new husband. If she had married one of the suitors proposed either by the Emperor of Byzantium or by her cousin the King of Jerusalem, she would have found herself married to yet another high-status lord, who owed gratitude for the gift of her hand to the emperor or the king, rather than to her. She would most likely have found herself politically side-lined and dismissed, just as she had been in her first marriage to Raymond. In marrying a relatively obscure knight, who owed the blessing of their marriage entirely to her, Constance's position in her own household rose immeasurably. Her husband would look up to her, rather than vice versa.

Now aged in her early twenties with two male heirs, two marriageable daughters and several years of political experience in her arsenal, Constance was in a far more powerful position than she had ever been before. Beyond that, she had the ear and support of Patriarch Aimery as well. It is easy to see why she was in no rush to forfeit this position of power through an arranged political marriage. In choosing her own husband, a man of inferior rank to herself, she was safeguarding her own position within the marriage and had a greater chance of sharing power with her husband.

If this was a factor in her choice of Reynald, it is clear the gamble paid off to some degree. Every single charter issued by Reynald is accompanied by Constance's name and consent, in contrast to the sporadic mentions of the princess in the surviving charters from her first husband's reign. However, whether this was merely an acknowledgement of her authority rather than tangible evidence of her power, is harder to discern.

Shortly after their marriage in 1154, Constance gave birth to Reynald's only child, a daughter christened Agnes. Despite the clear affection from which their marriage sprang, it is likely that Constance had cause to regret her choice of husband more than once during Reynald's primacy as Prince of Antioch. He was keen to assert his authority in his newly-won Principality.

One of his first acts as prince was the brutal persecution of Patriarch Aimery, who had hitherto been Constance's staunch ally. The Patriarch was Reynald's primary rival for power and influence within the Principality. Another point of bitterness between the two men was Aimery's vocal opposition to the match between Reynald and Constance. The Patriarch's frequent and free criticism of Reynald, in addition to the significant power and influence he wielded within Reynald's Principality, made him a great enemy of the new prince. Moreover, the Patriarch was a wealthy man holding the gold of the church in the city of Antioch, whereas Reynald was comparatively poor, even when taking into account his newly acquired position of prince.

While the revenues of a prince were great, the expenditure to maintain the city's defences could be greater still. On more than one occasion, Reynald found himself in need of gold from the Patriarch's coffers. When Aimery, quite legally, refused Reynald access to his treasury, Constance's new husband set his thugs on her former ally. The Patriarch was brutally beaten, and dragged kicking and screaming to the highest tower of the citadel of Antioch, positioned on a hill far above the city. Here, the brutalised churchman was thrown onto the top of the tower under the heat of the Syrian sun, stripped and his newly inflicted wounds were rubbed with honey to attract the vicious attention of insects to further torment him. Some illustrations and sources suggest that Reynald's abuse of the Patriarch went still further, and that he was hung naked from the side of the tower.

This occurred less than one year after Reynald's accession to the rule of Antioch, indicating the simmering tensions present from the beginning of his reign. Such treatment of a senior churchman was unheard of in Outremer, and earned Reynald swift condemnations from Baldwin III and Queen Melisende, who must also have been angered by her niece's choice of husband. On receiving a strongly worded letter from the king, Reynald released Aimery from captivity, and allowed him to flee to Jerusalem, but not before relieving him of the funds he had been seeking.

Reynald was active as a military leader of Antioch, and, in response to the request of the Byzantine Emperor Manuel Komnenos, campaigned doggedly against the Armenians of Cilicia. Manuel promised to compensate him generously for the expense of the campaign. Reynald defeated the Armenians at Alexandretta in 1155 and ceded the lands conquered in the Belen Pass to the Knights Templar. However, the gold the emperor had promised to pay Reynald in exchange for this military effort was not forthcoming. This withholding of these funds was an insult but also put Reynald in a difficult position himself, as he needed to pay his soldiers. Enraged by both the symbolic slight and the practical difficulty thrown his way by the emperor, Reynald then turned his attention to the most counterproductive military expedition of his career. He decided to teach Emperor Manuel a lesson and allied with Thoros, King of Cilicia, to raid the Byzantine-held island of Cyprus.

Reynald mounted this campaign with such ferocity that the recriminations of this activity would haunt him until the end of his days. The combined Frankish and Armenian host sailed to the island, landed quickly and spread out across it, burning, pillaging and raping as they went.

Pandemonium reigned. Crops were burnt alongside houses, churches and convents. The population was harassed and those who resisted were killed. Eventually, when there were rumours of an imperial fleet fast approaching the island, Reynald's men allowed the citizens of Cyprus to buy back their lives and their freedom. This was with the notable exception of Emperor Manuel's nephew, John Doukas Komnenos, ruler of Cyprus, whom they retained as a hostage.

The actions of Reynald and his armies against the innocent Christian community of Cyprus shocked not only the Byzantines but also the entirety of Outremer. Had such an atrocity been inflicted upon an enemy Muslim community, it might have passed with relatively little notice, but perpetrated as it was by Christians upon Christians, it caused outrage throughout Christendom. There is no mention of Constance raising any opposition to this campaign, or of her conducting any particular penitence for it either.

The most immediate ramifications of this brutal attack came in the form of Emperor Manuel exacting vengeance. He could not allow such a barbaric and public attack on his authority to go unpunished. In an unprecedented demonstration of the power of the Byzantine Empire, Manuel marched his armies across Anatolia and into Antiochene territory. This was the first time since the foundation of the states of Outremer that the Byzantine Empire had mobilised their troops on this scale and invaded Frankish territory. Manuel chased out the Armenian lords of Cilicia, and held court at the town of Mamistra. He summoned Reynald to attend him there, and the chastened prince obeyed.

Reynald, quailing before the assembled might of Byzantium, hurried there to do humble penance and pay homage to Emperor Manuel. In a display of deep contrition and obeisance, Reynald dressed himself in simple slave clothes – a short tunic, barefoot, with a chain around his neck. Naked sword in hand, he crawled before the emperor and prostrated himself at his feet. Manuel was surrounded by his court and swathed in the gilded trappings of the imperial regalia: this was a visual representation of his power, and a warning to all of the fate that awaited those who disobeyed the Emperor of Byzantium – even fearless princes like Reynald de Châtillon. Savouring Reynald's grovelling and wishing to draw out his humiliation, Manuel feigned to ignore the prostrate figure at his feet for some minutes, and Reynald had no choice but to lie with his face in the dirt before the assembled nobles of Antioch and Byzantium, and wait for the Emperor's acknowledgement. Eventually, Manuel deigned to look at him and accepted the offered sword and Reynald's oaths of fealty.

Such a spectacle was abject shame and degradation for the mercenary-made-prince, but through biting his tongue and submitting to the ritual, Reynald was able to keep his crown. He would remain Prince of Antioch, but now as a vassal of the Emperor Manuel. In making this concession, Reynald failed to re-establish the independence of Antioch. Raymond of Poitiers had done fealty to Manuel in 1145, and Constance and the city's inhabitants might have hoped that their new red-blooded prince might have resisted making similar concessions. If so, at this ceremony they were sorely disappointed.

It seems that following this, Reynald enjoyed more favourable relations with Byzantium. Manuel rode in triumph into Antioch on 12 April 1159 at the head of a jubilant procession which included the cowed Prince of Antioch and also the King of Jerusalem following on foot, as a mark of their inferior status. Manuel's court remained in the city for at least a week and the emperor socialised with the Frankish court, and hunted with King Baldwin III. It is likely that during this visit he met, or at least glimpsed, Constance's eldest daughter, Princess Maria of Antioch. In two years' time Manuel would jilt Melisende of Tripoli in favour of Maria. At this time, she was just fourteen years old, but already would have been displaying the beauty for which she would be famed in later life. The sixteen-year-old Maria would board a ship to Byzantium to wed Manuel and become his empress, thus solidifying the links of friendship between the ruling families of Antioch and Byzantium.

Byzantine royal weddings were events of rare splendour: games and tournaments were held in the hippodrome, glorious spectacles were mounted throughout Constantinople, robes weighted down with treasure troves of precious stones and heavy pearls were worn by members of the court, and furniture made of silver and gold adorned the imperial palace. In describing the wedding of Emperor Manuel and Maria of Antioch's son Alexios to Agnes of France some years later, William of Tyre wrote that 'words would fail' to describe the 'magnificence of the nuptial splendour'. Doubtless Maria of Antioch's wedding celebrations surpassed those of all her female relatives hitherto described in this book.

Before this lavish wedding took place, a far more disturbing development befell the Principality of Antioch. Constance was once again robbed of a husband by the ongoing conflict between Antioch and Aleppo. Nur ad-Din struck again, only this time Constance's husband was not killed in battle and decapitated, but taken hostage. Reynald was captured during a skirmish in the region of Marash in November 1161. He was conveyed to the citadel of Aleppo, infamous for housing Frankish prisoners in appalling conditions, and left there to rot in darkness for fifteen years.

Following Reynald's capture and imprisonment, Constance once again found herself husbandless, with an underage son, and with the potential to take control in Antioch. Her position was a precarious one, and Reynald's capture must have precipitated her efforts to solidify an alliance with Manuel Komnenos through marriage with her daughter Maria.

Constance herself had once been considered as a potential bride for this same emperor, and so it must have been with mixed feelings that she considered sending her first child to wed him. However, it was impossible to ignore the fact that a marriage between her daughter and the man whose Empire straddled East and West would enhance Constance's position immeasurably. Moreover, if Emperor Manuel married Maria, he might be more inclined to pay the ransom for her stepfather Reynald. Manuel commanded legendary wealth, and if he were so inclined he would easily be able to extricate Reynald from captivity. This strengthening of her position alarmed the nobles of Antioch, who wanted the stability of an experienced and independent male ruler, not a female ruler who could not lead an army, backed up by alliance with their age-old nemesis the Byzantine Emperor.

William of Tyre has relatively little to say about the power vacuum created by Reynald's capture, other than that the Patriarch was put in control temporarily while the Principality waited for Bohemond III to come of age, which would take no more than a year. However, Michael the Syrian, the Patriarch of the Syriac Orthodox church, who travelled extensively in the region and spent a year at Antioch in the 1160s, told a more complex version of events, which involved Constance reliving her mother's legacy and attempting to claim the regency of the city for herself.

Michael relates that Constance attempted to take power. The situation was delicate, her husband was not dead, and therefore she could not remarry. The nobility and citizens of Antioch, perhaps after the disasters they remembered during her mother Alice's rebellions, wanted a male ruler rather than the princess to rule. It seems there were concerns that she would ally herself with the Emperor Manuel in order to bolster her position. So rather than endure the authority of the Byzantine Empire, the nobility of the city decided to expedite Bohemond III's accession to the throne, despite him still being a year underage.

In order to achieve this end, the nobility did something very surprising. The young prince and his nobles went behind his mother's back and turned to Thoros of Armenia for help. Together with him and his armies, they 'drove the queen from the city and confirmed her son on the throne'. The 1234 chronicle confirms this with the assertion that 'the first son of Raymond ruled at Antioch after chasing his mother out, who went to Latakieh.'

After this dismissal from office, with her husband in captivity and her son turned against her, nothing is heard of Constance. It seems she retired to Latakieh and lived quietly. It is difficult to date her death precisely, but it is known that she died before 1176. It is likely that she died earlier still, owing to her lack of involvement in the tumultuous events in Antioch in 1164.

Three years after Reynald's capture and Constance's dismissal from the city of Antioch, another disaster struck Outremer. King Amalric was involved in a struggle for control of lands in Egypt for much of his reign, and during his absence on one such campaign Nur ad-Din joined battle with the combined armies of Tripoli, Antioch, Edessa and Armenia outside the fortress of Harim, some twenty-five miles east of Antioch. Nur ad-Din's army seemed to be caught on the back foot by the Frankish army and made to flee the battlefield. Together the combined forces of Tripoli, Edessa and Antioch gave chase, against the frantic advice of Thoros of Armenia.

Whether they had been feinting their original retreat or simply found their courage once again is unknown, but the Turks wheeled their army around and caught the surprised crusaders in slaughter. All of the leaders, save the more prudent Thoros, were captured and taken hostage, including Constance's eldest son Bohemond III of Antioch, Hodierna's son Raymond III of Tripoli and Joscelin of Courtenay, titular Count of Edessa. It was a rich haul for Nur ad-Din: in a single battle he had bagged himself three of the four rulers of the states of Outremer. They were cast into the dungeon of the fortress of Aleppo alongside Reynald de Châtillon.

On hearing this news, Amalric abandoned his campaign in Egypt and rode north to secure Antioch. Constance is not mentioned in the events that followed, either for attempting to seize power, helping Amalric shore up the borders, or assisting in raising the ransom and negotiating for her son's return. For such a prominent figure, this was unusual. Even though his mother was unable to assist, Bohemond III was the only one of the three highest-status hostages that managed to secure a quick release. Nur ad-Din accepted Amalric's offered ransom, and Bohemond III was back in control of his Principality within a year.

William of Tyre himself expresses surprise at Nur ad-Din's leniency with the young prince, and offers two potential explanations. The first is that, as Bohemond III's sister Maria had recently become Empress of Byzantium, he feared interference he could not withstand from the Byzantine Emperor; and the second is that in Bohemond III he saw a weak Prince of Antioch, and he worried that if he kept Bohemond in captivity, Amalric might install a more competent general in his place, which would be to Nur ad-Din's disadvantage. Whatever his reasons, Bohemond III was released, and Raymond of Tripoli, Joscelin of Courtenay and Reynald de Châtillon remained in chains in Aleppo until the mid 1170s, where a shift in Christian–Muslim diplomacy resulted in a release of many hostages.

Bohemond III did not return to an easy state of affairs. In addition to his military obligations, a scandal was brewing at the centre of his own court. While three of Bohemond III's siblings had left for Constantinople, two to marry and one to serve the emperor, his elder sister Philippa remained unmarried at his court. Without the watchful eye of her mother supervising her actions, and with her brother's attentions focused on the military affairs of the Principality, it seems Philippa was left less closely supervised than was expected of Princesses.

A certain Andronikos Komnenos, whose career shall be examined in more depth later, arrived in Antioch. He was a member of the Byzantine ruling family, but had been banished by his cousin, Emperor Manuel, in the wake of a sex scandal involving Manuel's niece Princess Eudocia, who was incidentally also a niece of Andronikos himself. Andronikos was welcomed by Bohemond III, but shortly after his arrival he betrayed his host by using his hypnotic personal charms to seduce his sister. Niketas Choniates writes of Andronikos' time in Antioch:

> In Antioch, Andronikos gave himself over to wanton pleasures, adorned himself like a fop, and paraded in the streets [. . .] Henceforth Andronikos pursued his quarry, bewitching her with his love charms. He was lavish in the display of his emotions, and he was endowed moreover with a wondrous comeliness [. . .] Philippa, utterly conquered, [. . .] forsook both home and family, and followed after her lover.

Andronikos abandoned Philippa as suddenly as he had seduced her. The unhappy girl mourned him for a time before being hastily married – it seems against her will – to the much older widower, Humphrey of Toron, the Constable of Jerusalem. It was certainly not anywhere near as lofty a match as her sisters had made, and was clearly intended to hastily patch up the scandal of her youth. The marriage did not last long, with both husband and wife succumbing to disease shortly after being wed.

Ten years after this event, Reynald de Châtillon was finally released from captivity in 1176. He had spent fifteen years in jail, and was returning to a political world very different to the one he had left. Constance had died, and with her had died Prince Reynald's claim to Antioch. Bohemond III had taken control of the city, and Reynald's own daughter Agnes had sailed to Constantinople to marry King Béla III of Hungary, and Constance's second son Baldwin had accompanied her there also.

While Reynald might no longer be Prince of Antioch, he was still in a more powerful position than when he had arrived in the East as a landless mercenary from France. He had built a reputation for decisiveness and ruthlessness that would stand him in good stead in the coming turmoil in the Kingdom of Jerusalem. It was no small feat to survive fifteen years in a dungeon in Aleppo, and no small feat to seduce a princess of the blood in one of the most turbulent principalities on earth. Moreover, his stepdaughter Maria was now Empress of Byzantium, which doubtless had a hand in his ransom being paid, while his own daughter, Agnes, who had travelled to Constantinople to join her half-sister, was Queen of Hungary.

Constance's death did not mark the end of Reynald's career. He married again, shortly after his release, a woman almost as illustrious as Constance had been. Stephanie of Milly was twice widowed, and the heiress of Oultrejourdain, the wildest but largest territory in Outremer, and it was this land that she brought to her marriage with Reynald. It was mostly desert, relatively unsettled, but brimming with potential for a fierce ruler. It was dangerous and unstable. The main castles of the region were Kerak and Shobak, imposing fortresses situated high on hill-tops that still dominate the landscape to this day. It was also an important region, as through it ran both the King's Highway, a trade route of ancient importance connecting Africa to Mesopotamia, and the Hajj road, the route of Muslim pilgrimage. The Christian settlers had to co-operate with Muslim pilgrims and traders. For the most part they did. Reynald would earn himself a reputation as a breaker of the peace, harassing peaceful caravans, and he became a key antagonist against the Muslims.

Reynald had been released at around the same time as Joscelin III, the titular but landless Count of Edessa, and Raymond III of Tripoli. All three men were rewarded with either high-status positions or brides: Reynald received Stephanie and Oultrejourdain; Raymond III received the Lady Eschiva of Galilee, who brought with her the important city of Tiberias; and Joscelin III of Courtenay was made seneschal of Jerusalem.

One of the key changes that Reynald had to confront on his release from captivity was the shift of power in the Muslim world. His old enemy, Nur ad-Din, the son of Zengi, had died in 1174, an event that doubtless played a part in the decision to ransom the Frankish hostages. The great Muslim power in the East was now the sultan Saladin. The first Sultan of Egypt and Syria, Saladin would exploit Christian disunity and continue Nur ad-Din's punishing campaign against the Christians of Outremer.

Saladin had been born in the Iraqi town of Takrit, son of the governor of the city. His ethnicity was Kurdish, but he would grow up to become a hero for almost the entire Muslim world. This hero status has shown no sign of abating in the twenty-first century. Saddam Hussein identified himself with Saladin. Jinnah and Assad also aligned themselves with the legacy of Saladin. For centuries he has been the archetypal representative of Muslim power and military strength.

Rising rapidly from his relatively humble origins, Saladin became a subordinate of Nur ad-Din and from there became vizier to the Caliph of Egypt. He was acutely aware of the politics of rule in both Egypt and Syria, and demonstrated feline flexibility in manoeuvring himself into position to unite and rule both territories. He exploited disunity, the power vacuum left by the death of Nur ad-Din, religious fervour, and marriage to unify the hitherto separate territories of Aleppo, Damascus and Egypt under his control.

'Saladin' is the westernisation of his Muslim moniker. Where Nur ad-Din translates as 'Light of the Faith', Salah ad-Din translates as 'Righteousness of the Faith'. He was born Yusuf, but this name was quickly dropped by chroniclers in favour of the title that emphasised his position as a leader of Jihad against the Christians of Outremer. The image of Saladin that emerges from the chronicles, both Western and Eastern, is one of nobility, honour, and razor-sharp cunning and military capability. To what extent these impressions are accurate, it is impossible to fathom. Western sources wished to create him as an anti-hero, a worthy opponent to Richard the Lionheart, who would become his nemesis in later years. Muslim sources were keen to represent him as an avenging saviour, restoring order and Muslim dominance to the Holy Land. Saladin is presented always as a courteous host, a fair negotiator and a brilliant tactician. As historians, we must hope that a glimmer of accuracy has trickled down through these sources, and we can be hopeful that it has, given the relative uniformity across the chronicles.

He is also presented as a family man. Little is known of his relationships with women, except that he had many wives and concubines. His first son was born in Cairo in 1170, and he had another child with the same woman in 1177. It seems that Saladin had fathered twelve sons by 1178, with the grand total for his lifetime reaching as many as seventeen. One daughter is mentioned too. It is likely that there were more, but they were simply not deemed worthy of note. These children were born of at least five different women, whose names are likewise not recorded by history.

The woman most conspicuously absent from the chronicles is Ismat ad-Din Khatoun. These names are honorifics only; Ismat ad-Din means 'Purity of the Faith' while Khatoun translates roughly as 'princess' or 'noble lady'. Her given name has been lost. This woman was Saladin's wife, and perhaps the most significant female in his life, both emotionally and politically.

Saladin was not the first husband of Ismat ad-Din Khatoun. Before she met him, her husband was none other than Nur ad-Din, Saladin's supposed former lord. Nur ad-Din had married her in 1154 when he seized control of Damascus, with the aim of mollifying the city's inhabitants through creating an illusion of co-operation with the previous ruling family. When Nur ad-Din died, Saladin was struck by much the same idea. In marrying Nur ad-Din's widow, Saladin allied himself symbolically with the old regime.

Ismat ad-Din Khatoun was married, therefore, to the two greatest warlords of the medieval Muslim Middle East. She was the companion and confidante of two of the most impressive and powerful men of her generation, and must have had a unique understanding of the two leaders who shaped the fate of Islam in Outremer. She is a figure of great historical significance, despite the lack of information available about her personality, her appearance and her life. What is still more striking about her than her marriages is her role as a diplomat in negotiating with King Amalric of Jerusalem during the Siege of Banyas, after the death of Nur ad-Din and before her marriage to Saladin. For this episode, she earns the praise of William of Tyre, despite his typical disdain for Muslims and for women. He writes:

In the month of May, scarcely a month after this time, Nureddin, a mighty persecutor of the Christian name and faith, died in the twenty-ninth year of his rule [. . .] On learning of his death, the king [Amalric] immediately convoked all the strength of the kingdom and laid siege to the city of Banyas. At this, Nureddin's widow, with courage beyond that of most women, sent a message to this king demanding that he abandon the siege and grant them a temporary peace. She promised to pay a large sum of money in return. The king, however, in the hope of extorting a larger bribe, at first pretended to spurn her plea and continued the siege.

For about fifteen days he prosecuted the undertaking with vigour and zeal and caused his foe great trouble with his siege engines and in various other ways. Finally he perceived that the ability of the Turks to resist was steadily increasing and began to realise that he had no chance of success. Meanwhile the envoys of the noble lady kept insistently demanding peace. He finally decided to accept the proffered money, and on the release of twenty captive Christian knights in addition, he raised the siege with the intention of undertaking greater projects later.

From this source we can perhaps glean that the sultana was noble, courageous and determined. Saladin, despite fathering children with other women, was devoted to her. He corresponded with her with touching regularity while they were apart. When eventually she died in January 1186 while Saladin was on a military campaign, the sultan's advisors were so concerned about the effect that her death would have on him that they concealed the news from him until March. Imad ad-Din al-Isfahani, one of Saladin's most trusted advisers, was asked to censor the sultan's letters to prevent him finding out, and Imad ad-Din himself related that every day Saladin would write long letters to his wife.

Of all the women whom Saladin loved, Ismat ad-Din Khatoun seems to be the woman most cherished by him, and whose mind he valued alongside her body. A man with no respect for what a woman has to say does not take the time to exchange lengthy letters with her, especially when in the midst of a military campaign. Ismat ad-Din Khatoun, as she demonstrated at the Siege of Banyas, was intelligent, and knew something about war, just as her counterparts in Christian territory did.

7

AGNES AND SIBYLLA

The eventual success that Saladin would achieve was due in no small part to the breakdown of leadership in the Kingdom of Jerusalem and across Outremer. The Kingdom faced a succession crisis, due to the fact that after Melisende no reigning monarch of Jerusalem managed to produce healthy male heirs. While Melisende left an heir and a spare, neither Baldwin III nor Amalric fathered a healthy son. This led to the throne eventually being passed to Amalric's first daughter Sibylla, who was not well suited to the role of queen regnant. Critics would view this ill-fortune as an act of God, punishing the Kings of Jerusalem for their irreverence in every matter, from claiming the title 'King of Jerusalem' to their lackadaisical attitude to the sanctity of marriage.

Sibylla would reign as Queen of Jerusalem from 1186 to 1190. She had been born around the year 1159 to her father's first wife, the 'evil' Agnes of Courtenay. During Sibylla's lifetime great disasters would befall the Kingdom of Jerusalem and indeed all of Outremer.

Sibylla herself cuts a mysterious and forlorn figure in the chronicles. Her reign was dogged with woe, and there was very little time during her adolescence and maturity when she was not either pregnant, recovering from childbirth or mourning the loss of a child. She had five children, a son and four daughters, but none of them would live long enough to show her what sort of adults they would be. Sibylla only succeeded to the throne of Jerusalem over the bodies of her father, brother and only son. She ascended the throne just as Saladin, the first Ayyubid sultan, made ready to invade. She was queen regnant rather than queen consort and she held authority in the Kingdom of Jerusalem at a time when the government would fracture: the vicious internal politics reached boiling point under external pressures. Sibylla and her two surviving daughters would find themselves buffeted from fortress to fortress as Saladin's grip on Outremer tightened.

Sibylla's personal life was no more stable than her political life. For the ruling families of Outremer, family and politics were inextricably linked. Sibylla's relationships with those closest to her were fraught and deeply conflicted, perhaps none more so than with her mother, the much-maligned Agnes of Courtenay. In her later life, Agnes exerted a good deal of control over her daughter, and William of Tyre believed that she was instrumental in bringing about the collapse of the Kingdom of Jerusalem. William's testimony must once more be viewed with caution with regard to his withering portrayal of Agnes, given that he blamed her for the greatest slight of his career, a snub in the Patriarchal election of 1180. The latter part of Sibylla's life is murkier still than the lives of the other women examined in this book, as William of Tyre gave up writing in disgust in 1184, and died shortly afterwards. Thus his chronicles do not extend to cover the great misfortunes of Sibylla's reign, and historians must look to other texts to document this period.

Agnes, for all her manifold faults, can be cast as an intriguing and ambitious woman who refused to let the misfortunes of her life derail her career. She suffered many injustices, and her early life was as troubled as her daughter's. To fully understand the choices made by Sibylla during her reign, it is important to understand the mother whom she allowed to guide her, and whose suffering she was determined to avenge. The union between Sibylla's parents was at best unhappy, and at worst a hostage situation. Her father treated her mother badly, and witnessing this certainly had an effect on the choices that Sibylla made later in life, both in allowing Agnes influence at court, and with regard to her own view of marriage.

AGNES – THE QUEEN WITHOUT A CROWN

Agnes was born into the Courtenay family, the ruling family of Edessa, in 1136, during the reign of Melisende and Fulk. She spent the first years of her life enjoying the privileged position of princess of an important crusader state. Her father Joscelin II, in the tradition of Frankish rulers of Edessa, had sought to strengthen his alliance with his Armenian neighbours and married an Armenian princess named Beatrice: 'a woman of noble rank but of still more noble character.' The marriage prospered and the couple welcomed three children, Agnes and Joscelin III, both fair-haired despite their Armenian blood, and a second daughter, about whom little is known.

Unlike Melisende, Alice and Hodierna, Agnes and her siblings' early years were not spent in the central citadel of Edessa, but instead she was raised in Turbessel, a city some eighty miles to the west. Turbessel was more picturesquely situated than Edessa, amid fertile countryside with much opportunity for hunting and leisure activities. Joscelin preferred to be removed from the anxieties of his capital city and so had moved his family there, a choice that would prove his undoing and a point of thinly veiled criticism among his contemporaries.

While the Courtenays' dynasty was secure, their lands were not: Edessa was the least protected of the Frankish states in Outremer. Lying in modern-day Syria and Turkey, in the twelfth century the landlocked County may have bordered allies to the west and south – the Armenian Kingdom of Cilicia and the Principality of Antioch respectively – but its eastern and northern borders gave on to Muslim territory and were vulnerable to invasion. Just as it had been the first state in the East to fall to Frankish invaders, it would be the first to fall to the Muslim reclaimers.

As has been examined earlier, the capital city of Edessa, Agnes' home and place of birth, was captured with much bloodshed by Zengi in 1144. His capture of Edessa sent shockwaves across Outremer and throughout Western Europe, and was the catalyst for the Second Crusade.

The young Agnes, forced to flee her home and not yet even in her teens, was hastily married to a lord named Reynald who was significantly her senior. He was a competent military leader and Lord of Marash, another significant Armenian territory, and the marriage took place in order to cement an alliance and consolidate her father's position to attempt to retake Edessa. Like so many royal marriages in Outremer, the union was cut short after only a few years by Reynald's death in battle in 1149. He died alongside Princess Constance's first husband, Raymond of Antioch, in the Battle of Inab. Agnes found herself a widow at thirteen.

Tragedy followed tragedy and the following year Agnes's father Joscelin was captured by Turkomans while travelling to Antioch. He had lost Edessa for the second time, and was going to Antioch to seek aid. William of Tyre paints a portrait of an irresponsible man who was a disappointment to his noble father. According to William, Joscelin II first lost his capital through negligence and then got himself taken hostage through carelessness. Joscelin II set off for Antioch without a proper escort and was captured by brigands while relieving himself in the dark. Zengi's successor Nur ad-Din had Joscelin publicly blinded, before casting him into the dungeons of the fortress of Aleppo. The fortress stands to this day, a colossus dominating modern-day Aleppo. The citadel has been lucky among the city's medieval structures, surviving the centuries and the recent civil war, due to its enduring importance as a military stronghold. Its massive scale and strategic location rendered it invaluable to the modern Syrian government and the rebels in turn, preserving it from the destructive spree carried out in recent years. Aleppo never fell to Christian control and the ill-fated Joscelin would spend the remainder of his blighted days in the dungeons of the fortress.

Agnes' early life, then, was plagued with personal catastrophe, an experience she would come to share with her only daughter, Sibylla. Following the capture and mutilation of her husband, Agnes' mother, the Armenian princess Beatrice, threw herself into crisis-management mode. She was in the very relatable position of being a single mother with two young children to care for, and the somewhat less relatable position of having hordes of hostile Seljuk Turks banging at her gates and baying for her blood. She earned the enduring respect of the discerning William of Tyre by her immediate action to secure the rest of her realm, acting with a diligence that surpassed that of her husband. William writes:

> [Joscelin's] wife, a chaste and sober woman, one who feared God and found favour in his sight, was left with a minor son and two daughters.* With the assistance of the principal men still left in the kingdom, she tried to govern the people to the best of her ability; and far beyond the strength of a woman, she busied herself in strengthening the fortresses of the land and supplying them with arms, men, and food.

Having done all this, she assessed her circumstances and made a radical move that would no doubt have horrified her husband's ancestors. In a decision that was starkly practical, in contrast to the romanticised fanaticism and the desire to cling to lands and titles demonstrated by so many of her contemporaries in the Latin East, Beatrice prioritised the safety and security of her young family over honour and rank. She sold her husband's hereditary right to the County of Edessa to the Byzantine Empire for gold.

Her reasoning was straightforward. While it was certainly a sacrifice to sell her children's inheritance, she needed to secure their short-term safety before she could look to their long-term prospects. Short-term security over the chance of long-term gain was not a popular perspective for adventuring knights in Outremer. Beatrice was, however, in a tricky position: she was a widow to all intents and purposes, in that she

---

* This is the only mention of a second daughter and it is likely either William was mistaken as to the number of Beatrice's children or the second daughter died in childhood.

was deprived of her husband and protector, but with the proviso that she could not remarry, as her husband, while certainly lost to her, still lived. Without personal fortune or the option of marrying a new lord for wealth and protection, Beatrice was distinctly vulnerable. She and her children needed immediate funds with which to purchase security. There is no record of her attempting to raise a ransom for Joscelin, who, confined as he was in the Aleppo fortress and severely disabled, was probably viewed as beyond help. That said, other royal women successfully ransomed their husbands from Muslim forces. If Beatrice did attempt this, no record of it has filtered down to modern readers.

The Byzantine Emperor, believing he could retake Edessa, offered Beatrice a generous annual income that would support her and her children in comfort always, if she surrendered to him her remaining lands and fortresses. She accepted, despite resistance from nobles and the King of Jerusalem. She planned to move with her family to the fortress of Saône in the Principality of Antioch, her inheritance from her first marriage. King Baldwin III came to personally escort the countess, her retinue, and all the citizens of the surrendered cities who wished to travel into Frankish territory now their lands were under Greek control.

They were a sorry sight, weeping to leave their ancestral homeland, and they travelled laden down with furniture and personal effects. The road to Frankish territory was a hard one, and although heavily defended by cavalry from the Kingdom of Jerusalem, the refugees were continually harried by Nur ad-Din's men. Showers of arrows rained from the skies onto the limping citizens until 'all the baggage bristled with darts like a porcupine.'

Beatrice and her children survived the exodus, and they retired to Saône as planned. Safe behind the city's high walls, she protected the then fourteen-year-old widow Agnes from another marriage for eight years, allowing her to complete her disrupted adolescence in relative peace and security.

The next record we have of Beatrice and her family is of their appearance in Jerusalem in 1157, when the now twenty-one-year-old Agnes had grown to become one of the most desirable women in Outremer. Her family capitalised on this. Without lands, a beautiful, fertile and impeccably bred woman was their most valuable commodity and presented their best chances of social advancement. There were many suitors to choose from, but at first the favoured candidate seemed to be Hugh of Ibelin.

Hugh was one of the most attractive and eligible nobles of his day. He undoubtedly presented a good match for the landless Agnes. Although the Ibelins had come to Outremer from a background of relative obscurity, they had risen to become one of the most powerful clans in the region. They had achieved this through merit and opportunism, a path far more possible for adventurers in the East than in the West.

Following negotiations, Agnes was at the very least betrothed if not actually *married* to Hugh of Ibelin. The records vary as to the nature of the contract made between the pair; it is not clear whether it was a legally binding marriage or merely an engagement.

Shortly after this ambiguous ceremony took place between Agnes and Hugh, he was captured in battle at Banyas and dragged from the battlefield as a prisoner. During his time in captivity, Amalric, Queen Melisende's favoured younger son, took a fancy to the beautiful Agnes. Given Amalric's position, Agnes would have had little choice but to give in to his advances, and in 1157 the pair were married. History does not relate if Agnes was a willing participant, or another in a long line of coerced and cajoled brides. Queen Melisende must have had a direct hand in the brokering of this marriage and she personally stood as a formal witness to the ceremony. Agnes was an attractive prospect to Amalric, not only for her famed beauty, but also because, through both her parents, she was related to nearly every noble family in Outremer and also to the rulers of Armenia. Any children born to such a marriage would be among the best connected in the land.

Hugh of Ibelin, when finally released from captivity, instead of returning home to a patient fiancée/wife, found instead that he had been thrust aside in favour of the prince. The hierarchy being what it was, he had no option but to bite his tongue.

Given the circumstances of its creation, the marriage was unsurprisingly ill-fated. While it lasted six years, and produced two children who would both grow to become monarchs of Jerusalem, it ultimately ended in disaster and disgrace.

Following Queen Melisende's death from illness in 1161, her elder son Baldwin III continued his reign as expected. What was unexpected, however, was the death of the hale and hearty Baldwin just two years after his mother in 1163. He was struck down by an unexplained illness in the County of Tripoli: William of Tyre believed the cause to be poison. Baldwin III was childless, and his child-bride, the Byzantine Princess Theodora, now a widow at seventeen, swiftly withdrew from the politics of Jerusalem and retired to Acre.

Thus, Agnes' husband Amalric stood as the undisputed heir to the Kingdom of Jerusalem, and suddenly their two young children took on new status in Outremer: they too were heirs to the Kingdom. The nobles of the Haute Cour were prepared to accept Amalric as king, but only on the condition that he annul his marriage to Agnes. For reasons which are unclear, they did not want her to be their queen. One chronicler observed: 'she was no queen for a kingdom as holy as Jerusalem', and the reason they gave was that the marriage was unlawful on the grounds of consanguinity. This is unlikely to have been a real objection. It was not unusual for first cousins to marry and the church to turn a blind eye, and so this excuse must have been a façade, concealing some real and unexplained animosity towards Agnes on the part of the Latin Patriarch and other nobles of the region.

She had already begun garnering a reputation for expedience and manipulation, and it is likely that they considered her a dangerous candidate for power. In the years to come, William of Tyre would describe her as 'a most grasping woman, utterly detestable to God.' The council had also not forgotten the scandal surrounding their marriage and Hugh of Ibelin's prior claim to Agnes. While such an event might be tolerated for the brother of the king, the King of Jerusalem himself could not remain in such an uncanonical marriage.

Amalric was keen to avoid charges of bigamy for both his and Agnes' sakes, and thus the official reason he gave for consenting to the annulment was consanguinity. Further to this, he was adamant that the reputation and status of his two children Sibylla and Baldwin would not be tarnished by the dissolution of his marriage to their mother. Amalric stipulated that he would only consent to this annulment if their legitimacy was guaranteed. This was highly irregular, in addition to being illogical and uncanonical, but the clergy of Jerusalem had a history of cherry-picking from scripture, and so acquiesced. Thus at three years old Sibylla became both motherless and second in line to the throne of Jerusalem.

While treated badly, Agnes wasted no time in making the best of a bad situation. She remarried almost instantly. 'Remarried' is a particularly pertinent term, as the man of her choice was none other than Hugh of Ibelin, the man to whom she had been engaged/married at the time of her marriage to Amalric, now released from captivity and willing to take her back. The fact that she reunited with him so quickly after her dismissal from court suggests that the true reason for her divorce from Amalric was that she was already wed to Hugh. She left Jerusalem almost immediately and moved with him to his lands. How much agency she had in this sequence of events cannot be known, but if her later reputation for manipulation and puppeteering of circumstances is anything to go by, Agnes can be considered to have influenced her own destiny.

Agnes and Amalric's separation and Agnes' loss of favour at court had great personal consequences for Sibylla and Baldwin. Both children were taken from their mother's care and given to the tutelage of other guardians. Baldwin remained at court and was fortunate in the mentor he found in his tutor, none other than the prolific writer and historian William of Tyre, who has guided generations of readers through the history of Outremer. In contrast, as she had no close female relatives at the court of Jerusalem, Sibylla was bundled up and sent away to the Convent of Bethany, the very same order founded by her grandmother Queen Melisende on behalf of the Princess Yvette.

Yvette still ruled in Bethany, and it was there that Sibylla was to be raised by her formidable great-aunt, the veteran Princess of Jerusalem. Yvette was the last surviving daughter of Morphia of Melitene, and one of Sibylla's few surviving female relatives. Yvette was perhaps the shrewdest of all Morphia's daughters. Eschewing both politics and the company of men, she instead came to rule the foremost religious order in Outremer. Perhaps she, of all her fiery sisters, achieved the purest power: while lacking the secular authority the others all achieved, amid a community of women, a woman's power was second to none. She answered to no husband and no secular liege lord. She survived all her sisters, and while she had no descendants of her own, she played a key role in Sibylla's upbringing.

Sibylla grew up instructed in Christian doctrine and Latin, safe but isolated behind the convent walls. To be raised by nuns in Outremer was not a second-tier upbringing, particularly at Bethany. In both Europe and Outremer there was a long tradition of noblewomen entering convents in later life, and of orphaned noblewomen being raised there. The most famous example in Europe was Fontevraud Abbey, where Eleanor of Aquitaine and many other queens spent their final years. In Outremer there were several such establishments which had a reputation for royal inhabitants, including Bethany and St Anne's in Jerusalem. Alongside the Abbess Yvette, other high-status noblewomen lived in the cloistered walls of Bethany.

At the time of Sibylla's arrival, the next most significant woman living there was another Sibylla, her half-aunt, who had been half-sister to her father Amalric. This woman was King Fulk's daughter from his first marriage, who had accompanied him to Jerusalem in 1131, and thus became a stepdaughter of Queen Melisende. This lady, Sibylla of Anjou, had married Count Thierry of Flanders in 1139 in Outremer, before accompanying him back to Europe. When Thierry returned to the East as part of the Second Crusade, the pregnant countess was left behind and ruled the County as regent. During this time her lands were invaded by the Count of Hainault, and in record time after giving birth, Sibylla reassumed command of the army and put the invaders to flight.

Her steely tenacity led to much praise by contemporary chroniclers, with Lambert of Waterlos describing her as 'like a lioness gnashing her teeth in wrath'. She continued to wield political influence in Bethany, and in 1157 she had thrown her support behind Queen Melisende and Countess Hodierna's plan to rig the patriarchal election of Jerusalem. The young Sibylla of Jerusalem was certainly in exalted company at Bethany.

Sibylla of Flanders clearly thrived in her husband's absence, and although she later consented to join him in the East, when she arrived in Jerusalem she separated from him and steadfastly refused to return to Europe as his wife. Instead she took up residence in the Convent of Bethany alongside Yvette. While Sibylla of Flanders would certainly have met her half-niece Princess Sibylla when she came to Bethany, she died less than three years after Sibylla's arrival, so her influence on the Princess's upbringing would have been limited.

Princess Sibylla of Jerusalem was unlikely to inherit the throne, given that she had a brother and her father was likely to have more children. When she was seven years old her father had remarried at the urging of the Haute Cour. Amalric leveraged his new exalted rank of King of Jerusalem to broker a far more politically lucrative match for himself with Maria Komnene, the niece of the Byzantine Emperor Manuel Komnenos. Following the death of Baldwin III, the court of Constantinople was clearly keen to keep a Byzantine princess on the throne of Jerusalem, and the Haute Cour of Jerusalem wanted to maintain their links to the military and financial support that the Byzantine Empire could offer. After two years of wrangling over the terms of the marriage contract, the Princess Maria Komnene made her way to Jerusalem to step into Agnes of Courtenay's shoes and wed King Amalric. They married with much pomp and ceremony in Tyre on 29 August 1167. Maria was only about fourteen years of age at the time of the wedding – closer in age to her new stepdaughter than to her new husband, who was thirty-one.

The King's marriage to the teenage Maria was to mollify him during a sex scandal of such international significance that it might have derailed the carefully crafted alliance between Jerusalem and Byzantium. Maria's cousin, the dowager Queen Theodora, was at the centre of this furore.

THEODORA AND ANDRONIKOS – 'UNBRIDLED LEWDNESS' – THE SCANDAL OF CHRISTENDOM

While Amalric had been busy wedding his Greek child-bride, the previous Greek princess to be ferried to Outremer from Constantinople to wed a King of Jerusalem had begun raising hell in the north of the country. Theodora – the angelic innocent from Constantinople, so pale, beautiful and many years his junior, who had so besotted Baldwin III that he completely reformed his character and became utterly devoted to her – was now aged twenty-two, and beginning to become restless in her gilded cage at Acre.

Five years previously, at the time of her husband's death, Theodora had been left a widow and dowager queen at seventeen. The terms of her marital contract had been generous and ironclad. In the event that her husband predeceased her, Theodora was to be given the city and lands of Acre, to live out her days in isolated luxury. Had all gone to plan, Theodora would have stepped into this life at some point in middle age after a successful period as Queen of Jerusalem, making friends, accruing loyalties and learning all the skills needed to run a castle and a kingdom. She would have retired gracefully at a time when she was becoming ready for a quieter life, and would have had a swathe of sons ruling in Outremer to guard her interests, pay her visits and listen to her counsel.

Things did not go to plan. Baldwin III died suddenly after just five years of marriage, leaving Theodora childless, alone and with no influence in affairs of state. The couple had failed to found a dynasty and instead power passed from Theodora to her brother-in-law, Amalric. While he was obliged to treat her respectfully in order not to alienate her uncle the Byzantine Emperor, he was under no obligation to be kind to her on a personal level. He abided by the terms of her marriage contract, bequeathed her Acre, and promptly sent her away from the capital to set up her lonely household and keep out of the way.

Acre was not a pleasant city in which to be isolated without prospects of love. William of Tyre described the city as well situated between mountains and sea and possessing much fertile land in the surrounding region, but he was writing as a statesman and historian, with an eye to revenue and defensive strategy; he was not writing from the perspective of a resident or a curious visitor. Ibn Jubayr, the same Andalusian travel writer who recorded the details of a Christian wedding procession in Tyre, described Acre rather differently. He compared it to Constantinople for greatness, but went on to say that its streets were 'choked with the press of men, so that it is hard to put foot to the ground'. He went on to speak of the stench and filth of the city, in no small part due to the presence of excrement everywhere.

Today's Acre is in the far north of Israel, near to the Lebanese border. The Old City of Acre stands as a visual record of the city's war-wracked history: pointed Ottoman and crusader arches rub shoulders, and intricate Mamluk structures intermingle with the minarets and bell towers that populate the horizon. The smell of the sea is always close at hand. The masts of sailing boats cluster the harbour, a reminder that this was once the most important port of Outremer. The Hospitaller citadel looms large in the skyline of the city, an undecorated and imposing wall of sun-stained stone, peppered with the occasional arrow slit or crenel. The colours of Acre today are lighter than those of Jerusalem – blue, green and white. The blue of the sea and sky, and the painted metalwork and shutters; the green of mosque domes and minarets; and the bright white of the age-old stone. The city is unfinished in many places, a work in progress: concrete structures are emerging between the ancient arches. As in medieval times, Acre now has one of the most diverse populations of any Israeli city, including communities of Jews, Muslims, Druze, Christians and Baha'is.

For Theodora Komnene, crusader Acre represented a fate she did not want. It was assumed that this young woman would live out her days behind the high walls in boredom and solitude. In practice this fate was little different from being sent to a nunnery, and arguably worse, because in a nunnery she might have found solace in a community of sisters all committed to the same life. In the secular world Theodora was an aberration: a beautiful young woman whom nobody could marry.

As a Byzantine princess she had always been a foreigner in Outremer, speaking Greek rather than French or Italian as her first language. Moreover, her brother-in-law, the new King Amalric, would never allow her remarriage. The widowed dowager Queen Theodora, though theoretically holding Acre, owed allegiance to the king, and thus the crown retained control of the city. If she remarried, control of Acre would pass to her new husband, which would create a powerful potential rival to Amalric. From Amalric's point of view, it was a far safer decision to let Theodora live out her life in safety and obscurity. If she died single and without issue, her lands would revert to the crown.

Theodora therefore had little hope of happiness ahead of her and was doomed to a spinster's existence. However, immediately following Amalric's marriage to her cousin Maria, Theodora, previously as meek as a church mouse, would reveal hidden fire. Unwilling to accept the life of isolation assigned to her, she flung herself into a scandal of such epic proportions that it exceeded those caused even by Queen Melisende and Eleanor of Aquitaine.

The catalyst for her rebellious awakening came in the form of Andronikos Komnenos, a villain who embodied all the gifts and vices of the archetypal Byzantine. He was beautiful but crafty, romantic but hard-hearted, and ultimately overreaching. His hypnotic personal charm and manipulative mind enabled him to rise from fast living and the serial seductions of princesses, to become Emperor of Byzantium, before a rather nasty Icarian fall.

This was the same Andronikos who, shortly before, had alienated the good will of Bohemond III of Antioch by seducing his sister Philippa, before abandoning her. At this stage in his life, Andronikos was past fifty, but showed no sign of losing the personal attractiveness that had already succeeded in winning the hearts of numerous noblewomen in Byzantium and Outremer. He would come into Theodora's life, fleeing scandals in both Antioch and Constantinople, where he had seduced his cousin Eudocia, much to the wrath of their uncle, the Emperor Manuel. He escaped imprisonment and fled to Outremer, where rumour had it that aristocratic adventurers were welcomed with open arms. He was not disappointed.

Andronikos relied on his good looks and electric charm to persuade those around him to turn a blind eye to his obvious vices and the threat he posed. His progress went unchecked for almost two more decades, leaving a trail of destruction and broken lives in its wake.

After abandoning the desolate Philippa at Antioch, Andronikos travelled to Jerusalem, where his charisma and flattery impressed the new King Amalric, who granted him the Lordship of Beirut and also permission to undertake a 'family visit' to his niece Theodora in Acre. These acts of generosity proved to be grave errors of judgement.

Despite their nearness in blood relation and distance in age, Theodora fell in love with the smiling villain and embarked on an incestuous affair. He was her uncle, more than twice her age, and had a notorious past, yet Andronikos' magnetism triumphed. He was a mesmerising presence and Theodora, sheltered as she was and isolated from other Greeks, was no match for his persuasive influence. This relationship in many ways parallels the alleged affair between Eleanor and Raymond in Antioch: an unhappy young woman, isolated from her kin, takes refuge in the arms of a charismatic older man who offers her both an escape from a miserable existence and welcome familiarity. Andronikos spoke Greek with Theodora, just as Raymond spoke Poitevin with Eleanor. The powers of attraction and nostalgia, coupled with frustration at her present circumstances, succeeded in winning over Theodora.

Niketas Choniates writes: 'Like a horse in heat covering mare after mare beyond reason, his behaviour was promiscuous, and he engaged in sexual intercourse with Theodora.' While this initial seduction predictably fits with Andronikos' pattern of behaviour, that is where the similarities between his relationship with Theodora and his earlier affairs end. Theirs was a true love affair, and Andronikos would remain devoted to Theodora as long as she lived.

Regardless of the sincerity of his affection, Andronikos was once again committing the very serious crime of incest, and bringing further dishonour on the family of his cousin the Emperor Manuel. Theodora was his niece, and Andronikos' own niece at that. The emperor was incensed by yet another seduction of a princess of his blood. He dispatched a letter to the authorities in Syria, advising them of Andronikos' reprehensible character and demanding that he be captured and blinded for his sins of incest. The letter was dutifully conveyed to Acre, but it found its way into Theodora's hands instead of the constable of the city. She immediately warned her lover and Andronikos fled to Beirut, where he was safe in command of the city.

In spite of this separation, their affair was far from over, but the lovers' time in Outremer was limited. If news of the affair had reached Constantinople, it could not be long before King Amalric also heard of it and took action against them. The lovers devised a daring escape. Under the guise of returning hospitality to a relative, Andronikos formally invited the dowager queen to visit him in Beirut. Theodora set off with her entourage, crossing through the mountainous region in the north of modern Israel and passing into the south of modern Lebanon. On this route, Theodora travelled with only a small retinue because the journey was theoretically a safe one, for there were no hostile Muslims in these lands who might do her harm or abduct her. A plan had been hatched between the young queen and her older uncle, and he, informed of their movements and travelling plan, laid an 'ambush'. Somewhere in the hills of northern Israel he 'abducted' Theodora from her guards, and together the pair fled.

Nowhere was safe for the fugitive couple in Christian lands, and so the nephew of the Emperor of Constantinople and the former Queen of Christian Jerusalem fled to the arms of their enemies and took refuge at the court of Damascus. The scandal this caused cannot be overstated.

Theodora and Andronikos made a new life for themselves in Muslim lands, under the permission of Nur ad-Din. The pair burned every bridge they had with Christianity and sacrificed all the wealth they had not been able to smuggle away with them, forfeiting the immensely valuable cities of Acre and Beirut. The wealth of Acre, however, meant nothing to Theodora without personal freedom, and in escaping with Andronikos she had succeeded in making a new life for herself. She became his 'companion and fellow wanderer'.

That said, we must be sceptical of the nature of their relationship. Andronikos was, after all, a much older man preying on an unhappy young woman. Despite this, his regard and affection for her appears genuine and thorough. It seems that Theodora had this impact on all the men in her life. Baldwin III was similarly smitten by her, and even William of Tyre breaks from his usual sang-froid regarding women, describing her as 'a maiden of unusual beauty, both of form and feature'.

For the first time, Andronikos was faithful to a partner, and stood by Theodora for the next twelve years. She bore him a son named Alexios and a daughter named Eirene. His affection for his family remained strong, and together they travelled extensively in the East, living variously in Damascus, Baghdad and Harran, before eventually settling in a castle near Kolonea given to them by a Turkish emir. There they lived peacefully and quietly for many years, raising Alexios and Eirene alongside Andronikos' legitimate son John, who had travelled to join his father.

The true test of Andronikos' affection for Theodora came when Emperor Manuel managed to abduct Theodora and the children. Rather than cutting his losses and looking for a new princess to seduce, Andronikos finally stopped running, begged forgiveness of the emperor and did spectacular homage to him in order to be reunited with his mistress and children.

Despite the audacity and ingratitude of this elopement, King Amalric of Jerusalem took no action against the fugitives. There are a few reasons for this leniency. It would have been futile and more trouble than it was worth to attempt to pursue the couple into Nur ad-Din's territory; secondly, in their flight the control of Acre and Beirut had returned indisputably to his control; and thirdly, he was preoccupied with his honeymoon with his new teenage bride, Theodora's great-niece, Maria Komnene, who was destined to become the longest-living Queen of Jerusalem, and to die with her dynasty secured.

SISTER OF THE LEPER KING

Sibylla was seven years old at the time of her father's remarriage but, for all their closeness in age, her relationship with her new teenage stepmother was cool at best. Sibylla remained at the Convent of Bethany under the care of Yvette for several years after her father's remarriage. Maria Komnene had great cause for disliking her stepdaughter. Sibylla and Baldwin, given their carefully guarded legitimacy, were obstacles to the inheritance of Maria's own children and as such were her main rivals for their father's affection, political ambition and wealth. While Sibylla and Baldwin lived, Maria's children could never rule. She soon gave birth to a daughter of her own, Isabella, who would stand as Sibylla's rival for the rest of her life.

Sibylla had left the court of Jerusalem as a small child, with probably very limited understanding of her parents' separation and with a baby brother in whom all her father's hope was invested. When she returned, it was to a teenage Greek stepmother who greatly disliked her, a new baby sister who was to become her adversary, and that sweet baby brother who had offered so much promise when she left had been diagnosed with the most feared and stigmatised of all medieval diseases: leprosy.

It was Baldwin's tutor and our guide, William of Tyre, who first diagnosed Sibylla's younger brother's leprosy. He was in charge of the young prince's education and writes of his first suspicions and eventual identification of the boy's condition. He describes observing the young prince at play with the sons of other nobles, and how their games took a sadistic turn, driving nails and pins into each other's arms to test endurance. Despite his princely status, his friends did not spare Baldwin, and while the other boys cried out with the pain of the game, Baldwin endured it with a stoicism unusual in a child. While William hoped this was simply on account of his high pain threshold and admirable fortitude, he felt very uneasy and summoned the boy to him for examination. His right arm and hand were almost completely insensitive to pain: he could not feel pinching or even biting. William's account of this discovery is sobering to read to this day:

> It is impossible to refrain from tears while speaking of this great misfortune. For, as he began to reach years of maturity, it was evident that he was suffering from the terrible disease of leprosy. Day by day his condition became worse. The extremities and the face were especially attacked, so that his faithful followers were moved with compassion when they looked at him.
>
> Nevertheless, he continued to make progress in the pursuit of letters and gave ever-increasing promise of developing a loveable disposition. He was comely of appearance for his age, and far beyond the custom of his forefathers he was an excellent horseman and understood the handling of horses. He had a retentive memory and loved to talk. He was

economical but always remembered both favours and injuries. In every respect he resembled his father, not alone in face but in his entire mien; even his walk and the tones of his voice were the same. His intellect was keen, but his speech was somewhat halting. Like his father, he eagerly listened to history and was well-disposed to follow good advice.

Almost a thousand years later, William's genuine anguish at his pupil's fate echoes down the centuries. William had taken over charge of Baldwin's education in 1170 when he was nine years old, and Sibylla was ten. William did not make his diagnosis of Baldwin IV's disease straight away. It probably took a few months for him to notice the boy's symptoms and confirm the diagnosis, meaning that Amalric would have been informed of his son's condition just months before summoning Sibylla back to court. This doubtless was what precipitated her return. It was not an auspicious homecoming for the young Sibylla.

Her brother's diagnosis was to have serious implications for her fate. It was not only a personal tragedy for the Prince's family, but a nation-wide calamity for Outremer. Suddenly, Amalric's son and heir was not only handed an early death sentence, but it was clear that he would never have sons of his own. The succession was thrown into uncertainty. It seemed likely Sibylla would be the next queen, and whoever became her husband would be the next king.

The spotlight illuminating the future of the Kingdom swung from Sibylla's brother to her, a girl who had been raised in a convent away from the court. The choice of Sibylla's husband, while always important as an opportunity to forge a meaningful political alliance, changed dramatically in significance. Her marriage would no longer simply create an alliance, but would dictate the future of the Kingdom of Jerusalem. Whoever was given her hand would also be given the throne. It would no longer be feasible to attempt to marry her to a royal house, who would simply see Jerusalem as another land in an empire. It became imperative to marry her to a strong nobleman who instead of taking Sibylla to his court to reign beside him, would come to her court to reign beside her.

A match was arranged with the far older Stephen of Sancerre, an influential French nobleman whose wealth, experience and retinue of knights made him a worthy candidate to be Sibylla's husband. Stephen travelled east in 1171 alongside Archbishop Frederick of Tyre (William's predecessor in that position), who had travelled to France to raise funds. Stephen passed several months in Outremer, and was shown all due courtesy by Amalric, who believed that he would one day be his son-in-law and the heir to the Kingdom. Stephen was asked to decide on several court matters, in preparation for his upcoming status.

In a bizarre twist and for reasons unknown, Stephen ultimately declined to marry the adolescent Sibylla. He returned to Europe a bachelor still, despite the throne of Jerusalem offered as an incentive. This was a public insult to Sibylla and her family, and while at first glance this might seem a surprising decision on Stephen's part, there are many reasons why he might have decided to return to his lands in Europe. He may have found the child princess not desirable as a wife, or, after his brief stint assisting Amalric on the Haute Cour, he may have lost confidence in the future of the Kingdom of Jerusalem and preferred instead to return and rule his lands in Europe, with the comfort of the Mediterranean lying between him and Islam's approaching armies.

Although in Outremer the throne of Jerusalem presented the ultimate political prize, to a wealthy European it may have seemed more trouble than it was worth. It was a high-risk investment in an unstable region. Furthermore, Stephen may not have wished to ally himself with the House of Jerusalem after all. Baldwin IV's leprosy was interpreted in contemporary times as a blight from God, a curse visited upon an ill-fated and impious ruling family. Amalric's divorce of Agnes was often linked to the young Prince's condition and unhappy fate.

With Stephen's squeamish departure, the role of the heir to the Kingdom was still vacant, and Sibylla's hand was still available to the most suitable candidate. Perhaps reeling from the insult of Stephen's departure, Amalric did not rush to find a new match for his daughter. He was in his mid thirties at this time, and clearly believed he had plenty of time to secure the succession by begetting a healthy son with his new, young wife. However, following a skirmish with Nur ad-Din in 1174, Amalric contracted dysentery in a military camp. He returned to Jerusalem as quickly as he could and consulted the advice of Western, Syrian and Greek doctors, but none could cure him, and after suffering a fever for several days, he died at the age of thirty-eight.

He left three unmarried children: Sibylla, aged fourteen; Baldwin, aged thirteen and already diagnosed as a leper; and the little Isabella, aged just two. On his deathbed he bequeathed the fortress at Nablus to his widow Maria Komnene and their daughter Isabella. Maria, who had wielded next to no political power during her time as queen consort, clearly knew her tenure as Queen of Jerusalem was at an end, and as soon as her husband was buried she fled to Nablus with her daughter. This was wise. Once Baldwin IV was invested as king, he summoned his estranged mother, Agnes of Courtenay, back to court to step into the role of Queen Mother. Had Maria lingered at court, she would likely have found herself forcibly ousted.

AGNES – QUEEN MOTHER

Agnes' life had not ceased to be colourful with her departure from Jerusalem. She lived in relative harmony and quiet with her husband, Hugh of Ibelin, for six years, but somewhat counter-intuitively he decided to leave Outremer for a pilgrimage to Europe in 1169. He set out for Santiago de Compostela in Spain but died of disease on the journey. Following his death Agnes was very much alone in the world. Her brother Joscelin III of Courtenay had, following in the footsteps of his unfortunate father, been taken hostage by Turks in 1164. She remarried quickly, taking as her fourth husband Reynald of Sidon, and by virtue of this union was Countess of Sidon herself at the time of Amalric's death.

Reynald, an unattractive but erudite man with a flair for Arabic literature, was not a husband who could fulfil Agnes' desires. It was during her fourteen-year marriage to him that she began to gain a reputation for extramarital affairs. These included rumours of a liaison with Heraclius, the new Patriarch of Jerusalem no less, and with a French nobleman named Aimery de Lusignan. On her arrival in Jerusalem, Agnes set about rebuilding a relationship with her powerful children. From this point onwards she played a significant role in the politics of Jerusalem, accompanying her son Baldwin to meetings of the Haute Cour and exerting her influence in every way she could.

Baldwin had now been crowned Baldwin IV of Jerusalem. Ill as he was and only thirteen, he was given a regent to help him govern. The first regent, as dictated by his father's will, was a man named Miles de Plancy. Miles was a powerful man, married to Stephanie of Milly, by virtue of which he was Lord of Oultrejourdain. However, he died in mysterious circumstances shortly after becoming regent. He was replaced by Raymond III of Tripoli as regent, and by Reynald de Châtillon as husband of Stephanie and Lord of Oultrejourdain following his release from captivity. The appointment of Raymond as regent was the logical choice. He was one of the King's most powerful vassals, and his closest adult male relative. Ibn Jubayr, who certainly had no reason to love Raymond, wrote of him: 'He is worthy of the throne, for which he seems born and has remarkable intelligence and astuteness.' William of Tyre called him 'an indefatigable and thoroughly upright man'.

Despite being a confirmed and vocal supporter of Raymond III of Tripoli, William of Tyre gave his readers an unidealised description of his appearance. According to William, Raymond 'was a man of slender build, extremely spare, of medium height and swarthy complexion. His hair was straight and rather dark in colour. He had piercing eyes [...] was prompt and vigorous in action, gifted with equanimity and foresight.' He had no children of his own with his wife Eschiva, Lady of Tiberias, but was said to have loved her, and her four sons from her first marriage as if they were his own.

While certainly an ambitious and slippery figure, Raymond was also shrewd and politically and militarily adept. He represented the old nobility of Outremer, and was a grandson of Baldwin II and thus a cousin of Sibylla and Baldwin. He knew the region of Outremer perhaps better than any other nobleman, and knew the ways of their Muslim enemies from first-hand experience, after spending ten years as a prisoner-of-war in Aleppo. He was captured following defeat at the Siege of Haram, and alongside Agnes' brother he was 'chained like the lowest of slaves'. William of Tyre records that his time in prison was spent 'in beggary and iron', but despite the undeniable trials of this experience, it was also in captivity that Raymond became literate, something unusual for a secular lord, and began to gather a reputation for learning which impressed both Christian and Muslim chroniclers.

Raymond and Agnes co-operated at the beginning of Baldwin IV's reign. Both encouraged the young king to secure his succession by swiftly finding a suitable husband for Sibylla. Sibylla was still one of the most eligible princesses in Christendom for an ambitious suitor undaunted by adventure and adversity. The importance of the Kingdom of Jerusalem must not be overstated. For all its symbolic and religious significance, it was a territory the size of Wales, and its princesses would not attract kings or princes as husbands. As had been the case with Melisende, who married Fulk – an impressive man but a mere count nonetheless – Sibylla was unlikely to attract royal stock. That said, for the right candidate her unique pedigree and the instability of her Kingdom would provide an intoxicating opportunity for both status and adventure.

The next man to be tempted to the East by such a promise was William, Marquis of Montferrat, who came to Outremer to marry the young princess at the invitation of Raymond and Baldwin in 1176. William did not follow Stephen of Sancerre's example, and instead wed the princess as expected. Upon their marriage the new couple were gifted the counties of Jaffa and Ascalon, the lands traditionally held by the heirs to the throne.

William seemed confirmed as the future King of Jerusalem, and the Kingdom breathed a collective sigh of relief to have the succession secured at last.

William 'Longsword' Montferrat was a reliable, experienced choice as heir. He seemed a likeable match for Sibylla, and was described as a 'rather tall, good-looking young man [. . .] very generous and of an open disposition and manly courage'. William of Tyre certainly deemed him a suitable candidate to defend Jerusalem, noting that he 'had been trained in arms from his earliest youth and had the reputation of being experienced in the art of war. His worldly position was exalted – in fact, few could claim to be his equals.' However, despite his eminent suitability for the role, William Longsword never assumed the crown of Jerusalem, and never had the opportunity to either flounder or flourish in the controversial kingship.

While his marriage to Sibylla started positively, with Sibylla becoming pregnant within months, the conditions in Outremer did not agree with William, and after just five months of marriage he perished of malaria in April 1177 at the fortress of Ascalon. Less than six months after William's death, Sibylla gave birth to her first child, a son dutifully named Baldwin after his uncle, great-uncle and great-grandfather. Sibylla was no more than seventeen at the time.

William was the Marquis of Montferrat, a large and important territory in northern Italy, and he came from a powerful family. Through his father, William had been a cousin of King Louis VII of France, and through his mother, a cousin of the Holy Roman Emperor, Fredrick I. The loss of William as the next King of Jerusalem was a great blow to Outremer.

Following William's death, Baldwin IV was still in need of an active regent to help him rule, given his illness. He appointed Reynald de Châtillon, the controversial widower of Princess Constance of Antioch and now Lord of Oultrejourdain by virtue of his marriage to the widowed Stephanie of Milly. Reynald had recently returned from a successful diplomatic mission to Constantinople, where he had negotiated with the same emperor who had shamed him after his Cyprus raids almost two decades previously. Perhaps it was believed that Reynald's time in captivity had cooled his temper and taught him a thing or two about diplomacy. Even William of Tyre, usually a critic of Reynald, did not disapprove of the appointment, as he noted that Reynald was of unusually loyal character.

The tragedy of William of Montferrat's death was mitigated by a great Christian military victory later that year under Reynald's command – the

Battle of Montgisard. The crusaders' forces were greatly outnumbered at this battle but still won a decisive victory over Saladin, beating him back for the time being at least. Following this triumph, and the birth of Sibylla's son by the late William of Montferrat, King Baldwin IV, in a fit of generosity, allowed one of his barons, Balian of Ibelin, to marry his widowed stepmother, Maria Komnene, who until this point had been quietly residing at Nablus with her infant daughter. This was a great compliment to the Ibelin family and cemented their power in the region.

Despite riding with his forces at Montgisard, King Baldwin IV's leprosy was progressing ruthlessly, and it was as urgent as ever to secure the succession. Once again, all eyes looked to seventeen-year-old Sibylla, bereaved as she was and a new mother. Mere months after the death of her husband, the vultures were already beginning to circle. Her brother and William of Tyre managed to fend off some of the more offensive propositions, such as those aggressively made by Philip of Flanders, that she should marry a relatively obscure lord from his retinue.

Through the mercy of her brother, Sibylla remained single for some years following her first husband's death. There was a plan to wed her to the powerful Hugh of Burgundy, but this came to nothing. Hugh was likely the suggestion of King Louis VII of France, and was proposed as a candidate to marry Sibylla in answer to a poignant letter written by Baldwin IV to Louis, which gives rare insight into Baldwin's own feelings of helplessness and desperation in the face of his devastating disease:

> To be deprived of the use of one's limbs is of little help to one in carrying out the work of government. If I could be cured of the disease of Naaman, I would wash seven times in the Jordan, but I have found in the present age no Elisha who can heal me. It is not fitting that a hand so weak as mine should hold power when fear of Arab aggression daily presses on the Holy City and when my sickness increases my enemy's daring [. . .] I therefore beg you that, having called together the barons of France, you immediately choose one of them to take charge of this Holy Kingdom.

Despite Baldwin's appeal, and for reasons that are unclear, no suitable candidate was sent by the King of France to aid the weakening Baldwin IV. The next serious suitor to appear on the scene was Baldwin of Ibelin, the brother of Balian, who had previously wed Sibylla's stepmother Maria Komnene. Such a match would have been popular with the nobles of the region, but profoundly unpopular with Sibylla's mother Agnes, who was anxious about the Ibelins becoming too powerful.

It was with Baldwin that Sibylla seems to have had her first taste of teenage romance, including initial ardour, pining, then swift detachment when someone glossier and more attractive came along. According to the chronicler Ernoul, while her brother was marshalling forces to resist the rapidly uniting Muslim armies, Sibylla fell in love with a widower more than twice her age, conveniently named Baldwin, in the fashion of nearly all her male relatives.

Baldwin would have been a popular choice for heir to the throne, for despite the relatively humble origins of the Ibelins, his family had prospered in the East and risen to become one of the foremost noble families of Outremer. Beyond this, he had grown to maturity in Outremer, and was familiar with the politics and military tactics of the region. He was not popular with Sibylla's mother, who delayed a betrothal to great effect. Agnes heartily disliked Maria Komnene, who had replaced her as Queen of Jerusalem when her husband put her aside, and sought to quell Agnes' influence and subvert Sibylla's inheritance. The idea of marrying her one healthy child to Maria's brother-in-law would not be tolerated by Agnes. Her anxieties were quickly assuaged. Before any binding ceremony took place between the couple, Baldwin was captured in a skirmish at Marj Ayun.

He was imprisoned, as was the custom, with the aim of extracting ransom, but Sibylla wrote to him in jail, reaffirming her love and fidelity. She was not in a position to raise his ransom, and his family did not respond to the call either. This was not surprising: Saladin demanded 200,000 bezants – greater than the ransoms demanded either for Baldwin II or Raymond of Tripoli – a king's ransom, in fact. Raising such a sum was no mean feat. Baldwin's hands were tied. He must have been in anguish as he lay in that cell. The throne of Jerusalem, the highest honour in the land, was within his grasp, and he was losing his advantage every day he stayed in that cell. Every hour that he was away from court was an hour that Sibylla's mother could use to turn her against him, and an hour when other suitors could emerge from the woodwork.

Somehow he negotiated his release with the promise that he would pay the ransom retrospectively. His jailers must have shrugged, thinking that while they could not trust a Frank, he was doing them no good rotting in their dungeons. If money was not forthcoming from his relatives, it made greater sense to release him in the hope that he would make good his side of the bargain, and owe them a favour in the future. Baldwin rushed back to Jerusalem, eager to claim Sibylla as his bride, but instead of a devoted mistress patiently awaiting her love's return and ready to throw her arms around him, he found a coolly distant princess. Sibylla spurned him when he arrived in Jerusalem, saying that she could not possibly wed a man so in debt to the Muslim enemy.

Baldwin quit the city immediately, journeying with all speed to Constantinople. No one in Outremer would lend him such money in order to ascend a throne they probably sought for one of their own kin, and his own family did not have the funds to hand. His best chance of a gift or loan was to beg it from the Emperor Manuel in Constantinople. The emperor, seeing the wisdom of being owed a favour by the next monarch of Jerusalem and being all for grand gestures and spectacle in the manner of his Byzantine predecessors, sat the supplicant lord in a chair and covered him with all the gold coins required for his ransom. Encouraged if slightly bemused, Baldwin thanked the emperor, paid his ransom and headed back to Jerusalem to claim Sibylla's hand. The fact that Saladin demanded so great a ransom, and that Emperor Manuel agreed to pay it, indicates that Baldwin was widely believed to be on the verge of wedding Sibylla.

He was too late. When he finally arrived back in Jerusalem, a free man with his debts cleared, Sibylla was betrothed to another man. This man was a nobody from France whose elder brother had allegedly become the lover of Sibylla's own mother. This match was Agnes' handiwork, and the Ibelins were furious. So too, it seems, was King Baldwin IV. Sibylla's behaviour had insulted one of the greatest families in the land, and she had given herself to the landless fourth son of a French lord. Hardly a fitting choice for the heir to the Kingdom of Jerusalem.

SIBYLLA AND GUY

The landless fourth son in question was Guy de Lusignan, the younger brother of Aimery de Lusignan, who according to Ernoul's chronicle was the lover of the insatiable Agnes. While certainly not of the same rank as a princess, he had a certain crusading pedigree. His father, grandfather and great-grandfather had all been celebrated crusaders, two of whom died in the East. To the eyes of the local baronage, however, they were interlopers, reaching above their station and amassing an influence to which they had little right.

While her marriage was doubtless an affair of state, Sibylla was also growing up and discovering agency. She was found to no longer be the passive chattel she had appeared thus far. By this time she had spent ten years away from the cloisters of the Convent of Bethany, married a lord and become a mother. She had fulfilled her duties in every way and, even more remarkably, retained her health. Her status was increasing, and so was her confidence. Furthermore, following the death of her father, her mother Agnes had returned to court, and in Agnes Sibylla certainly found a role model for self-interest and rule-breaking, just as she would have done if Eleanor of Aquitaine, or her grandmother Melisende, or her great-aunt Alice, or her cousin Constance had appeared on her doorstep to dish out advice.

Egged on by Agnes during Baldwin of Ibelin's absence, Sibylla threw herself heart and soul into a romance with Guy and resolved to become his wife. Roger of Howden wrote of their romance: 'The king's sister, seeing therefore that this Guy was handsome, chose him to be her husband. But not daring to make her will known to her brother, she loved him secretly, and he slept with her.'

Ernoul similarly asserts that Guy seduced Sibylla, and that when her brother Baldwin IV found out, he was furious and wanted to sentence Guy to death for his crimes, but was brought round by the cajoling of his mother and the tearful entreaties of his sister. It is unclear how Agnes, her supposed lover Aimery and the newly arrived Guy managed to make Sibylla forget her promises to Baldwin of Ibelin, but between the three of them, it seems they made quite a success of it.

Baldwin IV's hands were tied: the seduction of a princess was a serious matter, and if it were publicly acknowledged and the man were punished, then she would be unlikely to make another match with an honourable house. It was better therefore to repair the damage with a hastily arranged wedding.

On hearing of the proposed marriage, Raymond III of Tripoli and Bohemond III of Antioch marched south towards Jerusalem with troops. Baldwin IV was persuaded by his advisors that they were coming to challenge his authority and prevent Sibylla's marriage. Some went so far as to assert that Raymond was coming with the intention of marrying Sibylla himself. The evidence for this plan is dubious, but in any case the news of Raymond III and Bohemond III's approach seemed to make Baldwin IV panic and accelerate the marriage, holding it in Holy Week in the lead-up to Easter, a week usually given over to contemplation of Christ's crucifixion and during which weddings were not celebrated. Regardless of whether they had planned to interfere with the wedding, it is certain that Raymond and Bohemond were vehemently opposed to the union.

This wedding polarised the court. Two clear factions emerged in

Jerusalem, both fighting for the ear of the king. On one side were those who would not endure being ruled by Sibylla and Guy de Lusignan, and thus supported Sibylla's half-sister Isabella of Jerusalem as heir to the Kingdom. The leaders of this group were Raymond III of Tripoli, Bohemond III of Antioch and the influential Ibelin clan, not to mention the vocal William of Tyre. The other side, who were supporters of Sibylla and Guy, was led by Sibylla and Guy, Reynald de Châtillon, Agnes of Courtenay and her scheming brother, the feckless Joscelin, who had been made seneschal of the Kingdom following his release from captivity.

Agnes' influence can be measured by the fact that it was she who brought about the two most significant (and disastrous) appointments of the day. Her meddling dictated both Sibylla's husband and the heir to the Kingdom, but also the appointment of the new Patriarch of Jerusalem. When Amaury, the aged Patriarch and a reedy voice of reason in the Kingdom, died that same year, Agnes proposed Heraclius, Bishop of Caesarea of doubtful reputation, to replace him. This appointment was made over the better-qualified and better-suited candidate, William of Tyre. It was rumoured that Agnes' sexual appetite influenced both of these crucial appointments, as it was widely believed that she was conducting affairs with both Guy's elder brother Aimery and Bishop Heraclius.

It is self-evident why both of these choices appalled the local nobility. Guy was obviously Sibylla's social inferior, and held no redeeming qualities to qualify him to be the next King of Jerusalem; and the Patriarch Heraclius was widely deemed to be the most unpriestly priest in Christendom, engaged in sexual affairs and virtually illiterate.

Guy de Lusignan had one strength that Baldwin of Ibelin lacked. The Ibelin clan did not command loyalties across the sea, whereas the Lusignans did. Following the recent defeats, the Kingdom of Jerusalem was in dire need of another crusade to come from the West to relieve their ever-worsening position. There was a chronic manpower shortage in the East, so a strategic match with a French noble who might be able to rouse troops from back home made good military sense.

Despite the opposition it aroused, Sibylla's marriage to Guy began happily enough, with her brother showing appropriate favour to her husband and treating the pair in such a way that it was clear that they were intended to be his heirs. Baldwin initially showed faith in Guy, allowing him to enjoy influence at court, witness royal charters and stand beside him at key events. He even went so far as to promote Guy's brother Aimery to be Constable of the Kingdom.

While we are told little of Guy's character and his relationship with Sibylla in the sources, we can deduce from his actions and achievements that he was charming, ambitious and strong-willed, qualities that may have caused Sibylla to become deferential to him in marriage. They had at least two daughters while Baldwin IV still lived, and there was between them a bond of unusual strength. Perhaps after all her years of displacement and bereavement, Sibylla was finally investing in the stability she believed she had found in Guy, staying close to him and their children. Nevertheless, the relationship between Sibylla's husband and her brother swiftly began to deteriorate. As the extent of Guy's incompetence, ego and unpopularity inevitably began to present itself, the ailing king began to regret his hasty decision to allow Sibylla to marry the man of her choosing. Three years into the marriage, as Baldwin IV saw his death approaching, he began to panic about the succession once again.

At this time in Outremer there existed a truce with Saladin, brokered by Raymond III of Tripoli during his time as regent for Baldwin IV. While for some this brought relief in the belief that they were secure, those with more foresight could see that this was the calm before the storm. Jerusalem was the prize, and the newly unified territory of Eqypt and Syria under Saladin would not be content to rub along with the Christians while the Al-Aqsa Mosque and the Dome of the Rock were under Christian control and dishonoured. During the crusader period the Temple complex was used first as a palace and then as barracks by the Templar knights, the most famous and ferocious of the Christian religious orders.

Saladin was using the respite created by the truce as a time to prepare his forces and solidify his position militarily and politically. The Christians, in contrast, were using this time to fight among themselves and tear apart their Kingdom, selfishly and ignobly trying to acquire land and power. This infighting, along with the severe lack of resources, was the Kingdom's undoing. Perhaps the reason why William of Tyre cannot find the stomach to praise Sibylla was because in choosing Guy as her husband and standing by him unwaveringly, she put her marriage above the welfare of the Kingdom, which her brother had dedicated his life to protecting. While never directly criticising or praising Sibylla, William was a vocal supporter of Raymond III of Tripoli. By speaking out in praise of Raymond, he was implicitly speaking in condemnation of Sibylla and Guy.

The new ruling faction in the Kingdom of Jerusalem, headed by

Sibylla, her husband and her mother and uncle, set about further alienating those already unwilling to accept their rule. Antioch and Tripoli, two of the most powerful and significant territories, were brought to the point of mutiny, despite their previous loyalty to Baldwin IV. Two years after Sibylla's marriage, this disunity and strife reached its nadir, with the more war-mongering of Baldwin IV's advisers almost succeeding in persuading him to declare war on Count Raymond, his most powerful vassal and previously his closest adviser. This was on the basis of rumours, testified to in both Muslim and Christian sources, that Raymond III himself was playing for the throne. Given the King's illness and the fact that he himself was a grandson of King Baldwin II, Raymond did indeed have a not insignificant claim to power in Jerusalem. It cannot be known whether he ever truly intended to supplant Baldwin IV or usurp his heirs, but there was enough rumour circulating to give Baldwin IV cause for concern.

William of Tyre, at this point nearly despairing of the situation, decided to do what he could to neutralise the brewing crisis. Since enduring the greatest snub of his career and seeing the oafish Heraclius promoted over him to Patriarch of Jerusalem, William had retired to relative isolation to write history and study. However, when seeing the land he loved poised on a knife-edge, he rallied and returned to court, rushing to the young king's side and persuading him to see sense. It seems this reconciliation was well on the way to resolution by April 1182, because the king made a significant gift to William, and issued it in a document witnessed by none other than Raymond of Tripoli, indicating that Raymond too was back at court and welcomed back to the fold.

Even though disaster was avoided at this juncture, the new ruling party in the court of Jerusalem had not been ousted and their aggravating influence had not abated. Time would tell what disasters this would bring.

8

THE BEGINNING OF THE END

MARIA OF ANTIOCH, THE ILL-STARRED EMPRESS

Meanwhile, as tensions were rising and hostilities were simmering in Outremer, something far more calamitous for the Latins was occurring in Constantinople. Andronikos Komnenos, lover of Theodora, was about to reappear on the stage.

Some years previously in 1161, Constance of Antioch's most beautiful daughter, the sixteen-year-old Maria of Antioch, had left her mother and her city for the final time. She took a ship from St Simeon to wed the Emperor Manuel Komnenos in a lavish ceremony in the Hagia Sophia, on Christmas Eve 1161. Her particular beauty was remarked upon, and the Greek chronicler Niketas Choniates described the young bride in terms of the highest praise: 'The woman was fair in form and exceedingly beautiful; her beauty was incomparable.' He went on to attribute to her the golden hair of Aphrodite, the white arms and gorgeous eyes of Hera, and the long neck and beautiful ankles of Helen of Troy.

Maria's primary role as empress was not to appear beautiful, but to provide an heir, and she struggled in this task from the early days of her marriage. It took five years for her to conceive, and in 1166 she miscarried a son. Three years later she finally bore the emperor a healthy baby boy, to be his cherished son and heir. He was christened Alexios by his jubilant parents.

While the court celebrated, the birth of Alexios had far less joyous implications for another royal Maria. Manuel had been married once before to a German princess, the very lady who had entertained Eleanor of Aquitaine and written her letters of encouragement during the Second Crusade. This woman, Empress Irene, had given her husband one daughter, Maria Porphyrogenita. Prior to Alexios' birth, this girl had been the heir to the imperial throne. With the advent of a new half-brother born to her father's foreign wife, Maria Porphyrogenita found herself ousted from the line of succession.

Indeed, Maria of Antioch's 'foreignness' swiftly made her enemies in Constantinople. She was known in the Greek-speaking world not as Maria of Antioch but as Maria-Xena, which translates roughly as 'Maria the Foreigner'.

These tensions, kept in check by the firm rule of Manuel, came to an abrupt end with his death in 1180. Following her husband's death, Maria of Antioch, legally or not, took charge of the government. The eleven-year-old Alexios, now the emperor, was content to hunt and play at sports while his mother and her associates ruled. Maria of Antioch was theoretically meant to enter a nunnery on her husband's death, but it quickly became apparent that she did not intend to follow through with this scheme. She was thirty-five years old at the time of Manuel's death, and still retained that ethereal beauty that had caused chroniclers to catch their breath when she first arrived in Constantinople. Instead of retiring peacefully to a convent, she seized the opportunity for freedom and agency left by her husband's death, and proceeded to flirt with the aristocrats who jostled for her favour, before taking the late Manuel's own nephew, Alexios Protosebastos, as her lover.

This brazen and unabashed affair on the part of the dowager empress scandalised the court and the population of Constantinople. The ruling couple were imprudent. Maria of Antioch allowed her new lover all political freedom, to the extent that he forced her son the emperor to decree that no new law or decree was valid unless it had Alexios Protosebastos' consent as well. For a long time it looked as though Alexios' and Maria of Antioch's stars were in the ascendant, and it seemed likely that they would marry and confirm Alexios Protosebastos as the young Emperor's stepfather and the power behind the throne. Objections to this were strong, not least because of the pair's autocratic style of ruling, which sold court offices for gold and excluded the rest of the Komnenoi from sharing in the governance of the realm. Similarly, Maria rode roughshod over the pride of the citizens of Constantinople. She openly favoured the Latin inhabitants and traders of the city over the native Greeks.

The regime was not sustainable, and in 1181 Maria Porphyrogenita, Maria of Antioch's bitter stepdaughter, led a revolt against her step-mother. It was foiled, and many of her co-conspirators either fled, were imprisoned or were put to death. Maria Porphyrogenita herself and her husband rushed to take refuge in the Hagia Sophia. From the safety of the church, under Justinian's great dome, they issued demands and prepared for a siege.

Officials arrived to escort the couple to trial but they refused to budge. Relations between church and state deteriorated to such an extent that at Easter 1181 fighting broke out outside the great church, and the mob showed its potential to get its way, baying for the blood of the Latins and the exile of Maria of Antioch and her damned lover Alexios Protosebastos. Startled and frightened by this rioting, Maria and Alexios sent imperial troops to disperse the mob. Open warfare raged in the city's streets. The imperial troops surrounded Maria Porphyrogenita and her closest supporters within the Hagia Sophia, and went so far as to occupy its porch, but they could not risk the public outcry that would come of desecrating the Great Church by forcing their way in and spilling blood on the sacred stones. The Hagia Sophia is to this day one of the most awe-inspiring interiors in the world, evoking reverence and wonder in its visitors, and it would have been a step too far for either Maria to dare to profane the sacred space.

The two Marias had therefore reached a stalemate, and a reluctant peace was negotiated along with an amnesty for Maria Porphyrogenita and her husband. Despite this 'victory' for Maria of Antioch and her lover, Maria Porphyrogenita still retained the support of the populace, whose force was not to be underestimated.

Among those faithful followers who had taken refuge alongside their mistress Maria Porphyrogenita in the Hagia Sophia was yet another young Greek woman named Maria. While there were undoubtedly many of these, this Maria had the distinction of being the legitimate daughter of Andronikos Komnenos, born before his elopement with Theodora. She was a courtier of the Greek court, strongly opposed to the Latin Maria of Antioch. On her escape from the Hagia Sophia, this Maria made her way to Sinope, where her father had settled with Theodora and his young family. Andronikos, despite his absence from the capital, had the love and support of the city's inhabitants. His charm and reputation as an intelligent and daring adventurer had won him popularity. To Andronikos, this no doubt seemed like the perfect opportunity to capitalise on this misplaced popularity and seize control of the city. He assembled an army and marched on the city, brooking no opposition and welcoming fearful turncoats as he went. As he approached the walls of Constantinople he issued his demands: that Alexios Protosebastos should be deprived of power and be held responsible for his crimes; that Maria of Antioch should be forced to enter a convent; and that her son the young Emperor Alexios should be freed to rule in his own right.

Protosebastos ignored the demands, but his defences crumbled about him. Eventually he was seized by his own men, conveyed to Andronikos and publicly blinded as punishment for his sins, before being sent to a monastery to live out his days in ignominy and darkness.

What followed was unchecked horror. The pent-up tension coursing through the citizens of Constantinople as they awaited Andronikos' arrival was finally released in a wash of slaughter. They raged through the streets of the city, killing any Latin they could lay their hands on. Men, women, children, sick and elderly, all fell prey to their violence. The ill were butchered in their hospital beds. The Latin clergy were particularly targeted, and the head of a prominent Latin priest was struck off and tied to a dog's tail to be clawed at and dragged through the streets amid tides of blood. Those Latins that could fled the city by sea.

A meeting then took place between Andronikos and the Patriarch of the city. Andronikos greeted him respectfully, having no personal quarrel with the priest. However, the priest rightfully mistrusted him, and while Andronikos spoke of his support for the young Emperor Alexios, the Patriarch replied that he already counted the boy among the dead. This was as close as he could come to openly accusing Andronikos of plotting the boy's murder.

What happened subsequently was a tragedy. Andronikos set about slowly and unsubtly assassinating anyone likely to oppose him. While making a show of treating both Maria Porphyrogenita and Maria of Antioch respectfully, both perished not long after he had claimed power and assumed the regency of the young Emperor Alexios. The rebellious and ambitious Maria Porphyrogenita and her husband died within months of each other of unexplained causes, most likely poison.

Maria of Antioch was accused of plotting against the Empire with her half-sister Agnes' husband, Béla III of Hungary. Andronikos 'convened a court sympathetic to his cause with judges certain to condemn, not try, the wretched woman', and following this show trial he sent her into captivity. There she was mocked and mistreated, living in hunger and fear, and haunted by premonitions of her own execution. Her fears were justified, for shortly after this Niketas Choniates relates that Andronikos forced her young son to sign her death warrant, 'as though with a drop of his mother's own blood.' Andronikos ordered his son and brother-in-law to hasten to her cell and carry out the execution, but both refused on moral grounds, claiming that the empress was innocent of the crimes of which she was accused. Scarcely containing his anger at this response, Andronikos quickly found other less conscientious agents, and these men crept up on Maria and strangled her. Niketas Choniates lamented her death with the words, 'she, who was the sweet light and a vision of beauty unto men, was buried in obscurity in the sand of the nearby shore.'

The misfortune of this family was not yet over. Before long, Andronikos had risen from being Alexios' regent to become his co-emperor, and not long after that the young emperor – Maria of Antioch's only son and Constance of Antioch's grandson – was murdered. He was strangled with a bowstring, and his body was brought before Andronikos. His corpse was mutilated, beheaded and buried at sea, without funeral or lamentation, and Andronikos began his reign as sole emperor. With these disasters, the support the Kingdom of Jerusalem could have relied on from the Emperor of Byzantium was abruptly ended.

Constance's daughters suffered hugely at the hands of Andronikos, for it should not be forgotten that the first Latin princess to fall victim to his seductions was Princess Philippa of Antioch, the unfortunate Maria of Antioch's younger sister.

The young Emperor Alexios, despite his youth, had been married to an even younger French princess named Agnes. When she had arrived in Constantinople she had been rechristened Anna. At the time of her husband's death, she was still not yet twelve years of age. Andronikos' beloved mistress Theodora had died the same year as Maria of Antioch, leaving Andronikos a widower and free to marry once again. Despite her protestations, this young girl, a stranger far from her home, was forcibly wedded to Emperor Andronikos, a man more than fifty years her senior. The chroniclers of this period did not hold back their disgust at such a union, Niketas Choniates writing that Andronikos 'was not ashamed to lie unlawfully with his nephew's red-cheeked and tender spouse, who had not yet completed her eleventh year [. . .] the shrivelled and languid old man and the rosy-fingered girl.'

Andronikos was soon to pay the price of his crimes. His megalomania only increased following these events, and soon the fickle city determined to be rid of him. A rebellion ensued, the result of which was the mutilation and execution of Andronikos in the Hippodrome, Constantinople's foremost political arena.

SKIRMISHES WITH SALADIN – THE SULTAN ADVANCES

Meanwhile the situation in Outremer, while always hanging in a delicate balance, was now on the brink of real crisis. The King's illness was worsening, the truce with Saladin had expired, the Byzantine Empire could no longer be relied on for support, and the realm was plagued with conflict, both between Christians and Muslims and internally between themselves.

The uneasy truce which had existed with Saladin thus far had been due to expire in May 1182. Following the expiration, Saladin began to advance into Christian territory. The Christians won a decisive victory against the Muslims at the Battle of La Forbelet. While this certainly bolstered the confidence of the Christian soldiers and their commanders, it must be regarded as a fluke success at the beginning of a string of defeats. The Christian army demonstrated great bravery and endurance, as did Baldwin IV, who was present at the battle. The summer sun was at its strongest and for anyone, let alone a young man in the final stages of leprosy, to remain on the field was a feat of huge and symbolic endurance and willpower. Indeed, it is recorded that at least one man died of heat exhaustion on the march back to Jerusalem – a monk carrying a fragment of the True Cross.

After this, Reynald de Châtillon in his role as commander of the armies (a position he had assumed following Baldwin IV's fall-out with Raymond III of Tripoli) launched a daring raid on the coast of the Red Sea and threatened to sack Mecca itself. This foray into Saladin's territory would earn Reynald the sultan's lasting enmity. This raid, the Battle of La Forbelet and several other skirmishes present fascinating examples of medieval military history and strategy, and insight into the prowess and tenacity of several of the figures described in this book. For a detailed narration of these events, turn to the works of Professor Hamilton or Professor Tyerman, for these events have been expertly covered by them, and were first and foremost the deeds of men, and this book is about the deeds of women.

By 1183, Baldwin's leprosy had accelerated its progress, and the king was now blind and so horribly deformed that he could not use his hands or feet. He would never again ride out with his army as he had so valiantly done previously, and Saladin's grasp was slowly tightening on the territories surrounding Outremer. He captured Aleppo, consolidating his position and unifying the Muslims of Syria. The Christian states of Outremer made ready for war. The king, aware of the gravity of the situation and his own approaching death, convened a council to decide the matter of appointing a regent and securing the succession. The great magnates of the realm flocked to the King's bedside, including Raymond of Tripoli, Reynald de Châtillon, the Ibelin brothers and Guy de Lusignan.

Since Guy stood as the heir apparent, Baldwin's hands were tied and he was forced to appoint his unpopular brother-in-law as regent. This was not a temporary measure, as it had been with the King's previous regents, Raymond and Reynald, but a permanent one because this time Baldwin IV did not expect to recover and take power again. Resigning the burden of kingship should have been a relief to Baldwin and a welcome respite, but this decision proved to be nothing of the sort. William of Tyre asserted baldly that Guy 'was unequal in strength and wisdom' to the duty of governing, and indeed he was ill-placed for this role, given that half of the most powerful barons in the land despised him.

As Guy stepped into his new office, Saladin launched his campaign. There was a poorly managed stand-off between the Christian and Muslim forces, and Guy began to reveal his true colours as not only an ambitious ingrate but a poor leader of men. As regent he was commander of the army, and in several of the skirmishes that took place during this period his personal unpopularity meant he was unable to rouse the other barons of the region to support his efforts at crucial junctures, resulting in a series of unsuccessful military endeavours including a standoff in Galilee, wasting resources and energy.

THE OTHER PRINCESS

While such vicious internal politics raged and the Kingdom of Jerusalem readied itself for war, changes were occurring in the King's family. Agnes of Courtenay, who with failing health had retired to Acre, finally died, her scheming to be carried on by her brother Joscelin. As one generation declined, the other matured. Baldwin and Sibylla's little half-sister, Princess Isabella of Jerusalem, was growing up.

Isabella's life started as many princesses' lives do, in the lap of luxury, nestled, secure and full of promise and potential. Her mother was Maria Komnene, a Byzantine princess, and her father was Amalric, King of Jerusalem. Despite this illustrious parentage, Isabella was never meant to inherit her father's Kingdom. Sibylla and Baldwin had had their legitimacy confirmed, and so it was only by stepping over their corpses that Isabella would succeed to the throne of Jerusalem. She existed as an afterthought and an alternative when it came to matters of succession. This was enough to raise the hackles of Agnes of Courtenay when she returned to court as Queen Mother following the death of the king. Agnes of Courtenay and Maria Komnene were rivals, and both were concerned primarily with advancing the interests of their offspring in the Kingdom of Jerusalem. One could only succeed at the expense of the other, and with the death of Amalric, Maria Komnene's star began to wane, just as Agnes' began to wax once more.

Maria Komnene withdrew to Nablus with her young daughter, but before long a decision was made in Jerusalem to forcibly separate the child Isabella from her mother, and thus remove her from her mother's influence and control. This controversial measure was achieved through a betrothal to a young lord, Humphrey IV of Toron, approved by Baldwin IV but perhaps engineered by Agnes. Humphrey was heir to the lordship of Oultrejourdain, the son of Stephanie of Milly and her first husband. He was a weak and malleable young man under the influence and control of those loyal to Agnes' faction in Jerusalem. Isabella was just eight years old, and Humphrey fifteen. With this done, Isabella was removed from her mother's household and sent to live with Humphrey's family in the desert fortress of Kerak.

Kerak was far from a hospitable environment for a young girl torn from her family. The fortress is one of the best-preserved castles of Frankish Syria. It soars high above the desert plains of Jordan, an imposing giant of stone perched on a plateau high above a ravine with sheer cliff faces on three sides. It was built by Pagan the Butler, a vassal of Baldwin II, who rose to become Lord of Oultrejourdain in the 1140s, and its position was strategically important not only as a frontier castle bordering Muslim territory but also due to the position it occupied on both the ancient King's Highway and the pilgrim routes to Mecca. This meant the castle was in a unique position to control trade and pilgrimage in the region and, given its prime defensibility and the natural topography of the region which played to its advantage, to act as a buffer between Christian and Muslim territory. It was a far cry from the royal palaces of Jerusalem or the unwalled city of Nablus.

When Isabella arrived at the desert stronghold, it was made a still more hostile environment because it was being ruled by its most ferocious incumbents yet, Reynald de Châtillon and his formidable wife Stephanie of Milly. Reynald was Humphrey's stepfather by virtue of his marriage to his mother. He must have been a terrifying stepfather. It is likely that he had the young lordling under his thumb. Reynald and Guy had likely lobbied for this match because it would tie Sibylla's only potential rival to a man under their influence. For good measure, they went a step further and prevented the young girl from having any contact with either her mother or her stepfather. Maria Komnene had married Balian of Ibelin, a man of rising influence in Outremer who had won a great coup and a good deal of wealth through his marriage to the dowager queen. Both Agnes of Courtenay and Guy de Lusignan were keen to curtail the sphere of influence of this couple, and removing the alternative heir to the throne from their charge was the first step.

For three years, then, Isabella grew up in Kerak. In 1183, following the death of Agnes of Courtenay and with Baldwin IV's health declining, a plan was made to turn her betrothal to Humphrey into a proper wedding and seal the deal. Humphrey was by now eighteen, and Isabella just eleven. The groom's stepfather, Reynald de Châtillon, offered to host the festivities at Kerak, and nobles and entertainers from across Outremer descended on the imposing desert fortress. Unbeknownst to the revellers, so too did Saladin.

Even as the young Isabella recited her marriage vows, Saladin's forces were aligning outside the citadel. He had arrived with a vast army and all manner of siege machines, fully intending to besiege the city, capture the valuable hostages within, and teach Reynald de Châtillon a lesson for daring to threaten Mecca and attack unarmed Muslim caravans. Reynald's brutality was legendary even in his own lifetime.

During the siege-wedding, the chatelaine of Kerak and mother of the groom, the steely Stephanie of Milly, clearly anxious for the safety of the young couple as trebuchets and mangonels battered the city's defences, extended a gesture of hospitality to the besieging sultan. She arranged for delicacies from the wedding feast to be sent to Saladin as a gift and sign of respect. Saladin, who was always partial to courtesy, having sent his own physicians to attend the Leper King, received this gift warmly and reciprocated by instructing his soldiers not to attack the tower in which the young couple would pass their wedding night.

A CHANGE OF WIND

The defence of the city was bungled by Reynald, and the king summoned a council to rearrange the management of the Kingdom and save Kerak. This marked a decisive change in the King's favour within his court. It was withdrawn from his late mother's faction, including Reynald and Guy, and given back wholeheartedly to Raymond of Tripoli, the Ibelins and the nobles allied with their faction. This decision perhaps indicates more clearly than anything else the influence Agnes of Courtenay had wielded over her son. Only after her death was Baldwin able to return power back to those worthy of it. While she lived, he had been blind to the reckless folly of Guy de Lusignan, but now the mist had cleared.

Despite his failing health and doubtless the protestations of Sibylla, Baldwin IV dismissed Guy as his regent and took back the reins of the

Kingdom into his own decaying hands. The fact that the king, a dying leper, unable to ride and almost blind, believed that he was more fit to govern than Guy, a nobleman in the prime of life, was a public indictment of Guy's lack of abilities and made it very clear that this man was no longer the King's choice as the heir to his Kingdom.

Politics and personalities aside, Guy had proven himself an incompetent general in the preceding years, and the king needed to send an effective leader to relieve the Siege of Kerak. His sister Isabella, a princess of the blood and one of his father's few precious heirs, was trapped inside.

Baldwin was done with taking risks with the future of his family and Kingdom. He took steps to assure that Guy was prevented from taking power in his own right, and made a bold decision to have his nine-year-old nephew, Sibylla's son Baldwin from her first marriage to William of Montferrat, crowned as his co-king and designated heir. So crucial was this step that Baldwin delayed sending a relief force to Kerak until the ceremony was completed. From this point onwards Baldwin IV and Baldwin V reigned together as anointed co-rulers.

Baldwin IV's next target as he attempted to preserve his Kingdom was Sibylla's marriage to Guy. If he were to die and leave his nephew a child-king, which was highly likely given his condition, then Guy and Sibylla would be well placed to exert influence over him and use him as a puppet while they themselves ruled. It was not his sister Sibylla's influence he objected to, but Guy de Lusignan's, and short of an outright assassination attempt, the best way to get Guy out of the picture was to dissolve his marriage to Sibylla. The king began consultations with the Patriarch of Jerusalem to see how this could be accommodated within canon law. However, this was a long-term plan and the more immediate and pressing concern was the relief of Kerak, where Isabella and her new husband were still trapped alongside Reynald de Châtillon and his citizens.

The army was mobilised to Kerak, and Baldwin, by herculean effort, accompanied the war host to the walls of the city himself. Too ill to lead and fight alongside his troops, he appointed Raymond of Tripoli as commander and put him in charge of the action. None took place, however, as Saladin took to his heels at the sight of the approaching army and Raymond's banner. Kerak was relieved without further bloodshed, and the young Princess's safety was secured. With his younger sister now safe, Baldwin could turn his attention to ridding his elder sister of her inadequate husband.

What Baldwin did not take into account was that Sibylla did not want to be rid of Guy, and would resist his efforts. She adored her second husband, and was prepared to fight to keep him. The Patriarch Heraclius, the old ally of Agnes, loyally pursuing her ends even after her death, evidently tipped off Guy about the King's plans to dissolve his marriage. Following the relief of Kerak, Guy slipped away to Ascalon and summoned Sibylla to join him there. She must have also sensed the danger they were in and rushed to join him.

King Baldwin summoned the couple to appear before a court in Jerusalem to try the validity of their marriage, but Guy and Sibylla refused his summons, Guy unconvincingly pleading ill health. The marriage could not be overturned in their absence and so the ailing king had himself carried to Ascalon in a litter and demanded entry. Guy closed the gates of the city against him. Baldwin IV physically knocked on the gates in the name of the crown of Jerusalem but was still refused admission. This was blatant insubordination and could not be tolerated. The king immediately deprived Guy and Sibylla of Jaffa, and seemed about to march on Guy and besiege him at Ascalon, when the pleas of his council prevailed and a ruinous civil war was averted.

Despite this leniency, Sibylla's husband overstepped the mark once again. Not only had he flouted the King's authority in refusing to answer his summons or to allow him entry into Sibylla's city of Ascalon; he then went a step further and broke the King's peace. Non-combatant Bedouin caravans were allowed by royal decree to roam the lands of Outremer unmolested, and shortly after this first disobedience Guy attacked one of these caravans, no doubt taking a leaf from the book of his friend Reynald de Châtillon. The King's already fraying patience snapped, and he appointed Guy's nemesis Raymond of Tripoli as regent, giving him command of the Kingdom.

This is the last event William of Tyre describes in his chronicle, before laying down his quill with a mixture of despair and and old age. It is likely he lived until 1186, but wrote no more of his history after 1184. He had foreseen the demise of the Kingdom that he loved, and could no longer bring himself to record its ruin. He expressed a hope that Raymond's wisdom could prove to be the Kingdom's salvation.

Saladin launched a fresh attack on Kerak in the summer of 1184, with much the same results as before. In September he attacked Nablus. The lord of the city, Balian of Ibelin, who had married Amalric's widow Maria Komnene, was absent and so his wife assumed command of the city. She preserved the lives of its inhabitants by garrisoning them in the citadel until a relief force arrived and the city was saved.

As Saladin's forces gathered and the King's health weakened, Baldwin once again summoned his council to decide the pressing issue of the succession. The council declared: 'We do not wish when the child has been crowned that his stepfather should be regent because we know that he would have neither the knowledge nor the ability to govern the kingdom.' The dying king heartily agreed with this, as he had already made clear by depriving Guy of his regency and seeking to separate him from Sibylla. He told the council to choose a regent for Baldwin V, and they confirmed that this should be Raymond of Tripoli. The council agreed that Raymond would rule on behalf of Sibylla's son until he was of age. This was a wise move, as they needed to appoint a man with a will of iron and a sharp mind, if he was to fend off Guy's bids for power over a ten-year period.

These decisions were confirmed by the lords present paying homage to Raymond and the little co-king Baldwin V. The boy then performed a ceremonial crown-wearing, to reaffirm his status as co-king and heir, and was carried on the shoulders of Balian of Ibelin. This was a physical metaphor for the power shift in the Kingdom, and indicated that from this point forward, the boy would be raised and advised by the Count of Tripoli and the Ibelins, rather than his stepfather Guy. It was also agreed that in the event of Baldwin V dying without a male heir, then the Kings of England, France and Germany, together with the Pope, would debate and choose whether Sibylla or Isabella should inherit.

Now that he believed he had at last made adequate provision for the future of his fragile Kingdom, safeguarding it from the meddling influence of Guy and his mother's faction, Baldwin IV, the Leper King of Jerusalem, closed his eyes for the final time in April 1185. His personal strength and perseverance during his reign were remarkable, perhaps uniquely so. He never shied from his duty in governing the Kingdom. His esteemed tutor William of Tyre wrote of him: 'Although his body was weak and powerless, yet he was strong in spirit, and made a superhuman effort to disguise his illness and shoulder the burdens of kingship.'

SIBYLLA'S SON, THE LEPER'S HEIR

The death of the Leper King triggered a landslide of disasters. Baldwin IV's painstakingly crafted strategy for the succession collapsed after less than two years. The child King Baldwin V succeeded, with Raymond of Tripoli as regent as planned, but after just one year and seven months as sole king, aged just nine, he died at Acre in August 1186.

How exactly this happened remains unclear and rumours of foul play spread thick and fast. The Jacobean historian Thomas Fuller asserts that Sibylla murdered her own son, and there was a wide school of thought that believed Sibylla to be evil and to have murdered her son for her own ends. Fuller writes: 'Sibyll [. . .] to defeat Reimund, first murdered all natural affection in her self, and then by poyson murdered her son; that so the Crown in her right might come to her husband Guy.' Fuller's claims do not stand up to scrutiny, as there is no other evidence to substantiate them. It is unclear where Fuller, writing several centuries later and in another country, came across this idea, as it is not recorded in any of the main texts of the period, even those which are critical of Sibylla, so it is likely to have been based only on conjecture.

William of Newburgh agreed that poison was involved but asserted that Raymond of Tripoli was the murderer, on the basis that he intended to seize the throne for himself, as Baldwin V's nearest male relative. This also seems unlikely. Raymond of Tripoli was legally established as the boy's regent for ten years, so to all intents and purposes he ruled the Kingdom already. Indeed, Baldwin V's demise threw Raymond's position into uncertainty.

There is a trend in medieval chronicles to attribute sudden deaths to poison. It was also claimed that William of Tyre was eventually poisoned by his enemies. Whereas today the sudden death of anyone, except someone very elderly, would be considered suspicious, in those days it was not, because mortality rates were considerably higher in the medieval period, and life expectancy was considerably lower.

There is likewise a trend to cast problematic or rebellious women as Medeas and viragoes. Women who subvert the natural order of male dominance or manage to anger the male clerics chronicling events are generally depicted as unnatural and unbalanced, and what could be more unnatural than a mother murdering her child for political gain? The accusations against both Sibylla and Raymond seem to be smear campaigns by their enemies and critics.

Little Baldwin V was buried in an elaborate tomb commissioned by his bereaved mother, and laid to rest in the Church of the Holy Sepulchre near the tombs of his ancestors. His funeral was officiated by Heraclius, Patriarch of Jerusalem, and attended by his mother, stepfather and paternal grandfather, who had journeyed to the East to protect the interests of his grandson. This was a relatively small group of nobles; a King's funeral was usually attended by a far greater proportion of the nobility, especially those to whom he was related. Raymond of Tripoli, his half-sister Isabella and the Ibelins were conspicuously absent.

Following Baldwin V's death, the Kingdom split again. Sibylla had little time to mourn her child, for already the nobility were mobilising against her under the command of Raymond of Tripoli. Instead of attending the young King's funeral, Raymond summoned the nobility, including Sibylla and Guy and their followers, to Nablus. This meeting was convened to decide the hotly contested issue of succession. Raymond finally seemed to be openly playing for the throne, but his plans were to come to nothing. Sibylla had her eye on her inheritance, and was aligning her cards to claim it. She and her supporters ignored Raymond's summons to Nablus and while in Jerusalem, ostensibly for her son's funeral, she installed a garrison in the city and called all her supporters to attend her there. Since her mother Agnes had died two years earlier, this faction comprised primarily Guy, Reynald de Châtillon, Patriarch Heraclius and the masters of the Templars and the Hospitallers. She was preparing for a fight.

The magnates who convened at Jerusalem for Baldwin V's funeral agreed that Sibylla had the strongest claim to the throne, and they proposed to crown her queen without the consent of the missing barons. This was in direct contravention of an earlier agreement that, should Baldwin V die childless, the Kings of England, France and Germany together with the Pope would make a decision about which sister, Isabella or Sibylla, should inherit the crown. Furious at this flagrant disregard for the law, Raymond of Tripoli and his followers refused to attend the coronation, and began hatching a plan to supplant Sibylla.

While Sibylla's supporters certainly supported *her*, they were not so optimistic as to believe the placement of a crown upon his head would transform Guy into an appropriate leader for a Kingdom in crisis. Indeed, it is evident that even Sibylla's supporters acknowledged that it would be disastrous to allow Guy to rule as her consort. A compromise was brokered whereby the barons made Sibylla an offer very similar to that made to her father Amalric twenty-two years earlier. She was offered the throne of the Kingdom of Jerusalem on the condition that she consented to divorce Guy. Sibylla countered this with the conditions that her daughters remained legitimate, that Guy kept his lands as a nobleman of the Kingdom, and that she be allowed to choose her next husband from among the nobility of the region. This was duly agreed, the consensus being that no one else could be as incompetent a king as Guy, and preparations began for Sibylla's coronation.

Sibylla's coronation was perhaps the most dramatically charged episode in the history of the Queens of Jerusalem. The coronation of a monarch was a sacred moment, when a hitherto mortal was transformed by holy ritual into the instrument of God on earth and a lightning rod for divine authority anointed with sacred oil. Religion formed the bedrock of society in Outremer. The lands Sibylla would rule had been forged in blood on religious principles and the enemies who threatened her borders would be religious enemies. The people's belief in the solemnity of this ritual and the transformation that would occur was absolute, and once the sacred oil had touched Sibylla and the crown had been settled on her brow, she was invincible in her court and had absolute authority. Even if others disputed her right to Queenship, once she was crowned the deed was done.

Not only this, but Sibylla's coronation was of unprecedented significance as the first time a woman would be crowned in her own right without a husband alongside her. Melisende had been crowned for her blood right, but jointly with two men, her husband and son. Other Queens had been crowned as consorts with their husbands, but here Sibylla was setting a precedent as an unmarried female monarch with the power to choose her own consort.

Her first deed as monarch was an act of daring brilliance that strikingly asserted her autonomy and power over her barons. Almost as soon as she felt the power of the oil on her skin and the crown on her head, placed there by her mother's old ally the Patriarch of Jerusalem, Sibylla stood. She 'invoked the grace of the Holy Spirit' and her loud voice rang out through the echoing halls of the Church of the Holy Sepulchre, where her great subjects were gathered to witness the miracle and pay her homage. She declared: 'I, Sibylla, choose for myself as King and as my husband Guy of Lusignan, the man who has been my husband.'

There must have been uproar as the barons heard these words. They would have cursed both their new queen and themselves for not having prevented this in the terms of their agreement. Sibylla had been very crafty indeed. Not only had she asked to be allowed to choose her next husband from among the barons of the land, but she had also ensured that Guy remained a baron by ensuring that he was allowed to keep her dower lands of Jaffa and Ascalon. She had further convincingly played the part of a woman parting ways with her husband by insisting that her children remain legitimate even after her divorce, thus projecting to the world the image of a woman who intended the divorce to proceed. By the terms of the agreement she had brokered, she was within her rights to choose Guy: she had artfully constructed a loophole and at her coronation darted through it triumphantly.

Over the fury that was undoubtedly breaking out at her words, Sibylla continued her speech, hammering home her point: 'He is a worthy man and in every way of upright character: with the help of God he will rule his people well. I know that while he lives I cannot, before God, have anyone else, for as the Scripture says, "Whom God has joined, let no man put asunder."'

Her choice of this quotation from scripture is particularly significant. It must be remembered that Sibylla was a convent girl raised at Bethany and that she had been sent there because, in parallel circumstances, her father had consented to divorce her mother and send her away in order to claim the throne of Jerusalem for himself. In this bold statement Sibylla appeared to be passing judgement on the moral laxity of her father and forebears within the Kingdom of Jerusalem.

She had a point. Was it not hypocritical that the Kings of Christ's Kingdom ignored Christ's laws in order to obtain the office? Baldwin I had committed much the same offence in his treatment of his wives. It is likely that as she spoke these words, Sibylla was thinking of her dead mother. Agnes' loss of favour had blighted the lives of both women, and it is possible that Sibylla, like so many others, believed that her brother's harrowing disease had been God's punishment of her father's divorce of Agnes and taking of another wife while she still lived.

Sibylla was not only declaring her love for Guy, but for her mother, and for God's law. She was making it clear that she was mindful of her marriage vows, which had included a solemn promise to submit to Guy and obey him. The coronation took place just metres from the days-old grave of her son, and the only slightly older grave of her brother. She must have been thinking about her broken family, knowing that Guy was all she had left.

THE REIGN OF SIBYLLA, AND THE COLLAPSE OF A KINGDOM

It is possible that Sibylla's first autonomous act of her reign was also her last. To what extent she ruled during her reign is a question open to debate, and one that, at its heart, raises questions about the nature and realities of medieval queenship and female political agency.

In conferring the crown on Guy in the way that she did at her own coronation, Sibylla seemingly signed away her power to him. She seems to have been entirely under his influence during the early part of her reign. Guy had a strong hold over his wife. It is unclear if theirs was a love between equals or a controlling and manipulative relationship. In any case, Guy seemed to act primarily in his own interests, and wished to rule in his own right. There are charters from Sibylla's reign issued in Guy's name only, without Sibylla's, but no charters issued in her name without Guy's, which suggests he was the senior partner in their relationship. This is in stark contrast to the documents surviving from Melisende's reign and suggests that while Sibylla may have been the source of Guy's authority, this did not necessarily translate to her wielding actual power. Power equated to the ability to rule, authority the right to rule. Sibylla, following her coronation, had the right to rule, but in practice was rarely able to assert solid power during her reign. Her grandmother Queen Melisende, on the other hand, had a dubious claim to authority once her son Baldwin III had come of age, yet still wielded immense power in the Kingdom of Jerusalem.

Sibylla's opponents were far from impressed with either her coronation or the stunt she executed in selecting Guy as her consort, and they openly declared against her and her husband. Raymond of Tripoli and his allies at Nablus began trying to organise a rebellion that would see Isabella, aged fifteen, and her twenty-one-year-old husband Humphrey of Toron, on the throne instead. This scheme had a good chance of success, but what they did not count on was the squeamishness (or perhaps the foresight) of Humphrey of Toron. While this plan was being hatched, he absconded in the darkness from Nablus and rode with all haste to Jerusalem. Once there, he begged an audience with the king and queen, confessed to the plot, begged forgiveness and paid homage to Sibylla and Guy. Raymond's attempted coup was over before it had begun and Jerusalem was stuck with Guy at the helm.

Unable to stomach the prospect of doing homage to Sibylla and Guy but clearly defeated for the time being, Raymond of Tripoli rode back to his own lands. While he remained openly disloyal and at liberty, he represented a smouldering firebrand of sedition. Guy could not ignore this, else others might rally to him and throw the Kingdom of Jerusalem into civil war – a conflict they could not afford, with Saladin strengthening his position all the time. In October 1186 Guy moved against Raymond, leading his army to Raymond's stronghold in Tiberias to dispossess him of his lands, on the legal grounds that he had refused to do homage to his king for them.

Guy clearly believed this would be a straightforward operation, as Raymond did not have the resources to resist the army of Jerusalem at Tiberias. Pushed to desperate measures, Raymond, not for the first time in his family's history, decided to ally with a Muslim lord to avoid the loss of territory. The leader to whom he reached out for support was none other than Saladin himself.

Later historians and Raymond's contemporaries alike were quick to point out that this was an act of treason, but so too had been Raymond's refusal to pay homage to Guy. He had sworn no oaths of loyalty to either Guy or Sibylla and he believed that they had claimed the throne illegally. Beyond this, he believed that they were greedy and incompetent and would destroy the Kingdom. Despite the grounds Raymond had for refusing to obey Guy's commands, it remained shocking that he allowed Saladin to march his troops through his lands unchecked, and Guy had little choice but to withdraw from Galilee.

The rift between Jerusalem and Tripoli would not be patched up for many months, and only then because of the impending doom of the Kingdom of Jerusalem. In 1187 Saladin mounted a far more serious invasion of the Kingdom and marched his armies through Raymond's lands unhindered, as per the terms of their co-operation agreement. Panicked by this and realising the danger he was in without Raymond's help, Guy sent intermediaries to begin peace negotiations with him. Unsurprisingly, these envoys were frostily received, and Raymond only agreed to accept Guy's rule for the greater good of Outremer following a harrowing defeat of crusader forces at the Battle of Cresson on 1 May. This battle saw the massacre of a Christian army of over a hundred knights, mostly from the military orders, and hundreds of infantry. Just four knights survived.

The devastation at Cresson was, however, merely a warm-up act for what would follow at the Battle of Hattin on 4 July 1187. It was on that barren and unwatered battlefield that the consequences of Sibylla's choice of Guy as a husband came to a head. The Battle of Hattin signified the destruction of the Christian forces in the East that set in motion a rapid string of territorial losses and defeats that would ultimately culminate in the loss of the holy city of Jerusalem itself.

With Saladin's forces moving fast through the Kingdom, the Christians had to devise a strategy to face him. Guy mustered the armies at Saffuriyah, gathering over 1,200 knights alongside an 'innumerable' infantry force. The chronicler Ernoul estimates the full size of the Christian host at Hattin to have been 40,000 men. Saladin's first move was to march on and besiege Raymond of Tripoli's fortress of Tiberias that he had gained from his marriage to his wife Eschiva. The territory was guarded only by Eschiva herself and a small garrison, as her four grown-up sons were all supporting Raymond in Guy's army.

Despite his obvious ties and responsibility to Tiberias, Raymond still advised against attacking Saladin's armies there, believing it to be a hopeless enterprise. He was upbraided severely for his lack of chivalry towards his trapped wife, and was overruled by his newly acknowledged king. As it happened, Eschiva would acquit herself well at the Siege of Tiberias, and while she surrendered the city, she and its inhabitants escaped with their lives.

Guy moved the Christian army towards Tiberias, into Galilee and – crucially – away from water. They were forced to break their journey and as they camped one night in the shadow of the now infamous 'horns of Hattin', exhausted and thirsty, Saladin's forces attacked them in the dark. The 'horns of Hattin' are the two peaks of an extinct volcano in the south of Galilee, and it was in the shadow of these mountains that the army of Jerusalem spent its final night. It was the height of summer and the already arid landscape was covered with tinder-dry grass that Saladin's men, sneaking up in the dark, set alight. The air was filled with smoke and fire, and in that environment and the chaos and confusion that reigned there, it must have felt to the Christian knights as though they were in hell itself. Ambushed, choked by smoke and blind in the darkness, they could not drive Saladin's forces back from their camp. Even as dawn broke over the horizon, they failed to rally: nearly the entire Christian army was slaughtered that day. The True Cross, which had symbolically been carried like a standard with the army, was lost and thousands upon thousands lay slain. Of the Christian leaders, only Balian of Ibelin and Raymond of Tripoli escaped alive from the fray.

The result was shock, panic and despair across Outremer. The Christians of Outremer had suffered setbacks and losses in the past, but this defeat was different. It was final. Their most treasured relic, the True Cross, was lost and their army annihilated. The fortresses of Outremer now had little or no hope of defending themselves against Saladin's armies sweeping up the coast. Raymond of Tripoli, despite escaping the battlefield, was left so distraught by the defeat that he died not long after the battle. All his ambitions had focused on the Kingdom of Jerusalem. With the loss of almost all of the Kingdom's defences in one battle, there would soon be no Kingdom left to defend or to rule: he lost the will to carry on.

Almost every other significant leader was either killed or captured at Hattin. Guy and Reynald de Châtillon were both captured and brought to an audience with Saladin. In a scene recorded by Ibn al-Athir among others and made famous by Ridley Scott's film *Kingdom of Heaven*, Saladin offered a drink of water to Guy, who in turn passed it to Reynald. The gesture, no doubt intended as little more than goodwill between comrades, angered Saladin. While Guy was an anointed king with whom Saladin was willing to extend diplomatic courtesy, Reynald to his eyes was little more than a brigand and upstart who had threatened to sack Mecca itself. Guy's gesture was a breach of protocol, for the offer of a drink was symbolic rather than practical, and while Saladin was willing to guarantee Guy's safety, he had no intention of doing the same for Reynald, having previously sworn to execute him personally.

He gave Reynald the option to convert to Islam, and when Reynald refused, he beheaded him on the spot with his own scimitar. This personal debt settled, Saladin marched his armies onwards.

Sibylla was more alone and more in need of advice than ever before. Her mother was dead, she was separated from Guy, Raymond of Tripoli was dead, and nearly all of her great nobles were in chains in Saladin's dungeons. Isolated as she was, Sibylla was forced to take charge of the defence of her Kingdom.

Saladin made his way up the Phoenician coast from Hattin, conquering fortress after fortress including Acre, Jaffa, Toron, Sidon, Nablus, Beirut and Jebail, among others. Some of these cities negotiated terms and submitted on the condition that their populations were allowed safe passage to other lands; others refused to negotiate and were taken by storm. The survivors of these courageous but short-sighted cities – men, women and children alike – were sold into slavery in Muslim lands. The chronicler Ibn al-Athir relates that he himself bought a Christian slave, a woman who had lost her husband and six children, at a slave market in Aleppo.

While Saladin was seizing these territories, an unlikely ally arrived on the shores of Outremer. Conrad, the brother of Sibylla's first husband, William Longsword of Montferrat, arrived aboard a Genoese ship at Tyre. With great energy and prudence, Conrad took the command of Tyre into his own hands and organised a robust defence of the city. Under his instruction, Tyre would be the first to check Saladin in his progress up the coast. He was not a supporter of Sibylla and Guy, and came to the Holy Land with his own agenda and aims, but his first goal was to resist Saladin.

The sultan's next target was not Tyre but Ascalon. This was one of Sibylla's castles, within her dower lands, and she was present at the siege. She had rushed there to fortify it with provisions and soldiers, and seemed ready to stand her ground. Saladin, however, played a clever trick. Instead of proceeding with normal siege warfare, which the city was well provisioned to withstand, he brought two of his most valuable hostages out before the walls: Guy de Lusignan, and Gerard de Ridefort, master of the Templars. He gave an ultimatum to Sibylla and the Templars assisting her in the defence of the city: surrender the city, or watch as he executed the two men on the spot.

From their piteous position at the point of a scimitar, perhaps the very same that had decapitated Reynald de Châtillon, Guy and Gerard both ordered the city's defenders to surrender to Saladin. Sibylla, no doubt guided by her love for Guy and her vow to obey him, agreed to surrender. The city capitulated, and while Gerard was released, Saladin hung on to Guy a little longer, imprisoning him at Nablus and Latakieh, both of which had fallen to his armies. While once again demonstrating Sibylla's unswerving devotion to her husband, this surrender was not the move of a shrewd military strategist. Not long after this, Saladin would parade Conrad of Montferrat's imprisoned father before him at a similar siege, and Conrad would stand iron-faced and unmoved and call the sultan's bluff. Saladin did not go through with his threat of slaughtering the old man.

Following his capture of Ascalon, Saladin progressed to the great prize of the Holy Land, Jerusalem itself, and arrived there on 20 September 1187. He began to set up his formidable siege engines, and his forces circled the city, searching for a weak spot in the defences.

Following the loss of Ascalon, Sibylla had gone to Jerusalem, where her stepmother Maria and the Patriarch Heraclius were attempting to prepare the city to withstand a siege. It was a hopeless situation. Maria Komnene's new husband Balian of Ibelin wrote to Saladin and begged leave to rush to Jerusalem in order to rescue his wife and convey her to safety. He was one of the few lords of Outremer who had escaped the massacre at Hattin alongside Raymond of Tripoli and was still at liberty. Saladin magnanimously consented to this request for safe conduct on the condition that Balian did not remain in the city, and did not take up arms in its defence. Balian accepted these terms and rode to Jerusalem with all haste.

This magnanimity proved to be a great error on the sultan's part. Upon reaching Jerusalem, Balian was so moved by the helpless plight of the Holy City that he once again wrote to Saladin, this time begging to be released from his oath because he could not in good conscience abandon Sibylla and the city to its fate. Saladin graciously consented, and while Maria Komnene was sent to safety, Balian stayed in the cornered city with Sibylla and Heraclius. This unlikely trio made ready for war.

Saladin besieges Jerusalem

It is greatly disputed what role Sibylla played in the strategy and defence of Jerusalem during the ensuing siege. Many historians have been loath to give her role much credit, but as demonstrated by her stepmother Maria Komnene at Nablus, and Raymond of Tripoli's wife Eschiva at Tiberias, and even Saladin's own wife at Banyas, it was not unknown for women to command a siege, and there is at least one source that places Sibylla in Jerusalem during its defence. She was queen regnant and the highest-status person in Jerusalem at the time of Saladin's attack; hence it is unreasonable to assume that, on account of her sex, she did not play an active part in the defence of her capital. It is far more likely that Sibylla, Balian and Patriarch Heraclius jointly commanded the city's defences: Sibylla had authority, Balian had military expertise and Heraclius had control of the city's funds.

Between them they made a robust defence against impossible odds. The city had been flooded with thousands of Christian refugees from neighbouring territories, thus the food stores and sanitation within the city were under great strain, and on top of this they had next to no knights or men-at-arms. Only a small garrison had remained in Jerusalem when Guy commanded the armies to assemble at Saffuriyah before their defeat at Hattin. The circumstances were desperate indeed, and there was no chance of a Christian victory: even if they could withstand the sultan's bombardment for some time, they could never repel his army and there was no relief force to come to their rescue.

One version of events of the plight inside the city comes from the hand of the monk Thomas of Beverley, transcribing the experiences of his elder sister, Margaret of Beverley, who had been trapped in the city during the siege. She had come to Jerusalem on pilgrimage, arriving just before Saladin's forces, and she paints a vivid picture of the desperation and suffering within the walls. Wearing a cooking pot on her head as a helmet Margaret manned the battlements. She brought water to the fighting men, and was herself injured by flying stones and masonry. She claimed that she tried to suppress her womanly fears and fight 'like a fierce virago'. While the cooking pot helmet sounds like an invention, the idea of women toiling on the walls during the siege and an absence of able-bodied fighting men rings true, and this account of Margaret's experiences is credible.

As fighting raged atop the walls, inside women cut their hair and barefoot processions were led by the panic-stricken population around the holy places, wailing, repenting for sins and begging to be saved. In a moment of inspiration, Balian knighted every man-at-arms in the city to infuse them with a sense of pride and purpose and to bolster their confidence. When, under the sultan's relentless bombardment, the walls began to collapse and resistance became futile, the three commanders decided to negotiate terms of surrender. A meeting needed to take place between the Christian commanders and Saladin. The one chosen to do the talking was Balian of Ibelin.

Many historians have chosen to read Balian's role as the envoy to Saladin as confirmation that Balian was the one really leading the defence of Jerusalem. However, this is too simplistic a view. It would have been impossible for Sibylla herself to ride out to meet with Saladin on the battlefield, even if she were in command of the city. That would have been a step too far even for the most courageous of medieval princesses, and it is unlikely Saladin would have been prepared to negotiate directly with a woman. Female commanders were expected to send deputies to negotiate on their behalf, as had been the case with Saladin's wife Ismat ad-Din Khatoun at the Siege of Banyas. Who better to relay the Queen's message to the sultan than the husband of her stepmother and her one remaining baron, Balian of Ibelin?

The best that Sibylla, Balian and Heraclius could hope for was the survival and freedom of the Christians within the city. They were not in a strong bargaining position. The inhabitants of the city had rejected Saladin's initial offer of a peaceful surrender, and now they had resisted as long as they could and were on the brink of defeat. This was plain for all to see, and Saladin knew that he had them in his power.

Saladin did not wish to be merciful. He recalled the slaughter inflicted by the Christians on the Muslim inhabitants of the city in 1099. He refused to accept Sibylla's offer of surrender in exchange for her liberty and the safety of the Christians. The city was woefully short of fighting men, and could not withstand Saladin's amassed armies. He said as much to Balian, and said that as a result he would not offer terms. Balian's stoic reply was that if Saladin did not offer terms, then the Christians inside had nothing to lose. If Saladin would not promise the defenders of Jerusalem their lives and the freedom of their queen, then the first thing his men would do would be to raze the city from inside out and destroy and desecrate the Muslim holy places. He warned that they would die fighting to a man, and in their desperation they would destroy Saladin's army, fighting with the fury of men who see their own death approaching.

Balian's words were clearly persuasive and Saladin was moved to reconsider. Jerusalem was surrendered to him without further bloodshed. He allowed the Christians within to buy their freedom, and Balian supplied the funds for the ransom of the city's poor. They were then given safe passage to Christian lands, and Sibylla was given permission to rejoin her captive husband. However, even with Balian providing what financial assistance he could, not every citizen was able to purchase freedom, and many were taken into slavery. Patriarch Heraclius was criticised for not reaching into his own pockets, and left weighed down with all the church treasure he could carry, while defeated Christians were marched in iron to slave markets.

Margaret of Beverley, the woman who had fought valiantly with a cooking pot on her head, was among those enslaved: she managed to buy her freedom at the end of the siege, but then she and her fellow refugees were captured as they walked to Laodicea. Eventually her freedom was purchased by a gentleman from Tyre, and she made her way alone across the harsh terrain towards Antioch. After many more sieges, captures, releases and adventures Margaret finally made her way back to England. The experiences of Margaret give a rare glimpse into the lives of ordinary Christian pilgrims caught amid the fighting in the Holy Land.

When Guy was eventually released from his captivity by Saladin, he summoned Sibylla to his side and the pair marched with their depleted retinue to Tyre, one of the very few cities that had resisted Saladin. Conrad of Montferrat, the brother of Sibylla's first husband William and uncle to her dead son, had arrived in the east aboard a Genoese ship and taken control of the city, refused to recognise Guy's authority and denied the disgraced couple entry into Tyre. Following the defeat at Hattin and the loss of Jerusalem, Guy had lost what little credibility and respect he once had. Sibylla's reign was over, and Ibelin and Montferrat were now the names that commanded loyalty in Outremer. They were the only men still living who had not thoroughly bungled their duty to defend the Holy Land.

Fuming at this insult, Guy and Sibylla set off for Acre and began to besiege the city. Richard the Lionheart and the armies of the Third Crusade would soon arrive in Outremer and swell the ranks of Guy's armies, and ultimately succeed in taking the city. Sibylla never saw this victory, nor the progress made by the Third Crusade and the arrival of the Kings of England and France in her Kingdom. In 1190 she and her two surviving daughters, Alice and Maria, perished from disease in her husband's military camp beneath the walls of Acre. They were among thousands to die of the pestilence, and the placement of their graves was never recorded. With the death of Sibylla, Guy lost his claim to the throne, and was forced out of the Kingdom of Jerusalem, fleeing to Cyprus, which he would eventually come to rule. This is the end of Sibylla's story. She was the last Queen of Jerusalem to reign in the city, for although Isabella was thereafter styled as Queen of Jerusalem, the Christians did not regain control of the holy city during her lifetime.

William of Tyre's chronicle is uncharacteristically silent on the appearance and disposition of Queen Sibylla of Jerusalem. He does not praise her or describe her, but reports her actions in painfully brief fashion. Other chroniclers have followed his example. Even the Arabic sources exclude reference to her in certain sieges and events, perhaps because to describe a woman facing Saladin in a siege would be to dishonour the sultan. William of Tyre had opinions on everyone, and he made these abundantly clear to his readers. When he disliked someone, as with Agnes of Courtenay and Guy de Lusignan, he did not disguise his disdain and disgust, and lambasted their characters. When he respected someone, as he did Baldwin IV, Amalric, Melisende and Raymond of Tripoli, his praise was compelling.

It is impossible to believe that he had no opinion of Sibylla, a highly divisive figure whom he had known from her infancy, so why then did he keep silent? Perhaps the greatest insult a historian can bestow is to omit, and he omitted Sibylla as much as he reasonably could. My inference from his refusal to describe or commemorate her is that he could not forgive her actions regarding her marriage to Guy and the resulting catastrophe for the Kingdom, but at the same time he seems unable to raise his pen to disparage her. He died the year Sibylla acceded to the throne of Jerusalem, and perhaps if he had lived longer and continued to write, he might eventually have become more vocal in his criticism. As it was, when William stopped writing, the full extent of Sibylla's mistakes was not yet apparent, and she had yet to seize agency herself. It is possible that while William was writing, he perceived Sibylla to be little more than a pawn manipulated by her mother, husband and uncle. Perhaps he simply pitied her, or was charitable towards her because of his devotion to her brother and the ruling family of the Kingdom of Jerusalem.

In order to construct a picture of Sibylla we are forced to rely on deductions based on a multitude of inconsistent sources. Despite these barriers, a picture still emerges. She was not a force of nature or a battleaxe in the way that some of her female antecedents were, nor was she a romantic heroine or a model of chastity and virtue. Sibylla was a complex individual who made many mistakes but who always had the odds stacked against her. Her childhood was tragic, she did not receive a military education, and she came under the influence of at least two highly questionable characters. Nor should we discount the death of all her children. The loss of a child is debilitating, and Sibylla lost five.

No such misfortunes happened to Queen Melisende or Princess Alice, nor Eleanor of Aquitaine or Morphia of Melitene, and to draw direct comparison between her more successful predecessors on the throne of Jerusalem is unhelpful in assessing her life and reign. Sibylla was just thirty when she died, and during her life she had little real time to develop her own voice or agency amid the politicking of her family members and the brewing storm that would eventually engulf her Kingdom. Despite all that, she displayed great fortitude, and on the day of her coronation she revealed a courageous streak.

With the death of Sibylla, a power vacuum formed in the collapsing Kingdom of Jerusalem. Guy lost his right to kingship when he lost his wife and daughters: he was treated as a king consort only and his authority derived entirely from the claims to the throne of his wife and daughters. Also, he had demonstrated himself to be a catastrophically inept leader, and the remaining citizens of the crumbling Kingdom had no desire to perpetuate his rule. Eyes turned to Balian of Ibelin, married to the dowager Queen Maria Komnene, and her daughter the Princess Isabella of Jerusalem. Balian had earned himself the gratitude of Outremer for his role in the defence of Jerusalem, Maria was a Byzantine princess and Princess Isabella, now aged fifteen, was the last surviving blood heir to the throne of Jerusalem. Support rallied behind her.

Isabella had been married to Humphrey IV of Toron at the age of eight. It was this marriage that was celebrated in Kerak castle during Saladin's bombardment of the fortress. Humphrey, like Guy, had been taken prisoner at the Battle of Hattin, and while his stepfather Reynald de Châtillon had been executed, Humphrey's release had been negotiated by his mother, Stephanie of Milly. This capture, along with his previous submission to Guy, had lost him any respect or support he might have had, and thus the remaining Christians in the East and the newly arriving soldiers from Europe were not anxious to put Humphrey on the throne of Jerusalem alongside Isabella.

The obvious candidate to be Isabella's husband and the next King of Jerusalem was Conrad of Montferrat, the seasoned soldier who had arrived from the West and secured Tyre against Saladin. This man had the unequivocal support of Maria Komnene and Balian of Ibelin, Isabella's mother and stepfather, who had readily stepped into the role of kingmakers through their influence over Isabella. Conrad and his supporters leaked the information that at the time of her marriage to Humphrey, Isabella had been too young for the marriage to be considered binding. This fact, combined with the general political hostility towards Humphrey, led to a farcical annulment being rushed through. Isabella was married to Conrad on 24 November 1190, just months after news of Sibylla's death broke. This hasty marriage was all the more dubious since Conrad was himself already married.

Despite the arrival of the Kings of Europe and the Third Crusade, Conrad and Isabella would never be crowned in the Holy Sepulchre or reign as monarchs in Jerusalem. The city was never retaken by Christian crusaders, despite seven more crusades in subsequent centuries. Less than two years after their marriage, Conrad would be assassinated and Isabella would be hastily married to Henry of Champagne less than a week after Conrad's death. When Henry died in 1197, she was married to the King of Cyprus. Isabella herself died at the age of thirty-three: she had had four husbands in her short life and left behind five daughters.

Among these girls was Maria of Montferrat, the next heir to the crown of Jerusalem. The lives of Maria and her four sisters Alice, Philippa, Sibylla and Melisende were as varied and full of intrigue as those of the women whose names they shared, the daughters and granddaughters of Morphia of Melitene. Alice became Queen of Cyprus, Philippa became Lady of Ramerupt, Sibylla became Queen of Armenia and Melisende became Princess of Antioch. They never stopped fighting to secure their inheritance, and played key roles in the crusades that set out from Europe to attempt to reclaim Jerusalem in the following decades.

EPILOGUE

The historical legacy of women rulers is subject to a variety of unpredictable forces: each of the women discussed in this book has received very different treatment at the hands of historians from the twelfth century to the twenty-first. Some have been turned into sexual fantasies, some have had achievements or crimes attributed to them for which there is little evidence, others have simply been ignored. Few have had any record of their lives accurately or sympathetically recorded, and even fewer have been celebrated.

This is changing. A new interest in medieval queenship has been piqued in the popular imagination in the last fifty years, and in academia more attention has begun to be paid to uncovering the lives of women and bringing their voices back into the narrative. Without this recent progress, led in particular by female historians, this book would not have been written.

For all this, the role played by women in ruling the Christian states of Outremer has been consistently overlooked by the majority of historians. The Queens, Princesses, Countesses and Ladies of this period and region have been reduced by writers to voiceless caricatures: virtuous maidens, scheming harridans and unnatural viragoes. Queen Melisende was one of the few women rulers approved of by William of Tyre, but even his continuators found fault with his decision to present Melisende's leadership skills alongside her feminine qualities. In the age of chivalry and romance literature, where the stereotypical notions of 'femininity' were chiselled still more deeply into Western culture, they attempted to gloss over his descriptions of Melisende's political agency by attributing to her the more commonly accepted female virtues of beauty and chastity, to make her better fit the mould.

Alice of Antioch has been lambasted by historians, Yvette of Bethany has been variously ignored or presented as a rape victim and Hodierna of Tripoli was remembered in literature chiefly as the distant fantasy of a troubadour. Hodierna's depiction as an exotic sexual object is not dissimilar to Eleanor of Aquitaine's portrayal in literature. These two women represent clear examples of politically active medieval women becoming the victims of sexual fantasy and orientalism to audiences both medieval and modern. One must only consider Katharine Hepburn's iconic portrayal of Eleanor claiming that she 'rode bare-breasted halfway to Damascus', or Eva Green's highly orientalist and sexual depiction of Sibylla in *Kingdom of Heaven* to see how hard-wearing these clichés have proven to be. Agnes of Courtenay and Sibylla of Jerusalem have been treated differently in different periods of history; sometimes Sibylla has been presented as a mother who murdered her son and destroyed a Kingdom, but in other centuries she has been seen as the paragon of wifely virtue and loyalty, who upheld the sanctity of marriage. These varying presentations bear little relation to evidence and hinge instead on the popular tastes of the time.

Morphia's daughters and granddaughters represented a dynasty of formidable women with a thirst and talent for political agency. All, if only for a brief period, attained autonomous rule in their various territories. Even the Byzantine Princesses Maria and Theodora Komnene, who served as Queen Consorts of Jerusalem, made marks on the Kingdom of Jerusalem through the dowries and political alliances they brought with them. Both women showed some flair in their choice of second husbands, Maria marrying Balian of Ibelin and Theodora eloping with Andronikos Komnenos.

A look at the lives and reigns of these women has carried with it a necessary contemplation of the distinction between authority and power. Authority equates to political legitimacy: the right to rule. Power is the tangible ability to accomplish goals, either through authority or subversion of it: the ability to rule. Queen Sibylla had authority, but little power. Her grandmother had each in turn, and variously both and neither. Her relatives struggled in the fight for both. In this book I have tried to consider the gulf between authority and power, and the remarkable lives of women who sought to cross it. In the history of Outremer, women are portrayed as ever present but always in the shadows: my aim in writing this has been to bring their experiences and achievements into the light.

BIBLIOGRAPHY

NOTE ON RESOURCES

Below is a list of the sources that have most directly informed my work or been referenced in the text. However, as this list might appear dense to the general reader – but sparse to the academic – I think it is useful to explain which texts I have worked with most closely.

William of Tyre and his continuators have been my main primary source for the history of the Latin Kingdom of Jerusalem, balanced of course by the perspective and testimony of other medieval chroniclers. The writings of Matthew of Edessa and Michael the Syrian were invaluable to my study of the County of Edessa, and Niketas Choniates and Anna Komnene were key sources for understanding the court of Constantinople and its relationship with the ruling houses of the crusader states. Ibn Al-Athir's chronicle and the *Damascus Chronicle* were the main Arabic texts I consulted. Any unattributed quotations in the body of the text are taken from William of Tyre's chronicle.

Regarding secondary work, for understanding the wives of Baldwin I and the role Morphia of Melitene inherited as Queen Consort of Jerusalem, Susan Edgington's book on Baldwin I was essential. For understanding the accession and reign of Queen Melisende, Hans Eberhard Mayer's seminal essay 'Studies in the History of Queen Melisende of Jerusalem' was the most important source. For a consideration of the Melisende psalter and Melisende's cultural patronage, I consulted the work of Jaroslav Folda and Helen Gaudette. For Alice of Antioch, Thomas Asbridge's essay on her rebellions was key; and similarly for Constance, A.V. Murray's essay was the starting point of my own research. For understanding William of Tyre's treatment of these women, I looked to Andrew Buck's essay listed below. For Agnes of Courtenay and Queen Sibylla, Bernard Hamilton's book *The Leper King and His Heirs* was crucial, as was his essay 'Women in the Crusader

States: Queens of Jerusalem', which gave a brief overview of the lives of several of the subjects of this book. Helen Nicholson's work on Sibylla was also very thought-provoking and helpful. For Eleanor of Aquitaine, there was not one particular source that stands out as more useful than the others, but Jonathan Phillips' book on the Second Crusade was the one I relied on to understand that period. For the Kingdom of Jerusalem and the crusading movement as a whole, Christopher Tyerman's works *God's War* and *The World of the Crusades,* and Malcolm Barber's *The Crusader States* have been constantly at my side. In attempting to further understand the role of women in the crusader states and crusading narrative, I looked at *Women, Crusading and the Holy Land in Historical Narrative* by Natasha Hodgson.

For understanding the Armenian presence in Jerusalem and the other ethnicities and minorities living in Outremer, I relied on the work of Andrew Jotischky and George Hintlian, both of whom went the extra mile and had many conversations with me to enrich my understanding. For crusader archaeology and the physical layout/appearance of the Kingdom of Jerusalem, I relied on the primary source *The City of Jerusalem* and Adrian Boas' book *Jerusalem in the Time of the Crusades.* Adrian's advice and corrections to my chapters about Melisende's impact on the city were crucial. Christopher Tyerman read and corrected the completed manuscript, and any errors that remain are the result of my own bullishness rather than his oversight.

PRIMARY SOURCES

Anonymi auctoris Chronicon AD A.C. 1234, trans. A. Abouna, ed. J.M. Fiey (Louvain, 1974).

Albert of Aachen, *Historia Ierosolimitana*, ed. and trans. Susan Edgington (Oxford, 2007).

Ambroise, *The History of the Holy War: Ambroise's Estoire de la Guerre Sainte,* ed. and trans. Marianne Ailes and Malcom Barber, 2 vols (Woodbridge, 2003).

Anna Komnene, *The Alexiad*, ed. Peter Frankopan, trans. E.R.A. Sewter (London, 2009).

Baha' al-Din, *The Rare and Excellent History of Saladin*, trans. Donald S. Richards (Aldershot, 2002).

Bernard of Clairvaux, *The Letters of Saint Bernard of Clairvaux*, trans. Bruno Scott James, 2nd edition (Stroud, 1998).

Caffaro, *Caffaro, Genoa and the Twelfth-Century Crusades,* trans. Martin Hall and Jonathan Phillips (London, 2013).

Le cartulaire du chapitre du St Sépulcre de Jérusalem, ed. Geneviève Bresc-Bautier (Paris, 1984).

Cartulaire général de l'Ordre des Hospitaliers de Saint-Jean de Jérusalem, 1100–1310, 4 vols, ed. J. Delaville Le Roulx (Paris, 1894–1905).

Chartes de Terre Sainte provenant de l'abbaye de Notre-Dame de Josaphat, ed. F. Delaborde (Paris, 1880).

Chronique d'Ernoul et de Bernard le Trésorier, ed. Louis de Mas Latrie (Paris, 1871).

The City of Jerusalem, ed. and trans. C.R. Conder (London, 1909).

La continuation de Guillaume de Tyr 1184–1197, ed. Margaret R. Morgan (Paris, 1982).

The Conquest of Jerusalem and the Third Crusade, Sources in Translation, trans. Peter. W. Edbury (Aldershot, 1996).

L'estoire d'Eracles empereur, in RHC Occ., Vols 1 & 2 (Paris, 1884–1859).

Estoires d'Outremer et de la naissance Salehadin, ed. Margaret A. Jubb (London, 1990).

Fulcher of Chartres, *A History of the Expedition to Jerusalem, 1095–1127*, trans. F. Ryan, ed. H. Fink (Knoxville, TN, 1969).

——, *Chronicle of the First Crusade: Fulcheri Carnotensis Historia Hierosolymitana*, trans. Martha Evelyn McGinty (Philadelphia, 1941).

Felix Fabri, *The Book of the Wanderings of Brother Felix Fabri*, trans. A. Stewart, Part of Palestinian Pilgrims' Text Society (London, 1893).

Gabrieli, F., *Arab Historians of the Crusades*, trans. E.J. Costello (Berkeley and Los Angeles, 1969).

Giraldi Cambrensis Opera, ed. J.S. Brewer, J.F. Dimock and G.F. Warner (London, 1868).

Gesta Francorum: Histoire anonyme de la Premiére Croisade, ed. L. Bréhier (Paris, 1924).

Gesta Francorum et Aliorum Hierosolimitanorum, ed. and trans. Rosalind Hill (Nelson's Medieval Texts) (London, 1962).

Gregory the Priest, *Continuation of Gregory the Priest*, in *Armenia and the Crusades, Tenth to Twelfth Centuries: The Chronicle of Matthew of Edessa*, trans. A. Dostourian (Lanham, MD, 1993).

Guibert of Nogent, *Dei gesta Per Francos et cinq autres textes*, ed. Robert B.C. Huygens (Turnhout, 1996).

Guillaume de Tyr et ses continuateurs: texte français du XIIIe siècle, ed. and annotated Paulin Paris (Paris, 1879).

Henry of Huntingdon, *Historia Anglorum*, ed. and trans. Diana Greenway (Oxford, 1996).

Ibn al-Athir, *The Chronicle of Ibn al-Athir for the Crusading Period from al-Kamil fi'l-ta'rikh*, Parts 1 & 2, trans. D.S. Richards (Crusade Texts in Translation) (Aldershot, 2006, 2007).

Ibn al-Qalanisi, *The Damascus Chronicle of the Crusades*, trans. H.A.R. Gibb (London, 1972).

Ibn Jubayr, *The Travels of Ibn Jubayr*, ed. and trans. R.J.C. Broadhurst (London, 1952).

Imad ad-Din al-Isfahani, *Conquête de la Syrie et de la Palestine par Saladin*, trans. Henri Massé (Paris, 1972).

Itinerarium Peregrinorum et Gesta Regis Ricardi, ed. Helen Nicholson (Aldershot, 1997).

John Kinnamos, *Deeds of John and Manuel Comnenus*, trans. Charles M. Brand (New York, 1976).

John of Ibelin, *Le livre des assises*, ed. Peter W. Edbury (Leiden, 2003).

John of Salisbury, *Memoirs of the Papal Court*, ed. and trans. Marjorie Chibnall (London, 1956).

——, *Historia Pontificalis*, ed. and trans. Marjorie Chibnall (Oxford, 1986).

Kamal al-Din, *Extraits de la Chronique d'Alep par Kemal ed-Dine*, in RHC Or. Vol. 3 (Paris, 1872).

——, *La Chronique d'Alep*, in RHC Or., Vol. 3 (Paris, 1872), pp. 571–690.

Matthew of Edessa, *Armenia and the Crusades, Tenth to Twelfth Centuries: The Chronicle of Matthew of Edessa*, trans. A. Dostourian (Lanham, MD, 1993).

Matthew Paris, *Chronica Majora*, ed. Henry Richards Luard (London, 1872–83).

Michael the Syrian, *Chronique de Michel le Syrien, patriarche Jacobite d'Antioche (1166–1199)*, ed. and trans. Jean Chabot (Paris, 1899–1924).

Niketas Choniates, *O City of Byzantium: Annals of Niketas Choniates*, trans. H.J. Magoulias (Detroit, 1984).

Odo of Deuil, *De Profectione Ludovici VII in Orientem*, ed. and trans. Virginia Gingerick Berry (New York, 1948).

Orderic Vitalis, *The Ecclesiastical History of Orderic Vitalis*, ed. and trans. Marjorie Chibnall (Oxford, 1969–80).

Otto of Freising, *The Two Cities: A Chronicle of Universal History to the Year 1146 A.D.*, trans. C. C. Mierow (New York, 1928).

——, *Gesta Friderici I. Imperatoris auctoribus Ottone et Ragewino praeposito Frisingensibus*, ed. R. Wilmans (MGHSS, Vol. 20) (Hanover, 1925).

Ralph of Caen, *The Gesta Tancredi*, ed. and trans. Bernard S. Bachrach and David S. Bachrach (Aldershot, 2005).

Raymond d'Aguilers, *Le Liber de Raymond d'Aguilers*, ed. John Hugh and Laurita L. Hill (Paris, 1969).

Richard of Devizes, *Chronicon*, ed. and trans. John T. Appleby (London, 1963).

Roger of Howden, *Chronica*, Vols 1–3, ed. William Stubbs (London, 1868–71).

St Jerome, et al. *The Holy Land in the Middle Ages: Six Travelers' Accounts* (New York, Italica Press, 2017), retrieved 29 June 2020 from www.jstor.org/stable/j.cttɪt88tqq

Suger, Abbot of St-Denis, *Vita Ludovici Grossi Regis*, ed. and trans. Henri Waquet (Paris, 1964).

——, *The Deeds of Louis the Fat*, trans. Richard Cusimano and John Moorhead (Washington, 1992).

——, 'The Illustrious King Louis VII, Son of Louis VI', in *Selected Works of Abbot Suger of Saint-Denis*, trans. Richard Cusimano and John Moorhead (Catholic University of America Press, 2018).

Thomas Fuller, *History of the Holy Warre* (Cantabrigiae, 1639).

Tudebode, Peter, *Historia De Hierosolymitano Itinere*, ed. John Hugh and Laurita L. Hill (Paris, 1977).

Usama ibn Munqidh, *An Arab-Syrian Gentleman and Warrior in the Period of the Crusades: Memoirs of Usamah Ibn-Munqidh*, trans. P.K. Hitti (Princeton, NJ, 1929).

Walter the Chancellor, *The Antiochene Wars*, ed. Thomas S. Asbridge and Susan B. Edgington (Crusade Texts in Translation) (Aldershot, 1999).

William of Malmesbury, *Gesta Regum Anglorum*, ed. and trans. Roger A.B. Mynors, completed by Rodney M. Thompson and Michael Winterbottom (Oxford, 1998–9).

William of Newburgh, *Historia Rerum Anglicarum*, in *Chronicles and Memorials of the Reigns of Stephen, Henry II and Richard I*, ed. R. Howlett (London, 1884).

William of Tyre, *Deeds Done Beyond The Sea*, ed. and trans. Emily A. Babcock and August C. Krey (Columbia University Press, 1943).

SECONDARY SOURCES

Asbridge, T., *The Creation of the Principality of Antioch, 1098–1130* (Woodbridge, 2000).

——, 'Alice of Antioch: A case study of female power in the twelfth century', in *The Experience of Crusading*, Vol. 2, *Defining the Crusader Kingdom*, ed. P. Edbury and J. Phillips (Cambridge, 2003), pp. 29–47.

Avray, D. L. d , *Papacy, Monarchy and Marriage, 860–1600* (Cambridge, 2015).

——, *Dissolving Royal Marriages: A Documentary History* (Cambridge, 2014).

Baldwin, M.W., *Raymond III of Tripoli and the Fall of Jerusalem (1140–1187)* (New York, 1936).

Barber, M., *The Crusader States* (Yale, 2012).

Boas, A., *Crusader Archaeology: The Material Culture of the Latin East* (London, 1999).

——, *Jerusalem in the Time of the Crusades: Society, Landscape and Art in the Holy City Under Frankish Rule* (London, 2001).

Boehm, B.D. and Holcomb, M., eds, *Jerusalem, 1000–1400: Every People Under Heaven* (New York, 2016).

Brundage, J.A., 'Marriage Law in the Latin Kingdom of Jerusalem', in *Outremer: Studies in the History of the Crusading Kingdom of Jerusalem Presented to Joshua Prawer*, ed. B.Z. Kedar, H.E. Mayer and R.C. Smail (Jerusalem, 1982), pp. 258–71.

Buck, A., 'William of Tyre, Femininity, and the Problem of the Antiochene Princesses', in *The Journal of Ecclesiastical History*, 70 (4), pp. 731–49.

Cahen, C., *La Syrie du nord à l époque des croisades et la principauté franque d'Antioche* (Paris, 1940).

Carne, J., *Syria, The Holy Land, Asia Minor &c., illustrated. In a series of views drawn from nature by W. H. Bartlett, William Purser (Thomas Allom), &c. With descriptions of the plates by J. Carne* (London, 1853).

Castor, H., *She-Wolves* (London, 2011).

Chambers, F., 'Some Legends Concerning Eleanor of Aquitaine', in *Speculum*, 16, no. 4 (1941), 459–68. Retrieved 30 June 2020 from https://www.jstor.org/stable/2852844

Diehl, C., 'Les Romanesque aventures d'Andronic Comnène', in *Figures Byzantines* (Paris, 1928).

Downey, G., *A History of Antioch in Syria from Seleucus to the Arab Conquest* (Princeton, NJ, 1961).

Duby, G., *Women of the Twelfth Century, Volume 1, Eleanor of Aquitaine and Six Others*, trans. Jean Birrell (Oxford, 1997).

Edbury, P.W., 'Propaganda and Faction in the Kingdom of Jerusalem: the Background to Hattin', in *Crusaders and Muslims in Twelfth-Century Syria*, ed. M. Shatzmiller (Leiden, 1993), pp. 173–89.

——, *John of Ibelin and the Kingdom of Jerusalem* (Woodbridge, 1997).

—— and J.G. Rowe, 'William of Tyre and the Patriarchal Election of 1180', in *English Historical Review*, 93 (1978), pp. 1–25.

Edgington, S., *Baldwin I of Jerusalem, 1100–1118* (London, 2019).

Elisséeff, N., *Nur-ad-Din. Un grand prince musulman de Syrie au temps des Croisades, 511–569H., 1118–1174* (Damas, 1967).

Evans, H.C., 'The Armenian Presence in Jerusalem', in *Jerusalem, 1000–1400: Every People Under Heaven*, ed. B.D. Boehm and M. Holcomb (New York, 2016).

Evans, M.R., *Inventing Eleanor: the Medieval and Post-Medieval Image of Eleanor of Aquitaine* (London, 2014).

Folda, J., 'Images of Queen Melisende in Manuscripts of William of Tyre's History of Outremer, 1250–1300', in *Gesta*, 32, no. 2 (1993), pp. 97–112.

——, *The Art of the Crusaders in the Holy Land, 1098–1187* (Cambridge, 1995).

——, 'Melisende of Jerusalem: Queen and Patron of Art and Architecture in the Crusader Kingdom', in *Reassessing the Roles of Women as 'Makers' of Medieval Art and Architecture*, ed. T. Martin, Vol. 1 (Boston, 2012), pp. 429–77.

——, 'Sharing the Church of the Holy Sepulchre During the Crusader

Period', in *Jerusalem, 1000–1400: Every People Under Heaven*, ed. B.D. Boehm and M. Holcomb (New York, 2016).

Frankopan, P., *The First Crusade: The Call from the East* (London, 2012).

Friedman, Y., *Encounter Between Enemies: Captivity and Ransom in the Latin Kingdom of Jerusalem* (Leiden, 2002).

——, 'Peacemaking in an Age of War: When were Cross-Religious Alliances in the Latin East Considered Treason?', in *The Crusader World*, ed. A. Boas (New York, 2016).

Gaudette, H.A., *The Piety, Power and Patronage of the Latin Kingdom of Jerusalem's Queen Melisende* (PhD Thesis, City University of New York, 2005).

——, 'The Spending Power of a Crusader Queen: Melisende of Jerusalem', in *Women and Wealth in Late Medieval Europe*, ed. T. Earenfight (New York, 2010).

Gerish, D.E., *Constructions of Royal Identity in the First Kingdom of Jerusalem* (Dissertation, University of California, 1999).

Gibb, H.A.R., *The Life of Saladin from the Works of 'Imad ad-din and Baha' ad-Din* (Oxford, 1973).

Gibbon, E., *The History of the Decline and Fall of the Roman Empire*. Ed. D. Womersley (London: 2000).

Gillingham, J., 'Roger of Howden on Crusade', in *Richard Coeur de Lion: Kingship, Chivalry and War in the Twelfth Century* (London and Rio Grande, 1994), pp. 141–53.

Hagenmeyer, H., 'Chronologie de l'histoire du royaume de Jérusalem: Règne de Baudouin I (1101–1118)', in *ROL*, 9 (1902), pp. 384–465; *ROL*, 10 (1903–4), pp. 372–405; *ROL*, 11 (1905–8), pp. 145–80, 453–85; *ROL*, 12 (1909–11), pp. 68–103, 283–326.

Hamilton, B., 'The Elephant of Christ: Reynald de Châtillon', in *Studies in Church History*, 15 (1978), pp. 97–108.

——, 'Women in the Crusader States: The Queens of Jerusalem (1100–1190)', in *Medieval Women*, ed. D. Baker (Oxford, 1978).

——, 'The Titular Nobility of the Latin East: the Case of Agnes of Courtenay', in *Crusade and Settlement*, ed. P. Edbury (Cardiff, 1985), pp. 197–203.

——, *The Leper King and His Heirs: Baldwin IV and the Crusader Kingdom of Jerusalem* (Cambridge, 2000).

——, 'The Old French Translation of William of Tyre as an Historical Source', in *The Experience of Crusading*, Vol. 2, ed. M. Balard, B.Z. Kedar and J. Riley-Smith (Aldershot, 2001), pp. 199–207.

Harris, J., *Byzantium and the Crusades* (London, 2003).

Hintlian, G., *History of the Armenians in the Holy Land* (Jerusalem, 1989).

Hodgson, N.R., *Women, Crusading and the Holy Land in Historical Narrative* (Woodbridge, 2007).

Humphreys, R.S., 'Women as Patrons of Religious Architecture in Ayyubid Damascus', in *Muqarnas*, Vol. 11 (1994), pp. 35–54.

Hunt, L.A., 'Art and Colonialism: The Mosaics of the Church of the Nativity in Bethlehem (1169) and the Problem of "Crusader" Art', in *Dumbarton Oaks Papers*, 45 (1991), pp. 69–85.

Huneycutt, L.L., 'Female Succession and the Language of Power in the Writings of Twelfth-Century Churchmen', in *Medieval Queenship*, ed. J.C. Parsons (New York, 1998).

Huygens, R.B.C., 'Guillaume de Tyr étudiant: Un chapitre (XIX.12) de son "Histoire" retrouvé', in *Latomus*, 21 (1962), pp. 811–28.

Jordan, E.L., 'Hostage, Sister, Abbess: The Life of Iveta of Jerusalem', in *Medieval Prosopography*, Vol. 32 (2017), pp. 66–86.

Jotischky, A., 'Ethnographic Attitudes in the Crusader States: The Franks and the Indigenous Orthodox People', in *East and West in the Crusader States: Context – Contacts – Confrontations*, Vol. III, *Acta of the Congress Held at Hernen Castle in September 2000*, ed. K. Ciggaar and H. Teule (Louvain, 2003), pp. 1–19.

——, *Crusading and the Crusader States* (Harlow, 2004).

Kedar, B.Z., 'The Patriarch Eraclius', in *Outremer: Studies in the History of the Crusading Kingdom of Jerusalem Presented to Joshua Prawer*, ed. B.Z. Kedar, H.E. Mayer and R.C. Smail (Jerusalem, 1982), pp. 177–204.

——, 'On the Origins of the Earliest Laws of Frankish Jerusalem: The Canons of the Council of Nablus', in *Speculum*, 74 (1999), pp. 310–35.

Lambert, S., 'Queen or consort: rulership and politics in the Latin east 1118–1228', in *Queens and Queenship in Medieval Europe – proceedings of a conference held at Kings College London, April 1995*, ed. Anne J. Duggan (London, 1997).

Lawrence, T.E., *Crusader Castles* (Oxford, 1988).

Lay, S., 'A leper in purple: the coronation of Baldwin IV of Jerusalem', in *Journal of Medieval History*, 23 (1997), pp. 317–34.

Lewis, K.J., *The Counts of Tripoli and Lebanon in the Twelfth Century: Sons of Sainte-Gilles* (London, 2017).

——, 'Countess Hodierna of Tripoli: From Crusader Politician to "Princesse Lointaine"', in *Assuming Gender*, 3:1 (2013), pp. 1–26.

Mayer, H.E., 'Studies in the History of Queen Melisende of Jerusalem', in *Dumbarton Oaks Papers*, 26 (1972), pp. 95–182.

——, *Bistümer, Klöster und Stifte im Königreich Jerusalem* (Stuttgart, 1977).

——, 'Jérusalem et Antioche sous le règne de Baudouin II', in *Comptes-rendus des séances de l'Académie des Inscriptions et Belle-Lettres, année 1980* (1981), pp. 717–33.

——, 'The Concordat of Nablus', in *Journal of Ecclesiastical History*, 97 (1982), pp. 721–39.

——, 'The Double County of Jaffa and Ascalon: One Fief or Two?', in *Crusade and Settlement*, ed. P. Edbury (Cardiff, 1985), pp. 181–90.

——, 'The Succession to Baldwin II of Jerusalem: English Impact on the East', *Dumbarton Oaks Papers*, 39 (1985), pp. 257–65.

——, 'Angevins versus Normans: The New Men of King Fulk of Jerusalem', in *Proceedings of the American Philosophical Society*, 133 (1989), pp. 1–25.

——, *The Crusades* (Oxford, 1998).

Minella, A.-G., *Aliénor d'Aquitaine* (Paris, 2004).

Mitchell, P.D., 'An Evaluation of the Leprosy of King Baldwin IV in the Context of the Medieval World', in B. Hamilton, ed., *The Leper King and His Heirs: Baldwin IV and the Crusader Kingdom of Jerusalem* (Cambridge, 2000), pp. 245–58.

Möhring, H., *Saladin: The Sultan and his Times, 1138–1193*, trans. D.S. Bachrach (Baltimore, MD, 2008).

Murray, A.V., 'The Origins of the Frankish Nobility in the Kingdom of Jerusalem, 1100-1118', in *Mediterranean Historical Review*, 4 (1989), pp. 281–300.

——, 'Baldwin II and His Nobles: Baronial Factionalism and Dissent in the Kingdom of Jerusalem, 1118–24', in *Nottingham Medieval Studies*, 38 (1994), pp. 60–81.

——, 'Sex, death and the problem of single women in the armies of the First Crusade', in *Shipping, Trade and Crusade in the Medieval Mediterranean. Studies in honour of John Pryor*, ed. R. Gertwagen and E. Jeffreys, (Farnham, 2012).

——, 'Constance, Princess of Antioch (1130–1164): Ancestry, Marriages and Family', in *Anglo Norman Studies XXXVIII, Proceedings of the Battle Conference 2015*, ed. E. van Houts (Woodbridge, 2015).

Nicholson, H., 'Women on the Third Crusade', in *Journal of Medieval History*, 23 (1997), pp. 335–49.

——, '"La roine preude femme et bonne dame": Queen Sibyl of Jerusalem (1186–1190) in History and Legend, 1186–1300', in *Haskins Society Journal*, 15 (2004), pp. 110–24.

Oldenbourg, Z., *The Crusades*, trans. Anne Carter (London, 1998).

Pacaut, M., *Louis VII et son royaume* (Paris, 1964).

Park, D.E.A., 'The Power of Crusaders' Wives in Narrative and Diplomatic Sources, c.1096–1149'. Retrieved 29 June 2020 from http://blogs. reading.ac.uk/trm/files/2014/03/GCMSDanielle-Park.pdf

Pernoud, R., *La femme au temps des croisades* (Paris, 1990).

Phillips, J., *Defenders of the Holy Land: Relations Between the Latin East and the West, 1119–1187* (Oxford, 1996).

——, *The Second Crusade: Extending the Frontiers of Christendom* (London, 2007).

——, *Holy Warriors* (London, 2009).

——, *The Life and Legend of the Sultan Saladin* (London, 2019).

Prawer, J., *Histoire du Royaume Latin de Jérusalem*, 2 vols, trans. G. Nahon (Paris, 1969).

Pringle, D., *The Churches of the Crusader Kingdom of Jerusalem: A Corpus*, 4 vols (Cambridge, 1993–2009).

Pryor, J.H., 'The *Eracles* and William of Tyre: An Interim Report', in *The Horns of Hattin*, ed. B.Z. Kedar (London, 1992), pp. 270–93.

Richards, D.S., 'Imad al-din al-Isfahani: Administrator, Littérateur and Historian', in *Crusaders and Muslims in Twelfth-Century Syria*, ed. M. Shatzmiller (Leiden, 1993), pp. 133–46.

Runciman, S., *A History of the Crusaders*, 3 vols (Cambridge, 1975).

Schein, S., 'Women in Medieval Colonial Society: The Latin Kingdom of Jerusalem in the Twelfth Century', in *Gendering the Crusaders*, ed. S. Edgington and S. Lambert (Cardiff, 2001), pp. 140–53.

Sebag-Montefiore, S., *Jerusalem: The Biography* (London, 2011).

Smail, R.C., *Crusading Warfare, 1097–1193* (Cambridge, 1956).

Turner, Ralph V., *Eleanor of Aquitaine: Queen of France, Queen of England* (London, 2009).

Tutunjian, J., 'Fascinating Jerusalem', in *The Armenian Mirror-Spectator* (July 2017).

Tyerman, C.J., *God's War: A New History of the Crusades* (London, 2006).

——, *The World of the Crusades* (New Haven, 2019).

Walker, C.H., *Eleanor of Aquitaine* (Chapel Hill, 1950).

——, 'Eleanor of Aquitaine and the Disaster at Cadmos Mountain', in *The American Historical Review*, 55, no. 4 (1950), pp. 857–61.

Weir, A., *Eleanor of Aquitaine* (London, 2008).

INDEX

Page numbers in *italic* refer to images